Futures of
Digital Scholarly
Editing

Futures of Digital Scholarly Editing

Matt Cohen, Kenneth M. Price, and
Caterina Bernardini, Editors

University of Minnesota Press
Minneapolis • London

The University of Minnesota Press gratefully acknowledges the financial assistance provided for the publication of this book by the University of Nebraska–Lincoln.

Portions of chapter 12 are adapted from "Sparrow Data: Dickinson's Birds in the Skies of the Anthropocene," *The Emily Dickinson Journal* 30, no. 1 (2021): 45–84.

Copyright 2024 by the Regents of the University of Minnesota

Futures of Digital Scholarly Editing is licensed under a Creative Commons Attribution-NonCommercial-NoDerivatives 4.0 International License (CC BY-NC-ND 4.0): https://creativecommons.org/licenses/by-nc-nd/4.0/.

Published by the University of Minnesota Press
111 Third Avenue South, Suite 290
Minneapolis, MN 55401-2520
http://www.upress.umn.edu

Available as a Manifold edition at manifold.umn.edu

ISBN 978-1-5179-1667-1 (hc)
ISBN 978-1-5179-1668-8 (pb)

A Cataloging-in-Publication record for this book is available from the Library of Congress.

Printed in the United States of America on acid-free paper

The University of Minnesota is an equal-opportunity educator and employer.

Contents

Acknowledgments   vii

Introduction
MATT COHEN, KENNETH M. PRICE, AND
CATERINA BERNARDINI   ix

PART I. TRANSFORMATIONS OF TEXTUAL SCHOLARSHIP

1. Distant Editing: The Challenges of Computational Methods to the Theory and Practice of Textual Scholarship
ELENA PIERAZZO   3

2. Beyond Social Editing: Peer-to-Peer Systems for Digital Editions
JULIA FLANDERS   13

3. Creative Ecologies: The Complete-Works Edition in a Digital Paradigm   DIRK VAN HULLE   33

4. Charles W. Chesnutt and the Generous Edition: Collations, Annotations, and Genetic Histories
STEPHANIE P. BROWNER   51

5. Computational Literary Studies and Scholarly Editing
   FOTIS JANNIDIS 73

6. The Walt Whitman Archive at a Quarter of a Century
   ED FOLSOM 89

PART II. THE CONVERGENCE OF DIGITAL ARCHIVING AND SCHOLARLY EDITING

7. Digital Archival Ethics: Representation, Access, and Care in Digital Environments   K.J. RAWSON 101

8. Categories of Freedom: Colored Conventions, End-Movement Discourse, and the Nineteenth-Century Black Protest Tradition
   SARAH LYNN PATTERSON 121

9. Not Reading the Edition
   CASSIDY HOLAHAN, AYLIN MALCOLM, AND WHITNEY TRETTIEN 145

10. Indigenous Publishing, Scholarly Editing, and the Digital Future   ROBERT WARRIOR 169

11. Preserving the Walt Whitman Archive   NICOLE GRAY ... 197

12. Unsilent Springs: Dearchivizing the Data Choirs of Dickinson's Time-Shifted Birds   MARTA L. WERNER ... 217

    Afterword   JOHN UNSWORTH 243

    Contributors 249

    Index 253

Acknowledgments

This book emerged from an in-person event that took a small village to make happen. Thank you to Erin Chambers, Marco Abel, Claire Parfait, William G. Thomas III, Bob Wilhelm, Kevin McMullen, Brett Barney, and the staff of The Oven. Attendees of the symposium and the faculty and staff of the University of Nebraska–Lincoln's Center for Digital Research in the Humanities also influenced the essays that follow: thanks to Steve Ramsay, Melissa Homestead, Karin Dalziel, Greg Tunink, Laura Weakly, Brian Pytlik Zillig, Carrie Heitman, Andy Jewell, Liz Lorang, and Emily Rau.

We are grateful to the staff of the University of Minnesota Press for their vision, guidance, support, and talent. Thank you, Doug Armato, Zenyse Miller, Terence Smyre, Mike Stoffel, Carla Valadez, and Eric Lundgren. We are grateful to Daniel Fielding for an insightful index. Thank you to Trevor Owens and an anonymous external reader for suggestions that improved the collection.

The publication of this book and its Manifold version was supported by a University of Nebraska–Lincoln College of Arts and Sciences research development grant. The symposium at UNL that preceded it, "The Walt Whitman Archive and the Futures of Digital Scholarly Editing," was supported by the College of Arts and Sciences, the Office of Research and Economic Development, the university libraries, the Department of English, and the Hillegass University Professorship.

Introduction

MATT COHEN, KENNETH M. PRICE, AND
CATERINA BERNARDINI

Digital Scholarly Editing's Situation

It's a golden age of edition-making. Search the World Wide Web for "digital edition" and you will find hundreds; Patrick Sahle's list of electronic scholarly editions alone featured 821 in February 2023.[1] With comparatively little time, some simple web tools, cheap web hosting, an out-of-copyright copy text, and an argument to make about it, almost any academic can become a digital scholarly editor, in the broadest sense of that phrase. There are plenty of books in the library and guides online to help you on your way and introduce you to the dizzying history of scholarly editing in print and electronic media.[2]

But of course, tools, knowledge, and texts are not the only considerations. "Designing an edition, digital or otherwise, is not a straightforward process of tool-building," Alan Galey writes, "but a creative act bound up with the cultural history of a text."[3] This sense of the imbrication of past and present, when centered in the editorial process, impacts the conceptualization, development, and maintenance of an edition. The present digital environment is changing, and so are the times, raising questions that call for a rethinking of both the design and the public role of the scholarly editorial project in electronic form. New technologies, platforms, and user expectations are emerging rapidly. On another front, the politics of digital work and its significance in the academy are being called into question. And on still another front, demands for public-serving, ethical, and political engagement are increasingly being articulated by critics of digital projects and by review panels, as funding institutions adjust to both the maturing of the digital humanities and shifting political, social, and economic conditions. When we consider the technical and aesthetic challenges of designing editions for the age of portable or ubiquitous computing; the dedication of major resources for the study of canonical authors in the age of Black Lives Matter, Water Protectors, and #MeToo; and the troubled yet powerful leverage offered by social media in channeling the public outreach of scholarly work, we can't help but recognize a sea change in the world to which digital scholarly editing must address itself.

The landscape of editing is feeling the impact of linked open data (LOD), the development of application programming interface (API), the widespread adoption of GitHub, and other pathways for exposing, accessing, and repurposing data. In the historical and literary humanities in particular, the contributions of scholarly digital-editing projects to informatics and cultural analytics have been both controversial and revelatory. "The suggestion that quantitative research should count as a typical form of humanistic inquiry is still hotly debated," writes Ted Underwood; "In the past, it was broadly right to assume that numbers couldn't address the interpretive questions at the center of humanistic disciplines," but "the rules of that game have genuinely changed."[4] Underwood has used such techniques to show that literary historians' assumptions about the durability of literary reputation, the evolution of genres, and the participation of women in the literary marketplace have been off the mark. And the very recent past has witnessed the "mainstreaming"— exciting, troubling, and disruptive—of artificial intelligence (AI) in the form of everyday tools for generating a wide range of visual or textual representation. Still, digital scholarly editions have often imagined themselves, in tune with their print past, as mere primary sources for computational analysis. Are there ways to make such work more integral with the task of editing, and if so, what might be the costs of that convergence? Where are the most likely sites or frameworks for scholarly editors to focus their effort and imagination in this domain?

The rise of Black and Latinx digital humanities, together with decolonial approaches to archival preservation, has led many to rethink the goals and structures of scholarly digital projects. The convergence of scholarly interests with those of particular communities based on historical experiences of inequality points to ways of rooting editorial efforts in particular publics beyond mere textual recovery. Take the award-winning Colored Conventions Project (CCP) as a vivid example: The CCP digitizes the records of nineteenth-century black political conventions, and as such is a leading editorial project. But the CCP's declared first principle is not textual-editorial, but rather "to enact collective organizing principles and values that were modeled by the Colored Conventions Movement."[5] To this end, the project among other activities involves local communities in transcription projects and serves as a hub for a read-a-thon on Frederick Douglass Day. Nonacademic community members and groups help generate the archive, rather than just using it; community is built rather than just represented by it. This takes a step toward what in other areas of preservation work is called "post-custodial archiving": the shift from scholars, universities, or libraries owning and authorizing materials to those entities serving as instruments for community needs and as expert consultants on the futures of materials.

At the same time, the CCP takes a stance that qualifies the desirability of text as data. "Data has long served in the processes and recording of the destruction and devaluation of Black lives and communities," the CCP staff note, so they "seek to avoid exploiting Black subjects as data." Can editorial projects more generally learn from that ethical caution, which is not limited to racialized communities?[6] Such questions extend beyond choices of subject matter and into labor practices, crediting, and the goals of editing in the first place. When it comes to labor, unanswered questions remain about wages and conditions for the graduate students and post-docs doing much of the work in academic editorial projects. Crowdsourcing has question marks, too: clearly Amazon's Mechanical Turk platform raises serious ethical red flags, but it is less obvious what it means either to the integrity of a university-based preservation project (given also that large percentages of university cloud-storage systems are hosted by Amazon) or to the community contributor in a crowdsourcing arrangement that is unpaid and open to all who want to participate. And when it comes to accessibility, most digital editions still struggle to provide access both for those with disabilities and for a multilingual audience. More broadly, as Johanna Drucker has observed, digital interfaces in the humanities tend to "carry with them assumptions of knowledge as observer-independent and certain, rather than observer co-dependent and interpretative."[7]

In an age of increasing awareness of the human impact on climate change, sustainability takes on many levels of significance. "What is the place of Digital Humanities (DH) practice in the new social and geological era of the Anthropocene?," asks Bethany Nowviskie; "What are the DH community's most significant responsibilities, and to whom?"[8] Editorial projects in the past have had to worry about leadership transitions, but seldom their carbon footprints. In a compelling, synoptic effort to frame emerging issues in digital preservation, the Santa Barbara Statement on Collections as Data embraces many of the issues described above, listing key fundamental components or stances that preservation initiatives must consider for sustainability not only during the design phase but in the structure and daily activities of projects. A fundamental implication of the statement is that the technological and financial sustainability of a project are inseparable from its social sustainability, and that the latter requires as careful cultivation as the former.[9]

How can humanities scholars imagine and enact editions that will respond to the insights and challenges of declarations such as these? *Futures of Digital Scholarly Editing* gathers together an international, interdisciplinary group of scholars to pursue that question. Long-standing struggles in textual scholarship are addressed in new ways in these pages: the definitions of work, text, variation, the author and authorial intent, textual genetics, or the phenomenology and technology of reading; the role of judgment and approach in the editorial act; the nature of collaboration; the relation between authorial pasts and editorial present; or the erosion of editors' scholarly authority. But the emergences described above form the more pressing occasions for this volume. The insights of feminist, queer, African American, Native American, Disability studies, and postcolonial scholars about the problems associated with re-presenting the cultural-historical record have begun to have a widespread effect on editorial imaginations.[10] Those insights began with a focus on canonicity and text selection, but have evolved to challenge more fundamental editorial operations: citation, funding, annotation, marketing, the composition of editorial staff, the relationship of editorial projects to interested communities, and much more. The ethics of care advocated by much of that scholarship may also be found in the increasing focus on the durability of digital editions, a focus that has intensified as climate change impacts the largest framework for sustainability (that of all human endeavors) and transformations in the hardware, software, and human capabilities of digital scholarship increasingly teach us about the difficulties of maintaining any digital project.

And beyond maintenance is, of course, preservation, for if, as Jerome McGann has argued, stasis is an illusion in the print-based textual world, it seems almost antagonistic to the digital one.[11] As the affordances of non-print-based editions are increasingly explored and editions that are more dynamic and more integrated with other resources are created, the long-term lives of those projects come into question. "What are editors, publishers, and librarians to do with the conundrum of preserving for scholars of tomorrow the fluid text of today?," asks Marilyn Deegan.[12] It may seem clear that libraries are historically best equipped to do this preservation, but given the tidal wave of digital materials beginning to inundate them, the shortage of funding to hire digital archivists, and the accelerating proliferation of data formats, platforms, software, and hardware, the actuality is considerably more muddy.[13] Deegan observed in 2006 that scholars simply hadn't had to consider the long-term preservation of their editions in the print era. But the maturing of the digital editorial field means that this question converges with the new problematics, both ethical and technical, of textual scholarship in digital environments.

After all, digital preservationists and archivists are as concerned about how to do their work in an ethical, community-sustaining way as they are in coming up with technical ways to manage the tidal wave of digital materials headed their way. Librarians, archivists, and editors are increasingly collaborating, not least because the basic means of storage and requirements for display of digital assets have converged in searching software, image hosting, metadata norms, and flexible and accessible display frameworks. And so the question of how the priorities, imperatives, and limitations of digital preservation in libraries are beginning to shape those of digital editing gives fundamental structure to this volume. Digital archives studies has for some time been at the forefront of reckoning with the shifting role of academic institutions in cultural preservation—most recently and influentially evidenced by Michelle Caswell's *Urgent Archives*.[14] The librarian F. Gerald Ham heralded what he called the "postcustodial era" of archival policy in an influential address over four decades ago. Archivists' rethinking of their roles in sociopolitical conflict has been constant ever since, led by provocations like Joan M. Schwartz and Terry Cook's essay "Archives, Records and Power" and Verne Harris's framework of memory for justice. Recently, across the globe, there has been a proliferation of postcustodial partnerships with Indigenous tribes and community organizations.[15] Postcustodial effort goes beyond doing preservation in new ways or with new priorities, or providing access for audiences previously blocked from the archives: it seeks to return control of the documents and their representation to descendant communities and interest groups. This reckoning has begun to shape editorial work as well, not merely on noncanonical writers whose work still bears crucial importance for descendant communities, but on major figures whose work treated or was enabled by colonialism, slavery, genocide, and other histories not always considered in traditional editorial treatment. *Futures of Digital Scholarly Editing* evidences a growing exchange of ideas across the professions of archivist and academic editor with respect to transformations happening in the realms of both technological development and professional ethics.

Digital Scholarly Editing's Many Futures

The essays published here emerge from a conversation about the futures of scholarly editing and archival projects at a symposium titled "The Walt Whitman Archive and the Futures of Digital Scholarly Editing," which took place at the University of Nebraska–Lincoln in spring 2021. To foster a conversation among field leaders about the future of scholarly editing and archival projects that could be of use to the entire community of people working on the preservation of literary-cultural resources, we assembled a list of contributors diverse in methodological outlooks, professional contexts (scholars, administrators, librarians), national backgrounds, and length of experience in the field. The contributors were asked some hard questions: How can projects like the Whitman Archive update aging technical infrastructures, configure innovative next-generation plans, and maintain mutually beneficial relationships with the technical partners (usually in libraries and archives) necessary to their survival? How can electronic editing projects imagine new collaborations, both within and beyond the humanities world? Share data in a forward-looking, maintainable, but also ethical way? Expand on international partnerships, global outreach, and social media participation, but again, within a framework oriented toward inclusiveness and justice? As headlines about lawsuits against tech industry leaders like Uber, Google, Amazon, and Apple remind us seemingly every week, the challenges faced by technology innovators have less to do with machines and more to do with human relationships and social responsibility. How can the creators of digital scholarly editing projects respond to crucial questions about ethics and about cultural, linguistic, and gender diversity, questions that are increasingly raised not just in the academy but also in public conversations about technological development? And, ultimately, in an age of mixed feelings about technology, how can such projects continue to play a leading role in shaping questions about what literature and culture are, and how these can be represented and studied in a world both linked and fragmented by digital media?

The editors and a few contributors to the volume are affiliated with or veterans of the Walt Whitman Archive. The Whitman Archive is an excellent example of a long-standing, heavily accessed digital archival project that raises all the questions discussed above about politics, organizations, relations between scholars and archivists, and more. Yet, in conversations at the symposium, it became clear that in many ways it is simply unrepresentative. As evidenced in Ed Folsom's chapter, the Whitman Archive, though free to the end user, has been and remains expensive to build, is dependent on grants, and is not replicable in other institutional contexts. Moreover, while the Whitman Archive has rendered the Good Gray Poet a less monolithic, unitary, single-author figure, nonetheless it could be argued that the canonicity matrix that makes Whitman a representative author for champions of U.S. democracy, queer folk, and innovators of literary form across the globe also benefits the Archive by making it difficult to erode the aura of the author, irrespective of how the Archive is structured. We have tried in these essays to diversify the material evidentiary bases from which contributors argue about the potential futures of digital editorial practice and at the same time to engage both the merits and the faults of projects like the Whitman Archive that have become canonical and materially contributed to the expansion of the field of digital scholarly editing.

The book is divided into two parts, the first focusing on transformations of textual scholarship and the second on the convergence of digital preservation and scholarly editing. This collection was not designed to capture a consensus but rather to stage a conversation—sometimes conflictual, sometimes simply divergent, and occasionally convergent—about many possible futures of digital editing. It is also far from exhaustive. Its dialogic approach is expanded in the Manifold edition of *Futures of Digital Scholarly Editing*. There can be found, in addition to these essays, reflections on the volume by commentators Morris Eaves, Michelle Caswell, Katherine Bode, and John Young, who have experience in areas that weigh on or usefully refract the ideas and positions represented in the collection: scholarly editing, ethical approaches to digital preservation, digital methods for textual recovery, Black and Indigenous textual scholarship, and digital archiving and preservation.

Each chapter enacts a reconsideration of digital scholarly editing, calling for a reconfiguration of its intellectual nature, realm, and stakes. To put it in a Gramscian way, all the chapters in this collection inquire about how to work and what to do for the creation and preservation of organic intellectual ecosystems, rather than traditional and hegemonic hierarchical structures and infrastructures, for digital projects to develop and to persist. All chapters, then, crucially ask readers to shift their thinking. Julia Flanders, Dirk Van Hulle, Stephanie Browner, and Marta Werner ask us to leave aside any monumental conception of an Ur-text (or "cabinet of curiosities," as Werner puts it) and the related teleology of an everlasting, authoritative edition, and to concentrate on textual fluidity and broad cultural heritage, in order to show the ever-changing agencies, relationships, and nonneutral practices (in lieu of static categories) that make and mediate texts. This fluidity exposes the complexity, relationality, and sociality that texts inevitably embody in a co-textual, contextual, paratextual, extra-textual sense. Ephemerality, Werner argues, can even be shown to be an essential quality of the work: a poetic but also editorial *desideratum*.

While Browner points out the complementarities of print and digital formats for authors that have not yet received the intense treatment of scholarly editing, she also notes that scholarly editing and textual-critical trends aren't universally applied to all literatures, and that this differential is important to account for in thinking about scholarly editing as an activity in the broadest sense. Flanders observes that the "idea of a distributed or community-based or 'social' edition can thus take many different forms which, though geometrically analogous in a superficial way, are conceptually quite different in the ways they imagine agency and relationships, and also in the way they imagine human virtue." Ethics vary; the work that would reflect them consequently varies, and the theory that connects the two varies. Her example of rethinking authorial intent from the standpoint of empathy is striking: to respect the author's deletions and deliberate silences rather than "recovering" them would be "to situate the author's work as something other than an object of study, and to orient the editorial enterprise as a whole toward goals other than scholarship as currently understood."

With the proliferation of open-access digital editions, the pressures being brought to bear by communities of interest on the representation of and access to the cultural-heritage record are already being felt by scholarly editors. As several of our contributors note, Michelle Caswell and Maria Cifor propose that archivists think about the affective attachments that a range of readers have to archival documents, and therefore embrace an audience much wider than the academic.[16] Is this true of scholarly editing as well? After all, it's long been the case that specialized audiences and their publication venues produce, from time to time, extraordinary knowledge that would never have been attained without the space granted to complex, and frankly tedious, analysis and debate. Even if one acknowledges with Elena Pierazzo that "pursuing a large readership is not necessarily a desirable outcome for research editions," many of the essays here suggest that scholars of race, sexuality, gender, and identity make arguments that strike deeply at the roots of traditional editorial habits, from the choices of works, texts, and collaborators to funding patterns, the establishment of standards, and questions of copyright.[17] The practices of African American and Indigenous editors increasingly reflect their embedment in particular communities and their traditions, rather than in a professional situation with its own ethos. "The archivist has an ethical obligation to empathize with all parties impacted by archival use," writes Caswell and Cifor (38–39). But does the Black archivist whose work may negatively affect those empowered by White supremacy have to have that universal sympathy? And does the Indigenous archivist need to empathize when wrestling with documents that may help revert control of U.S. territory to a tribe? The same question might be turned to editorial empathy, since by definition the scholarly is, at the moment, regulated by a professional ethos rather than one operating extramurally from the academy. It seems likely, as Flanders implies, that the field of digital scholarly editing will witness a struggle over how to respond to the demand for a broadened ethos of care, attentiveness to communities, and responsibility to a wide audience.

Editors' roles are deeply questioned and revised in these essays. For Van Hulle, the editor is a maker of what Browner calls "generous" connections (which are, as Browner demonstrates, in urgent need of excavation and study in the case of Black literature), and the notion of complete works to be represented has to be fundamentally revised as "oeuvre in motion." Folsom describes the Whitman Archive as an event and part of a field that will soon, he predicts, simply be called "collaborative humanities" instead of "digital humanities." And Nicole Gray, while asking the profound postcustodial question of what and why to preserve, and what and why to let go, reflects on the value of the Whitman Archive not so much as a scholarly repository that documents and organizes the, at times, maddeningly complex compositional and publishing work of a single author, but as a continually changing methodology of understanding and representing that world qua world. While accessibility remains a central issue to be promoted and investigated, so is how to facilitate and empower a revolutionized, community-oriented agency of users and co-creators. At the core of K. J. Rawson's, Sarah Patterson's, and Robert Warrior's reflections are attempts at deconstructing old protocols of metadata and annotation practices, by interrogating their ethical and representational implications for inclusion and exposure in order to avoid new forms of oppression, violence, and dispossession. These shifts involve developing new models centered in an ethics of care directed primarily at people and community and less at objects and documents. Interrogating the "scholarly" is not just a matter of thinking about the scope, content, labor model, or rhetorical stance of a project, as Rawson's piece points out: "When contextualized within the extensive history of cisgender researchers benefiting from studying trans people (often with considerable harm done to trans people)," Rawson notes, "it becomes clear that the DTA [Digital Transgender Archive] can contribute to this problematic legacy if we rely too heavily on scholarly engagement as a central indicator of our project's impact." The dream of SNAC (Social Networks and Archival Context), mentioned in John Unsworth's afterword—of a central, free-access repository of information about people—is profoundly complicated by the observations in Rawson's essay, not least by the reflection that "beyond the individualized impacts of sharing more information about specific trans people, both alive and deceased, our project itself contributes to the increased cultural visibility of trans people that can elicit a violent response." With Rawson's piece and several others, we see two developments that complicate the traditional regime of critical judgment. First, they claim that critical judgment is a matter of collaboration, and not only among editors and, in a sense, with the intentions of past subjects or "authors," but with audiences. Second, there is a sense that the potential implications of that critical judgment have widened, to include *not* editing in certain circumstances as a result of this collaborative analysis of a historical subject or text.

Fotis Jannidis's chapter aims at breaking rigid boundaries between editors and audiences but also between the subfields of scholarly editing and computational studies, exploring the promising results of their combined efforts. Elena Pierazzo, sympathizing with this aim but complicating its prosecution, discusses the potentials but also problematic implications of distant editing. Pierazzo sees us in a developing "prolegomena of a computational revolution in editing." The automatic recognition of handwritten text and other computer vision advances. But the dark side, she warns (echoing Alan Liu's caveats in his essay on data and transcendence), is that development of these technologies is happening rapidly in the private sector and not as fast among humanists.[18] Jannidis is certainly one of those humanistic developers, but while providing a vivid example of the potential mutual benefits for computational literary studies (CLS) and editorial practice, he concurs that field conditions are not yet ideal for the evolution of this kind of work. Noting, for example, the divergent "error culture[s]" within which computational linguists and editors work, he calls for the kind of mutual appreciation of working methods and timelines that facilitates interdisciplinary collaboration and, indeed, the very imagining of new projects. Jannidis's examples of the utility of CLS for editors suggest that, in the near future, thanks to advances in natural language processing (NLP) techniques, editors may be leaving some of the textual marking they have traditionally done to computers, but also that editors may need to start thinking about what features are markable that, at least for the moment, elude or exceed the AI capacities available to most of us. Put another way, editors, depending on their goals, may not need to tag place names or rhymes, but might want to tag features of the text that would allow for CLS analysis in or across large textual objects. A number of other issues to be mobilized and rethought emerge from the collection: Cassidy Holahan, Aylin Malcom, and Whitney Trettien discuss how digital platforms like Manicule can bring to light and facilitate new (but also old) practices of "not-reading," by consulting, touring, visualizing, and experiencing texts nonlinearly. Warrior's essay would reframe thinking about such platforms in the light of sovereignty histories. Warrior asks us to consider what it would mean to archive the products of Indigenous presses and to account for the particular material necessities for doing that archiving, but also audience relations, project imperatives and benefits, and questions about who receives those benefits. But one might derive from his observations a yet more challenging suggestion: to think about how *any* activity of archiving and editing could be oriented toward the restoration of Indigenous land, self-determination, and political primacy. The question is raised by postcustodial archival theorists in many cases, but it's one that has yet quite to register at the level of editorial work based in questions of textual materiality. What would it mean to ground the work more literally in questions of land, dismantlings of settler colonialism, and reconfigurations of agency and authority? Any editorial project might be thought about in terms of what populations it benefits. Imagine a digital edition of Shakespeare whose goal was to center Indigenous sovereignty and the land-back potential of editorial work, a decolonizing stance both material and intellectual. It's less hard now to imagine such editions of Native materials, thanks to the Mukurtu platform, or to Siobhan Senier's editorial work, or to editions like Blaire Morseau's of Simon Pokagon's birch-bark books.[19] But what happens when, at least for U.S.-based projects or materials, it is a matter of the organization and orientation of the entire enterprise, rather than merely about the content?

What Goes Unsaid

"If you listen closely to editors editing," writes Eaves, sagely, "you will hear the harsh sounds of primal conflict as visionary aspirations clash with reality."[20] While the essays here are informed in part by the conversations we had at the symposium, those conversations also revealed some areas of concern not covered in this volume, and others that, if not quite reaching the level of primal conflict, were shared by the contributors but difficult to resolve, often involving that tension between vision and reality. We report them here without having fully formed addresses to or stances in relation to them, in the spirit of continuing the dialogue with a broader audience.

To make relationality, communities, and contexts the foci or axes of editorial initiatives is a major shift, called for by some of the contributors here, in the spirit of those feminist and antiracist intellectual interventions. But what, other participants wondered, are the practicalities involved with being more "social" and more community engaged? And how do we redescribe *editing* or *scholarly* differently in order to do that? Our colleagues in rhetoric and composition studies and public history, to say nothing of libraries doing postcustodial initiatives, might have some guidance for us.[21] For starters, if the community is a key editorial partner, and the resource being built is a valuable one in that community, then thinking about an edition or archive's sustainability—thinking about its ending, as Gray asks us to do from the start—has to involve factors and structures beyond those of hardware/software sustainability or finding an institutional home for the data.[22]

Two factors in that thinking emerged in discussion: First, it was clear from Rawson's and Gray's work, for example, that the conversations that go into the editorial decisions are a key site of intellectual contribution, and not just in the sense that a good conclusion worth reporting to the field is reached, but rather that, conclusion or no, hosting a difficult conversation requires its own foresight, careful navigation, protocol creation, and so on. Yet the methods, ethics, and rewards of reporting these to an academic readership are not, perhaps, as straightforward as the traditional "note on the text." Second, given this more socially immersed but still text-interested vision of editorial work, how will the training of students be structured? By what means can ethics and employability, and textual historical rigor and the navigation of community politics, be taught together? Participants also wondered whether it was only a matter of individual scholars or their working groups declaring and enforcing ethical standards, or whether some structural change might be imagined. Librarians and archivists have gathered collectives to generate not only the best protocols (comparable to Text Encoding Initiative [TEI]) but also guidelines for professional ethics. Might a coalition of text scholarship groups (e.g., the Association for Documentary Editing, the Bibliographical Society of America, the European Society for Textual Scholarship, the Society for Textual Scholarship, and the Society for the History of Authorship, Readership, and Publishing) think collectively about establishing ethics protocols for editions (broadly defined)? Even were it to fail, the effort could be valuable for what it might tell us about the kinds of investments in the representation of works and texts from the past.

These questions also haunted the discussion of computational approaches to text analysis and representation. Jannidis's essay speaks to the convergence of edition-making with NLP techniques innovated by computational linguists. On the one hand, another path away from TEI encoding as a standard seems to emerge in thinking of the data-table representation of a text and the dream of automatic collation advances.[23] On the other hand, the questions asked about accessibility, the ethics and politics of edition-making, and sustainability loom the larger as we contemplate that other path. One attendee, Melissa Homestead, for example, asked whether canonicity remains a problem with CLS, given the kinds of resources the method requires: it's convenient to have not only an enormous amount of carefully corrected text but also generations of human observations against which to measure computational findings. Do we not then risk perpetuating canonical tendencies? And the question was raised of whether the semantic level of analysis is, from an editor's standpoint, only a first step in computational analysis. How far can we go toward automating *meta* patterns, not just semantic ones, to generate the kind of evidence needed to make humanistic claims about authors and their evolutions in terms of craft methods?

Pierazzo's essay provocatively asks us to think comparatively about the shifts in editorial theory and practice in the digital age, drawing on the history of linguistics as a field. It was noted in conversation that the pressures on computational linguistics were coming from outside the academy, from Google and other search engine developers, Amazon, medical insurance analysts, and so on, and that this had the double impact of thinning the professorial field (as graduates went into industry instead of the academy) and impacting, in a range of ways, the kind of research that was valued in dissertations, articles, and the like. Might this, too, be instructive as we think about how digital humanities and textual scholarship are evolving, and might evolve in the future? In general, it was noted that the pedagogical questions raised by the contributions could be treated much more deeply.

Interoperability seems self-evidently valuable, and is lauded widely in digital humanities literature and best-practices documents. Yet both Patterson and Rawson raise the question of what happens when not just metadata categories but their underlying ethics differ or are so highly mobile or capacious that individual editorial projects struggle to employ them. One thinks not just of the attempt to bring Library of Congress metadata standards into dialogue with, say, those of the Homosaurus or emerging Native American data nomenclatures, but with other synoptic resources like SNAC.[24] And for all its potential and the effort involved to enact it, interoperability does not guarantee re-use, and so we return to the question of interface, both social and technical. Yet, as Pierazzo and others have observed, interfaces, with their many technical and contextual contingencies, are "extremely fragile and very hard to sustain in the long term."[25] Fragility emerged, then, in our discussions of funding, interface design, preservation, and metadata standards.

Fragility seemed significantly a financial matter for many participants. In looking to the future of digital editions, it is clear that more attention needs to be paid to economics. To produce an open-access edition is not the only way to proceed, but it remains a widely embraced ideal, though a challenging one. Ambitious open access sites are free to the end user, but they are typically expensive to produce. For scholars wishing to create fully realized digital editions, freely available and comprehensive in scope, the difficulties are daunting. Lacking a revenue stream from sales, and with institutional support limited in volatile financial times, and with the fit between a project's goals and the shifting priorities of funding agencies varying from project to project, editors have much to juggle as they strive to build, maintain, and preserve their editions. In fact, the financial landscape is inadequately understood because of a lack of overarching studies of the economics of digital editions. Digital editorial work is still relatively new, takes multiple forms, and treats material of wide-ranging scope and complexity. As the editors of the 2006 anthology *Electronic Textual Editing* put it, "[past] scholarly debates over what sorts of editions to produce—whether favoring the textual object, the author of the text, or the text's reception history—were driven as much by economics as by ideology. Quite simply, one could not have it all."[26] "I do not see," wrote Kathryn Sutherland a few years later, "that the economics (in a wide sense) of the thing really add up as yet." Over a decade later, today's advocates of minimal computing would agree.[27] Grant funding and the priorities of agencies and foundations matter a great deal if open-access publishing of truly ambitious work is to flourish. Literary scholars hardly want the digital realm to reinscribe a conservative canon. Still, it is possible that the "significance" question that is often the opening question faced by editors when drafting grant proposals can inadvertently serve to reinforce established reputations and hierarchies. To put this another way: who decides what matters? What risks might there be in having foundations and federal agencies take such an oversized role in shaping what from the past can thrive in the present and thus live in the future?

Finally, the valence of the term *scholar* in scholarly editing often seemed interrogated in thinking about the implications of the contributors' visions of the future. Do we need to rethink or move away from it? In literary studies, this rethinking was initiated by the postcritical movement; Eve Sedgwick, Bruno Latour, and more recently Rita Felski have been considered the avatars of the movement, but it was started long before by African American and feminist scholars of the 1960s and 1970s, criticizing and reworking the habitual hierarchies of the academy.[28] One could think in many ways about this redefinition of the scholar. On the one hand, for example, one could celebrate public humanities, a return to the big media relevance of scholarship—perhaps scholars could win back their cultural authority from the post-truth movement. On the other hand, it could be argued that such a move is a capitulation to neoliberal audience shifts that administrations are currently encouraging, particularly in public universities but not exclusively so, in order to recalibrate the university's activities not to intellectual or ethical goals but quite openly to instrumental, capitalistic ones. In any case, despite the affordances of the academic institutional environment, it is hard to ignore the vast and powerful gatekeeping apparatus (which functions both passively and actively and not always positively) that underwrites the term "scholarly."

Why "digital" scholarly editions? In part, this term signals our focus on a subset of the ongoing conversation about textual scholarship and edition-making more broadly. If it may have looked briefly as if digital editions would become the only editions, recent years have witnessed not only the strength of the print edition but the rise of "hybrid" editions (like this one) in both print and digital formats.[29] Our focus is on the ongoing impact of and potentials for digital affordances in the work of textual representation. But many of the issues discussed by our contributors, particularly with respect to the work of the editor and the ethics of editorial work in a shifting political, economic, and intellectual landscape, speak more broadly to the question of scholarly editing's futures as a practice in any format. "To even talk about *digital* editions as one particular type of edition is debatable," asserts Mats Dahlström.[30] The point is fair, and perhaps the essays here only underscore the practical nature of our choice of title phrase, to focus on editing more than editions.

In 2006, the editors of *Electronic Textual Editing* made an observation that still rings true:

> Even if we start the history of electronic scholarly editions with Father Busa's punch-card Aquinas in 1949, we are not many decades into developing an understanding of how to make and use electronic documents in general, let alone electronic scholarly editions in particular.[31]

The subtitle of Peter Shillingsburg's 1986 *Scholarly Editing in the Computer Age: Theory and Practice* indicates a consequent theme appearing in the many tomes on scholarly digital editing that would follow it: finding themselves in a fast-evolving computational environment, editors of volumes precedent to ours often tried hard to keep up with the present (sharing resources, software solutions, and detailed case studies) even as they thought about what could be to come.[32] *Electronic Textual Editing* included a CD-ROM containing the TEI guidelines, as the editors noted that experience with digital editing to that point tended "to be shared in the form of theoretical speculation rather than as practical guidance" (12). *Futures of Digital Scholarly Editing* does feature some concrete examples of projects doing new things and taking new stances toward editorial activity, stances that at times explicitly or implicitly part ways rather than offering a speculative catechism; but it offers no practical standards or guides, and does a good deal of speculating about potential, and potentially diverging, futures. "From time to time editing is admitted to be a subjective activity," Shillingsburg wrote back in 1986, "and if that is so, arguments may never cease" (5).

The shibboleth in textual scholarship that denies objectivity in editing has a long pedigree. What is interesting about the recent insights from critical race theory, postcolonialism, feminism, and queer studies, however, is that it's not only the impossibility of an objective stance that Hans-Georg Gadamer long ago warned of that we must consider, but the negative effects, racist and otherwise, of the belief in, pursuit of, and advocacy for objectivity, however impossible. A version of this debate has played out recently in the circles of digital humanities, particularly over the question of the role of big data or computational corpus analysis in literary scholarship.[33] Part of the difficulty is that, the wider the audience for our editorial work, the more likely some part of it will desire a totalizing authority claim for our version of a work or archive of texts. The practitioners of Black bibliography, feminist bibliography, and queer bibliography ask us to embrace the difficulties presented by the web's widening of audiences for scholarly work as an occasion to change our approaches, rhetorics, and collaborations in ways that will fight patriarchy, white supremacy, xenophobia, homophobia, ableism, and other forms of prejudice and inequality.

"The scholarly editor is interested in the remains of the past and in what those remains tell us about the origin and transmission of texts," writes David Greetham. Yet decisions about editing, he goes on to say, "must always rest on a careful and articulate assessment of past and present."[34] This yoking of past and present signals a more sophisticated sense of the historicist mentality than, say, G. Thomas Tanselle's dichotomy of "historical" and "nonhistorical."[35] Not only backward looking, and far from a simple opposition of presentism and historicism, Greetham's sense of "assessment" involves the scholar's choice of contextual focus in the past and awareness of the present-day impetus, which indelibly marks any act of historicism. If an editor chooses to assess the past as, say, Christina Sharpe does—slavery's context extending into the present, in a struggle to extend itself into the future—then she may think differently about everything from punctuation to copy text from how she would if she believes that was then and this is now.[36] Scholarly editors, steeped in this navigation of past and present, may also be good guides, whether cautionary or utopian, to potential futures during fraught times, and we hope these essays help foster both conversation and experimentation to that end.

NOTES

1. Patrick Sahle, *A Catalogue of Digital Scholarly Editions,* updated 2023, digitale-edition.de/.

2. Just a few of those helpful works, in addition to those cited later in this volume, include Daniel Apollon, Claire Bélisle, and Philippe Régnier, eds., *Digital Critical Editions* (Champaign: University of Illinois Press, 2014); Elena Pierazzo and Matthew James Driscoll, eds., *Digital Scholarly Editing: Theories and Practices* (Cambridge: Cambridge University Press, 2016); Darcy Cullen, ed., *Editors, Scholars, and the Social Text* (Toronto: University of Toronto Press, 2012); Elizabeth Bergmann Loizeaux and Neil Fraistat, eds., *Reimagining Textuality: Textual Studies in the Late Age of Print* (Madison: University of Wisconsin Press, 2002); Richard J. Finneran, ed., *The Literary Text in the Digital Age* (Ann Arbor: University of Michigan Press, 1996); Peter Robinson, "What Is a Critical Digital Edition?," *Variants* 1 (2002): 43–62; Paul Eggert, *Securing the Past: Conservation in Art, Architecture and Literature* (Cambridge: Cambridge University Press, 2009); Eggert, *The Work and the Reader in Literary Studies: Scholarly Editing and Book History* (Cambridge: Cambridge University Press, 2019); and Jerome J. McGann, "The Rationale of HyperText," *Text* 9 (1996): 11–32.

3. Alan Galey, "Signal to Noise: Designing a Digital Edition of *The Taming of a Shrew*," *College Literature* 36, no. 1 (2009): 42.

4. Ted Underwood, "Dear Humanists: Fear Not the Digital Revolution," *Chronicle of Higher Education* 65, no. 29 (2019), chronicle.com/article/dear-humanists-fear-not-the-digital-revolution/.

5. Colored Conventions Project, coloredconventions.org/.

6. "Colored Convention Project Principles," Colored Conventions Project, coloredconventions.org/about/principles/. See also Jacqueline Wernimont, *Numbered Lives: Life and Death in Quantum Media* (Cambridge, Mass.: MIT Press, 2019).

7. Johanna Drucker, "Humanities Approaches to Graphical Display," *digital humanities quarterly* 5, no. 1 (2011), digitalhumanities.org/dhq/vol/5/1/000091/000091.html.

8. Bethany Nowviskie, "Digital Humanities in the Anthropocene," *Digital Scholarship in the Humanities* 30, supplement 1 (2015): i4–i15.

9. "Santa Barbara Statement on Collections as Data," collectionsasdata.github.io/statement/.

10. To cite just a few of these, from a vibrant and widespread conversation: Sylvia Wynter, "Unsettling the Coloniality of Being/Power/Truth/Freedom: Towards the Human, after Man, Its Overrepresentation—an Argument," *CR: The New Centennial Review* 3, no. 3 (2003): 257–37; Autumn Womack, "Reprinting the Past/Re-Ordering Black Social Life," *American Literary History* 32, no. 4 (2020): 755–80; Kate Ozment,

"Rationale for Feminist Bibliography," *Textual Cultures* 13, no. 1 (2020):149–78; Derrick Spires, "On Liberation Bibliography: The 2021 BSA Annual Meeting Keynote," *Papers of the Bibliographical Society of America* 116, no. 1 (2022): 1–20; Christen A. Smith, Erica L. Williams, Imani A. Wadud, Whitney N. L. Pirtle, and The Cite Black Women Collective, "Cite Black Women: A Critical Praxis (A Statement)," *Feminist Anthropology* 2, no. 1 (2021): 10–17; Clare Mullaney, "Dickinson, Disability, and a Crip Editorial Practice," in *The New Emily Dickinson Studies*, ed. Michelle Kohler (Cambridge: Cambridge University Press, 2019), 280–98; Jeffrey Masten, *Queer Philologies: Sex, Language, and Affect in Shakespeare's Time* (Philadelphia: University of Pennsylvania Press, 2016); Daniel Heath Justice, *Why Indigenous Literatures Matter* (Waterloo, Ontario: Wilfred Laurier University Press, 2018); Phillip H. Round, *Removable Type: Histories of the Book in Indian Country, 1663–1880* (Chapel Hill: University of North Carolina Press, 2010); and Roopika Risam, *New Digital Worlds: Postcolonial Digital Humanities in Theory, Praxis, and Pedagogy* (Evanston, Ill.: Northwestern University Press, 2018).

11. See Jerome J. McGann, *The Textual Condition* (Princeton, N.J.: Princeton University Press, 1991).

12. Marilyn Deegan, "Collection and Preservation of an Electronic Edition," in *Electronic Textual Editing*, ed. Lou Burnard, Katherine O'Brien O'Keeffe, and John Unsworth (New York: Modern Language Association of America, 2006), 359.

13. James Smithies et al., "Managing 100 Digital Humanities Projects: Digital Scholarship & Archiving in King's Digital Lab," *digital humanities quarterly* 13, no. 1 (2019), digitalhumanities.org/dhq/vol/13/1/000411/000411.html.

14. Michelle Caswell, *Urgent Archives: Enacting Liberatory Memory Work* (New York: Routledge, 2021).

15. See F. Gerald Ham, "Archival Strategies for the Post-Custodial Era," *The American Archivist* 44, no. 3 (1981): 207–16; Joan M. Schwartz and Terry Cook, "Archives, Records and Power: The Making of Modern Memory," *Archival Science* 2 (2002): 1–19; Verne Harris, *Archives and Justice: A South African Perspective* (Chicago: Society of American Archivists, 2007); and more recently, Dorothy Berry, "The House Archives Built," *up//root*, 2021, uproot.space/features/the-house-archives-built. For an early rumination on postcolonial bibliography, see D. C. Greetham, "Textual Imperialism, Post-Colonial Bibliography, and the Poetics of Culture," in *Textual Transgressions: Essays Towards the Construction of a Biobibliography* (New York: Garland, 1998), 581–82.

16. Michelle Caswell and Marika Cifor, "From Human Rights to Feminist Ethics: Radical Empathy in the Archives," *Archivaria* 81 (2016): 23–43.

17. Elena Pierazzo, *Digital Scholarly Editing: Theories, Models and Methods* (Farnham, UK: Ashgate, 2015), 9. On copyright being held in part by communities, see Catherine Bell and Val Napoleon, "Introduction, Methodology, and Thematic Overview," in *First Nations Cultural Heritage and Law: Case Studies, Voices, and Perspectives*, ed.

Catherine Bell and Val Napoleon (Vancouver: University of British Columbia Press, 2008).

18. Alan Liu, "Transcendental Data: Toward a Cultural History and Aesthetics of the New Encoded Discourse," *Critical Inquiry* 31, no. 4 (2004): 49–84.

19. Mukurtu CMS, mukurtu.org/; Siobhan Senier, *Sovereignty and Sustainability: Indigenous Literary Stewardship in New England* (Lincoln: University of Nebraska Press, 2020); Blaire Morseau, ed., *As Sacred to Us: Simon Pokagon's Birch Bark Stories in Their Contexts* (East Lansing: Michigan State University Press, 2023); see also Kelly Wisecup, *Assembled for Use: Indigenous Compilation and the Archives of Early Native American Literatures* (New Haven, Conn.: Yale University Press, 2021).

20. Morris Eaves, "Multimedia Body Plans: A Self-Assessment," in Burnard, O'Keeffe, and Unsworth, *Electronic Textual Editing*, 221.

21. Among others, rhetoric and composition scholar Gabrielle Kelenyi has written about the praxis of adult writing instruction as benefitting from a formally distanced relation between the writing group and the university, as the university can be an antagonistic or inhibitive space for many people ("Our Writing Group: How Low-Income Adults Built a University-Adjacent Writing Community" [PhD diss., University of Wisconsin–Madison, 2023]). Critical-editorial initiatives already feature a range of institutional relations with academic institutions—a perhaps underappreciated realm of textual scholarly creativity—but a deliberate approach to questioning the effect of the university as a culture or setting seemed to be called for by a number of the interlocutors in our discussions.

22. This would presumably be the case irrespective of the location or common thread of the community, from, say, the Indigenous communities for which the Mukurtu platform was built to the space-distributed Trans Metadata Collective that informed, via Slack, the development of the Homosaurus.

23. For other interrogations of TEI, see John Lavagnino, "When Not to Use TEI," in Lou Burnard, Katherine O'Brien O'Keeffe, and John Unsworth, *Electronic Textual Editing*, 334–38; and Desmond Schmidt, "The Inadequacy of Embedded Markup for Cultural Heritage Texts," *Literary and Linguistic Computing* 25, no. 3 (2010): 337–56.

24. SNAC, snaccooperative.org/.

25. *Digital Scholarly Editing*, 9

26. Lou Burnard, Katherine O'Brien O'Keeffe, and John Unsworth, "Introduction," in Burnard, O'Keeffe, and Unsworth, *Electronic Textual Editing*, 11.

27. Kathryn Sutherland, "Being Critical: Paper-Based Editing and the Digital Environment," in *Text Editing: Print and the Digital World*, ed. Marilyn Deegan and Kathryn Sutherland (Burlington, Vt.: Ashgate, 2009), 25. Among other proposals, Sutherland suggests that digital editions consider print-on-demand capabilities to produce reading texts that might quickly saturate smaller readerships (24). For a thoughtful summary and questioning of the minimal-computing movement, see Quinn Dombrowski, "Minimal Computing Maximizes Labor," *digital humanities quarterly* 16, no. 2 (2022), digitalhumanities.org/dhq/vol/16/2/000594/000594.html.

28. Eve Kosofsky Sedgwick, *Novel Gazing: Queer Readings in Fiction* (Durham, N.C.: Duke University Press, 1997); Bruno Latour, "Why Has Critique Run Out of Steam?: From Matters of Fact to Matters of Concern," *Critical Inquiry* 30 (2004), 225–248; Rita Felski, *The Limits of Critique* (Chicago: University of Chicago Press, 2015); but see also bell hooks, *Feminist Theory: From Margin to Center* (1984; repr. London: Pluto, 2000); and Brittney C. Cooper, *Beyond Respectability: The Intellectual Thought of Race Women* (Urbana: University of Illinois Press, 2017).

29. On hybrid editions, see, among others, David Gants, "Drama Case Study: The Cambridge Edition of the Works of Ben Jonson," in Burnard, O'Keeffe, and Unsworth, *Electronic Textual Editing*, 122–37; Stephanie P. Browner and Kenneth M. Price, "Charles Chesnutt and the Case for Hybrid Editing," *International Journal of Digital Humanities* 1 (2019): 165–78; and Linda Bree and James McLaverty, "The Cambridge Edition of the Works of Jonathan Swift and the Future of the Scholarly Edition," in Deegan and Sutherland, *Text Editing*, 127–36.

30. Mats Dahlström, "The Compleat Edition," in Deegan and Sutherland, *Text Editing*, 29.

31. Burnard, O'Keeffe, and Unsworth, "Introduction," 20.

32. Peter L. Shillingsburg, *Scholarly Editing in the Computer Age: Theory and Practice* (Athens: University of Georgia Press, 1986). See also the later, 3rd edition, published by the University of Michigan Press in 1996. "I do not think editing is a science," Shillingsburg wrote, "nor do I think many editors undertake their onerous tasks for any reason other than love" (7).

33. Hans-Georg Gadamer, *Truth and Method,* trans. Joel Weinsheimer and Donald G. Marshall (New York: Continuum, 2004); Ted Underwood, "The Theoretical Divide Driving Debates about Computation," *Critical Inquiry* 46, no. 4 (2020): 900–912; Nan Z. Da, "On EDA, Complexity, and Redundancy: A Response to Underwood and Weatherby," *Critical Inquiry* 46, no. 4 (2020): 913–24; Lisa Gitelman, *'Raw Data' Is an Oxymoron* (Cambridge, Mass.: MIT Press, 2013); and Wernimont, *Numbered Lives.*

34. David C. Greetham, "Introduction," in *Scholarly Editing: A Guide to Research,* ed. David C. Greetham (New York: Modern Language Association of America, 1995), 6.

35. G. Thomas Tanselle, "The Varieties of Scholarly Editing," in Greetham, *Scholarly Editing*, 11, 18.

36. Christina Sharpe, *In the Wake: On Blackness and Being* (Durham, N.C.: Duke University Press, 2014). For a provocative recent meditation in this mode, see Bianca Swift, "'Time Enough but None to Spare': Chesnutt Alive in Today's Archive," *Scholarly Editing* 40 (2023).

PART I

TRANSFORMATIONS OF TEXTUAL SCHOLARSHIP

CHAPTER 1

Distant Editing

The Challenges of Computational Methods to the Theory and Practice of Textual Scholarship

ELENA PIERAZZO

Back in 2015, I published a couple of books about digital scholarly editing, in which I reflected hard and long about editing.[1] Now, only a few years later, I have the impression that I wrote these books in a completely different environment. What has changed in the meantime? For a start, I did not mention artificial intelligence (AI), deep learning, or computer vision. At the time, discussions of digital scholarly editing were centered around the representation of sources and how computers would help us better understand a variety of text-bearing objects. At the time, computational approaches were scarce and, for the most part, marginal to the core activity of editing documents and texts. The main exceptions were automatic collation and phylogenetic methods for stemmatology, and even these struggled to be accepted by digital editors: no matter how revolutionary we thought them to be at the time, these approaches, most of us concluded, yielded relatively few benefits for the initiated and were challenging for the average researcher.[2] For these approaches, we mostly discussed the "black-box" problem, the need to respond to communities of practice and their expectations, and the need to propose tools and methods that can be easily accessible, understandable, and verifiable by the researcher in the humanities.

The use of automatic collation, in particular, was opposed because the hand transcription of all extant witnesses seemed to be an unnecessary addition to the already heavy list of editorial duties. At the time, the idea that we could transcribe manuscripts with optical character recognition (OCR) was almost sci-fi, and even though the Transkribus project started in 2013, its results were limited and kept within the inner circle of the project members. On the other side, phylogenetic approaches were viewed with suspicion and stacked in a methodological loop: if we already know what the stemma looks like, how can we be sure that we are not influenced by what we know? And if we do not know what the stemma looks like, how can we trust algorithms and procedures that we cannot control?

The use of computational analysis was not unknown to digital humanities (DH) and particularly to literary scholars, of course: the work of Franco Moretti, Matthew Jockers, and Patrick Joula, to mention only a few, was making front-page news already. Distant reading and authorship attribution were getting to very important results, like the unmasking of Robert Galbraith, which also opened an allegedly new preoccupation for literary scholars: ethics. And yet, these approaches seemed far away from the digital editor's preoccupations, particularly because they almost completely ignored (when they didn't openly oppose) the very idea of adding markup to texts, which represents the methodological core of digital editing. Later, I will discuss this further. For many of us, the main preoccupations of digital editors were (and still are) text representation and presentation, the workflow of a digital edition, the taxonomy and recognition of the phenomenology of the written page, objectivity and interpretation, and the sustainability of our editions. Nevertheless, thanks to some pioneering researchers, we are now starting to see the prolegomena of a computational revolution in editing.

I will start this analysis by tackling the so-called handwriting text recognition (HTR) revolution and, in general, computer vision and deep-learning algorithms applied to images of ancient books. The development of the Transkribus platform and the first results produced by the Venice Time Machine, as well as the research done by Lambert Schomaker in artificial intelligence and pattern recognition, highlighted the enormous potential of computer vision applied to manuscripts;[3] a pioneering work produced by Mike Kestemont and published in *Speculum* wowed first the medieval studies community, and then everybody else.[4] In his work, Kestemont showed how a neural network could recognize and classify manuscripts by type of script, and within these scripts, group them by area of production. The impact of this research has been profound, and the community of medievalists has shown a new openness to this kind of research. Kestemont is now working on the manuscript production of Carthusian monks and showing how AI can "see" things that were overseen by editors, like a change of hands, for instance, thus unveiling writing practices that are likely to transform our understanding of how medieval scriptoria within monasteries worked.[5] Scholars of the Middle Ages understand that we know the content of only about 9 percent of all the medieval codices that still exist scattered in the world's libraries, and computational approaches promise to help us "read" them for the first time.[6] Libraries are making available online millions and millions of high-quality images of manuscripts. To paraphrase Greg Crane: what shall we do with millions of manuscript images?[7] This availability, the development of interoperable standards for harvesting data across countries and libraries (the development of international image interoperability Framework [IIIF] has been enormously important), and the standardization of data and metadata thanks to the Text Encoding Initiative (TEI) and the FAIR (Findable–Accessible–Interoperable–Reusable) protocol—all are contributing factors to the uptake of computational methods in manuscript studies. The transformative potential of this research can be seen via some examples based on medieval material, where these developments have been most impactful.

The work of Dominique Stutzmann has been groundbreaking. Stutzmann was, in fact, the person that launched the competition/hackathon that prompted Kestemont's research, and has been one of the first paleographers to engage with computational methods for transcriptions.[8] His most recent work is focused on quantitative codicology, and in particular on the use of AI and natural language processing for studying books of hours.[9] These prayer books for the use of the laity were the "bestseller" of the Middle Ages. Produced in large numbers from the thirteenth century throughout Western Europe and more numerous than the biblical manuscripts, they are a primary source for the history of religious sentiment and social practices, but also the circulation of texts and transmissions between different regions or even the processes of industrialization of book production, because they are largely standardized. Before the invention of printing in the West, they were the first so-called "shelf" books produced by booksellers outside of any religious order, shifting the book from an economy of demand to an economy of offer. These luxury books were often richly decorated and gave rise to the formalization of stable iconographic cycles, such as that of the Childhood of Christ.

Although they are known to all medievalists, especially to art historians, books of hours are often overlooked or despised as standard mass production: they are so abundant that nobody has ever dared to study them. From a textual perspective, they are impossible to manage: they are compilations of compilations, they are produced in series, and they transcend the idea of contamination. Using a combination of traditional techniques and computational approaches, the first results are merging, and they are mind-blowing: we can now see how distinctive groups of production, different offices, and different liturgical emphases serve different communities. Books of hours feature a huge variation, for instance, in handling psalms: some have one, some have 130; some psalms were very popular, others were barely known.

Another type of research using computational analysis is the one produced at the École Nationale des Chartes in Paris. The team is led by Jean-Baptiste Camps, but features other young scholars such as Ariane Pinche, Thibault Clérice, Elena Spadini, and Simon Gabay.[10] They have successfully applied stylometry and automatic collation to "noisy" medieval data. Their research earned them the Fortier Prize for the most innovative research at the DH conference in Utrecht in 2019.[11] What does "noisy" mean here? Namely that, for instance, in the tradition of the *Chanson de Roland* or of the *Roman de la Rose,* we count twenty-seven different spellings of the word "horse," or that in any given line of a medieval text we can see variations of spelling mixed up with substantial variation, making almost impossible the use of automatic collation. Here AI approaches are combined with linguistic models, which in turn are based on databases of dictionaries. The work championed by this team shows that, in fact, one can use marked-up text in TEI (or another markup system) to apply stylometric analysis, and that, contrary to some previous criticisms, it can be very useful. In fact, the annotation in TEI allows one, for instance, to normalize words, align versions, or establish equivalences. Camps is also responsible for elaborating the model of computational philology, bridging together in a coherent workflow all the "pieces" that we have seen so far: from digitizing and distributing images using IIIF to transcribing them automatically, to collating them, annotating them, re-collating them, proposing stemmas, and finally editing. At the end of his talks, he always asks the same question: are we really there yet? The answer is no, not quite, but we are getting there, one algorithm at a time.[12]

Peter Stokes and his teams at the École Pratique des Hautes Études in collaboration with the Institut National pour la Robotique et l'Intelligence Artificielle (INRIA), are working toward the democratization of these tools: the elaboration of eScriptorium,[13] an open source, free platform for the automatic transcription of manuscripts, is progressing in efforts to allow TEI downloads of transcribed texts that can be published via the TEI Publisher.[14] These tools are particularly developed to handle non-Latin, non-left-to-right scripts, but of course, they have been used for any kind of writing, including early modern and modern manuscripts.

With all this progress in new research, what are the implications for textual scholarship, and more specifically, what will scholarly editing look like in ten years? More pointedly, will we be put out of the editing business by computers? Not yet, anyway. Of course, I do not have a crystal ball, but I can look at the past and see what happened a few years ago when computational methods arrived in the germane field of linguistics, and use that as a way to outline some scenarios. To do so, I will use the words of Karen Spärck Jones, one of the leading researchers responsible for that uptake. In an article from 2007 that was published posthumously by her friends and colleagues, she reflects on the fact that, in mainstream linguistics journals, there is no trace of computational linguistics topics and vice versa—and then she candidly asked, "Does it matter?"[15] Reflecting on the early stages of the evolution of computational linguistics, she noted how, at first, the use of computational methods was hailed as an amazing innovation by many, but that only a few lucky ones were able to use them, since computers were scarce and their use was limited. From compartmentalization came suspicion and reciprocal misunderstandings. She argues that

> since then [the 1960s] there has been a divergence. On the computational side, ...research continued and expanded in the 1970s without much input from mainstream linguistics. It had to model process.... Thus, by the 1980s it was already clear that computational linguistics and natural language processing were advancing without referring significantly to mainstream linguistics or being significantly inadequate thereby.

She comes then to a realization: "As this historical summary implies, computational linguistics does not need mainstream, non-computational linguistics, whether to supply intellectual credibility or to ensure progress. Computational linguistics is not just linguistics with some practically useful but theoretically irrelevant and obfuscating nerdie add-ons." She concedes that this is a "comforting conclusion" if "perhaps more than a little arrogant." In her analysis of the field, Spärck Jones states: "The growth of computational linguistics or, more specifically, natural language information processing is increasingly being done by people with a computational rather than linguistic background; machine learning work needs a mathematical, not a linguistic, training." What Spärck Jones is clearly implying is not only that computational linguistics and mainstream linguistics have grown apart, but that there is basically no interchange between the two anymore. Computational linguistics is not linguistics done digitally, but the result of interdisciplinary research in which computer scientists are not at the service of linguists, but have "merged" with them or even taken their places. Finally, Spärck Jones concedes that "we should not forget that mainstream linguistics may have some things to offer us, even if not as many as linguists themselves may suppose."

Let us stop here for a moment. I think that the risk of disenfranchisement suggested here is real. Let us go back a few years and remind ourselves about what happened when Google Books was the fancy new toy that everybody wanted to play with. The development of the Ngram viewer, and particularly the closing keynote given at DH2011 in Stanford by Jean-Baptiste Michel and Erez Lieberman,[16] was welcomed very skeptically by our community, and rightly so: Ngram is trivial and doesn't do anything new, but those guys were able to publish the research results in all the right places (their core article was published on the cover of *Science*)[17]; they got all the media attention, including a TED talk,[18] and we did not; they were seen and depicted as the ones who brought the humanities into the twenty-first century, and they were doing it under our nose. We may not crave that kind of attention, but there is a problem here.

These algorithms and these techniques are hard to master, and while learning XML and TEI can be done quite easily by the average researcher in the humanities with a few hours of training, these cannot. As Spärck Jones said, "machine learning work needs a mathematical, not a linguistic [and editorial] training," and algorithms require a commitment and a drive that I can only try to imagine, or, better, a partnership and a division of labor, where a humanist matches up with a computer scientist. We are all for collaboration, but this could also be seen as an intellectual surrender, since it implies giving up control of one's research and putting it straight into the black box. Once we give the power to someone to decide what can and what cannot be done, then we give someone the power over our research, and we are back where we didn't want to be when we chose to get our hands dirty with code. Of course, we can work with trusted colleagues if we are lucky enough to find them, but what if things go wrong? Who ends up "owning" the research?

Another factor to consider is that computational approaches work only with large datasets, and therefore may not be applicable to most editorial projects, so we might think we are safe and that this revolution does not concern us. However, the fact that we are left out, so to speak, from the latest cutting-edge development may mean that we are no longer the coolest kids on the block and that research funding may prove harder to get; the significance of our research and of our scholarship may become less certain. We know that digital editing has been used as a way for textual scholarship to regain some academic momentum after many decades during which editing was seen as not being so cool or seen as a "service" to other scholars. The risk now is that the significance and standing of our research might decline. And, if the texts we care about are not amenable to computational approaches, they might end up not being edited at all.

I do not mean here to be alarmist about computational methods and editing. On the contrary: I think the potential of this research is inspiring, and as I said after hearing presentations by Kerstemont, Stutzmann, and Camps in October 2021 at a conference in Nijmegen,[19] my purpose in life may have been to attend that session! I can't wait to see what distant editing will look like: maybe we will be able to discover when we started to hyphenate words, which kind of Dante was read in the eighteenth century, which author most influenced the development of Renaissance in Europe, or even be able to edit texts such as the Bible or the *Commedia* by Dante considering their entire tradition, and not just a handful of witnesses. In short, the digital editing community should embrace these methods and see what we can do with them. The greatest risk here, in my opinion, is to be left behind instead of being at the forefront, as we used to be. This "embracing" must take many forms, and at the least, these:

1. We need training in and at least a basic understanding of AI concepts, methods, and techniques.
2. We need ideas, we need creativity: what can be done is what we will dream of doing, and then the technology will follow—we cannot be the ones to follow the technology.
3. We need to care about ethics.

As mentioned before, the "unmasking" of Robert Galbraith, to which we can add the unmasking of Elena Ferrante, that was done by members of our community has raised a series of questions, aired in major newspapers. The discussion has also taken a gendered flavor,[20] with men seen as unable to stand the success of women writers and treating their anonymity as a crime. But besides these considerations, the question that our community has not yet asked enough is the following: does the fact that we can do something mean that we always should do it? Does the fact that we can tell who is behind the name of Robert Galbraith mean that we are allowed to expose J. K. Rowling? Michele Cortelazzo, who led the team researching Ferrante, claims that using a pseudonym is an indirect call for publicity; therefore, he felt completely free to undertake this research.[21] Whether we agree or not with this statement, questions of ethics and deontology should be taken seriously, as other disciplines have done.

And here I am not talking about only authorship attribution. Methods like those discussed here are used worldwide for less than ethical reasons. Computer vision is used for face profiling, and textual analysis is used to influence elections and other social and antisocial behavior. Being at the forefront of research also means to be using and taking advantage of research that perpetuates human inequality and discrimination. Methods and tools are not neutral; they have agency and implications. And, since we recognize the fallacy of the slogan "guns don't kill humans, humans kill humans," we cannot accept comparable arguments in connection with computational methodology. Ethics, deontology, self-limitation, autoregulation—these are things that we associate perhaps with our work as teachers but not necessarily with our research. Since our authors are, for the great part, dead, we are less inclined to think that these things concern us.

So, we have some homework to do, I think. What will digital scholarly editing look like in ten years? Will editors do it, or will it be done by computer scientists and computer engineers? Will it still be called digital scholarly editing, or computational philology, or distant editing? It is too early to say, and maybe it will be a completely different thing altogether, but I think we will have to decide these things, or these things will be decided in spite of us.

Notes

1. See Elena Pierazzo, *Digital Scholarly Editing: Theories, Models and Methods* (Aldershot, UK: Ashgate, 2015); Matthew James Driscoll and Elena Pierazzo, eds., *Digital Scholarly Editing: Theories and Practices* (Open Book, 2016), doi.org/10.11647/OBP.0095.

2. See Heather F. Windram, Prue Shaw, Peter M. W. Robinson, and Christopher J. Howe, "Dante's *Monarchia* as a Test Case for the Use of Phylogenetic Methods in Stemmatic Analysis," *Literary and Linguistic Computing* 23, no. 4 (2008): 443–63, doi.org/10.1093/llc/fqn023. See also Christopher J. Howe, Ruth Connolly, and Heather F. Windram, "Responding to Criticisms of Phylogenetic Methods in Stemmatology," *Studies in English Literature 1500–1900* 52, no. 1 (2012): 51–67.

3. Mladen Popović, Maruf A. Dhali, and Lambert Schomaker, "Artificial Intelligence Based Writer Identification Generates New Evidence for the Unknown Scribes of the Dead Sea Scrolls Exemplified by the Great Isaiah Scroll (1QIsaa)," *PLOS ONE* 16, no. 4 (2021), doi.org/10.1371/journal.pone.0249769.

4. Mike Kestemont, Vincent Christlein, and Dominique Stutzmann, "Artificial Paleography: Computational Approaches to Identifying Script Types in Medieval Manuscripts," *Speculum* 92 (2017): 86–109, doi.org/10.1086/694112.

5. Wouter Haverals and Mike Kestemont, "Silent Voices: A Digital Study of the Herne Charterhouse Scribal Community (ca. 1350–1400)," *Queeste* 27, no. 2 (2020): 186–95, doi.org/10.5117/QUE2020.2.006.HAVE.

6. Mike Kestemont, Folgert Karsdorp, Elisabeth de Bruijn, Matthew Driscoll, Katarzyna A. Kapitan, Pádraig Ó Macháin, Daniel Sawyer, Remco Sleiderink, and Anne Chao, "Forgotten Books: The Application of Unseen Species Models to the Survival of Culture," *Science* 375, no. 6582 (2022): 765–69, doi.org/10.1126/science.abl7655.

7. Gregory Crane, "What Do You Do with a Million Books?," *D-Lib Magazine* 12, no. 3 (2006), doi.org/10.1045/march2006-crane.

8. See Kestemont, Christlein, and Stutzmann, "Artificial Paleography."
9. Amir Hazem, Béatrice Daille, Marie-Laurence Bonhomme, Martin Maarand, Mélodie Boillet, Christopher Kermorvant, and Dominique Stutzmann, "Books of Hours: The First Liturgical Corpus for Text Segmentation," *Proceedings of the 12th Conference on Language Resources and Evaluation (LREC 2020)*, 2020, 776–84, aclanthology.org/2020.lrec-1.97.pdf.
10. Jean-Baptiste Camps, "La Philologie Computationelle à l'École des Chartes," *Bibliothèque de l'École des Chartes* 176 (2021): 193–216.
11. Jean-Baptiste Camps, Thibault Clérice, and Ariane Pinche, "Noisy Medieval Data: from Digitized Manuscript to Stylometric Analysis, Evaluating Paul Meyer's Hagiographic Hypothesis," *Digital Scholarship in the Humanities* 36, supplement 2 (2021): 49–71, doi.org/10.1093/llc/fqab033.
12. Camps, "La Philologie Computationelle," 193–216.
13. See Peter A. Stokes, Benjamin Kiessling, Daniel Stökl, Ben Ezra, Robin Tissot, and Hassane Gargem, "The EScriptorium VRE for Manuscript Cultures—Classics@ Journal," *Classics@* 18 (2021), classics-at.chs.harvard.edu/classics18-stokes-kiessling-stokl-ben-ezra-tissot-gargem/.
14. See "LECTAUREP—L'intelligence artificielle appliquée aux archives notariales," lectaurep.hypotheses.org/.
15. Karen Spärck Jones, "Computational Linguistics: What About the Linguistics?," *Computational Linguistics* 33, no. 3 (2007): 437–41, doi.org/10.1162/coli.2007.33.3.437.
16. See "Conference Video: Closing Keynote by JB Michel and Erez Lieberman," *Digital Humanities*, June 19–22, 2011, dh2011.stanford.edu/?p=1385.
17. Jean-Baptiste Michel, Yuan Kui Shen, Aviva Presser Aiden, Adrian Veres, Matthew K. Gray, The Google Books Team, Joseph P. Pickett, et al., "Quantitative Analysis of Culture Using Millions of Digitized Books," *Science* 331, no. 6014 (2011): 176–82, doi.org/10.1126/science.1199644.
18. See Jean-Baptiste Michel and Erez Lieberman Aiden, "What We Learned from 5 Million Books," ted.com/talks/jean_baptiste_michel_erez_lieberman_aiden_what_we_learned_from_5_million_books.
19. The proceedings are being published now in a special issue of the *Journal of Data Mining and Digital Humanities*; see jdmdh.episciences.org/page/on-the-way-to-the-future-of-digital-manuscript-studies.
20. Patrick Juola, "The Rowling Case: A Proposed Standard Protocol for Authorship Questions," *Digital Scholarship in the Humanities* 30, no. 1 (2015): 100–113.
21. Arjuna Tuzzi and Michele Cortelazzo, ed., *Drawing Elena Ferrante's Profile: Workshop Proceedings* (Padova: Padova University Press, 2018).

CHAPTER 2

Beyond Social Editing

Peer-to-Peer Systems for Digital Editions

JULIA FLANDERS

Introduction

The symposium from which this book emerges invited a conversation about the "futures of digital scholarly editing," a phrasing that usefully puts the emphasis on the process of editing, and by extension on the human work and agencies involved, rather than on the monumentalism of editions as products. Although discussions of digital scholarly editing during my professional lifetime have often been driven by a fascination with technological possibility, and also an accompanying fascination with definition and redefinition—"what is a digital scholarly edition?"—the questions that most interest me now about the futures of digital scholarly editing are about how the idea of "editing" models, brokers, and informs human interactions: in effect, the social geometry and social entailments of the edition.

In order to understand fully what such a "social geometry" entails, we need to observe the forms of human agency that are present within the ecology that is created around an edition or an editorial process. These include formal practical roles such as author, editor, and reader, and also what we might call "ideological" roles, such as the "scholar" in "scholarly editing": not a person, precisely, but a name for a formation of authority. Another thing that needs to be made visible is the forms of agency that inhere in documents and editions themselves. Patrick Sahle gives us a great example of this kind of agency in his opening definitional essay in Matthew J. Driscoll and Elena Pierazzo's *Digital Scholarly Editing*:

> [Editions] *explore* the uncharted circumstances of documents, texts and their transmission. They may *correct* errors introduced by the conditions of production, copying and publishing. They *explain* what is not evident to the present-day reader. In short, they *bridge* a distance in time, a historical difference. Texts that are created today do not need to be critically edited. They can speak for themselves. Only historic documents and texts need an editor to make them speak clearly.[1]

The simplest "social geometry" of the scholarly edition consolidates these agencies: it accords to the *editor* an intellectual self-sufficiency and mastery to serve as the intellectual anchor and guarantor of an *edition* that fully explores, explains, and bridges the history and uncharted circumstances of an *author's* work to a *reader*. However artificial this consolidation may feel (we know the situation is never this simple!), as an archetype it is compelling enough that critics over the years have taken seriously the task of problematizing it, aiming in varied ways toward a more "social" or pluralized vision of the editorial enterprise. For example, in the space marked out for the author, critics in the tradition of D. F. McKenzie and Jerome McGann argue that we should attend to an array of different kinds of contributors whose forms of agency equally deserve attention. The Canterbury Tales Project in the 1990s opened up the possibility that a set of manuscript witnesses might constitute a set of potential editions rather than a single edition, with each edition making a provisional argument based on a set of choices rather than a definitive statement. Paths of proliferation like these were marked out early on and were animated by a variety of motives in several of the constituent competencies that contribute to the product we think of as the "digital scholarly edition." These include the study of digital publishing and its politics, which has put insistent pressure on concepts like definitiveness and proprietary information; they also include the study of digital archives, which addresses the question of how we amass the documents that might contribute to an edition, and what such gatherings represent in terms of power relations and agency. Strategic choices by the funding agencies that support digital editing have urged the creation of sharable repositories of source material (with the explicit goal of encouraging a divergent proliferation of editions). And technological developments over the decades have steadily improved the availability of tools for collaborative and distributed work: for instance, version control, annotation systems, and collaborative editing platforms. The idea of a distributed or community-based or "social" edition can thus take many different forms that, though geometrically analogous in a superficial way, are conceptually quite different in the ways they imagine agency and relationships, and also in the way they imagine human virtue.

The "Social Edition"

The term "social edition" in a digital humanities context seems to have been introduced by the INKE (Implementing New Knowledge Environments) collaborative team, including Ray Siemens, Cara Leitch, Megan Timney, and others, in a series of articles that discuss a social edition of the Devonshire manuscript, a commonplace book containing the poems of Thomas Wyatt but also writings by many other contributors, both men and women. The qualified term "*social* edition" explicitly draws attention to a set of differentiations and deliberately experimental practices that set this approach apart. Broadly, the INKE team situates the social edition in two ways. Historically, they position it as a further step in a genealogy of the digital edition that begins with the "dynamic" nature of the electronic text and the "hypertextual" nature of interlinked digital archives, a foundation of abundance and interactive bilateralism. Typologically, the social edition is characterized by the way it "blends traditional scholarly editing practices with ... digital social media environments," and by its debt to contemporary editorial theory (building on work by McGann and McKenzie), "which recognizes the inherently social form and formation of texts."[2] In their practical account of how this social edition was developed, the INKE team directs our attention to the components and work processes of the traditional scholarly edition to show us where they could be blown open. As in the "pluralized" geometry above, the social edition imagines multiple, negotiated agencies in places where the traditional edition tends to consolidate authority: for example, in the selection of documents and prioritization of texts (the result of transparent, but unilateral decision-making) and in the communicative circuit created by the edition, in which expertise is disseminated to be shared with other experts. The social edition also deliberately diminishes the effects of prestige in places where the traditional edition seeks to magnify it. These spaces of diminished prestige include the authorship of the text(s), the "work" itself as something worthy of attention—something that stands out from the much larger set of texts in existence as canonical or canonizable—and the scholarly editor as a credentialed and named figure. They also include the editing process, conventionally construed as a heroic "life's work," and the resulting monumentalism of the edition itself as a product, as well as the intellectual sponsorship conferred by the press that magnifies the monumental effect.

But the INKE accounts also draw attention to specific choices about project design and working environments that diverge from what we might call the "traditional digital scholarly edition." The first of these is the choice to edit a compilation rather than a single-author work:

> *A Social Edition of the Devonshire Manuscript* seeks to publish the contents of the original manuscript in their entirety, move beyond the limitations of an author-centred focus on Wyatt's contributions and concentrate on the social, literary and historical contexts in which the volume is situated as a unified whole.... *A Social Edition of the Devonshire Manuscript* aims to preserve the socially mediated textual and extra-textual elements of the manuscript that have been elided or ignored in previous work. These ostensible "paratexts" make significant contributions to the meaning and appreciation of the manuscript miscellany and its constituent parts: annotations, glosses, names, ciphers and various jottings. The telling proximity of one work to another, significant gatherings of materials, illustrations entered into the manuscript alongside the text and so forth all shape the way we understand the manuscript, but are often ignored when preparing scholarly editions.[3]

Mirroring the multi-author space of the compilation, the editorial team makes use of social media environments and collaborative authoring environments (rather than more local, internal working spaces) to "enable new editing practices," using Wikibooks, which situates users as "active authors rather than simply readers or consumers."[4] Drawing in a "community of individuals" to create the new edited text, the team uses TEI (Text Encoding Initiative) markup to make transcription and editing decisions visible, debatable, and revisable by the project team and its external audience. These editorial design decisions reinforce the team's emphasis on working in public and distributing editorial authority beyond the editorial team. The social edition "brings communities together to engage in conversation around a text formed and reformed through an ongoing, iterative, public editorial process. A central aim of the project was to facilitate knowledge transfer and creation between multiple editorial communities with varying values and priorities."[5]

These design choices are notable for being motivated by ethical rather than purely intellectual considerations, and they cohere around three distinct types of virtues. The first of these are what I would describe as "epistemological virtues" or virtues of enlightenment: enhancements to knowledge such as accuracy, clarity, transparency, distribution, access: "knowledge transfer"; "public editorial process." This kind of virtue is also evident in Sahle's definition of the mission of the scholarly edition: "correct errors"; "explore uncharted circumstances"; "explain what is not evident"; "speak clearly." This language is echoed in other definitional spaces such as the white paper "Considering the Scholarly Edition in the Digital Age" published by the Modern Language Association's Committee on Scholarly Editing, which identifies "a set of crucial features that we take to be fundamental to scholarly editing: transparency, accuracy, appropriateness of method, clear and responsible documentation, and the exercise of critical judgment in representing a full account of the textual situation at stake."[6]

The second set of virtues are what I would describe as "affective virtues" or virtues of empathy, such as enhancements of trust and strengthened social bonds. In the Devonshire manuscript scenario, this is evident in the way that knowledge transfer is being effected "between multiple editorial communities with varying values and priorities, . . . bringing communities together to engage in conversation." And the final group are virtues we might describe as "social virtues" or "virtues of empowerment": shared agency, equity, and inclusiveness. The INKE team describes their editing process as creating "active authors," "enabling new editing practices," "speaking for themselves." The work of "knowledge transfer" also operates as a virtue of empowerment, since what that transfer accomplishes is the transfer of agency as well.

If we imagine the world of the edition as a social network with a proliferating set of agents and interactions, we can see how these virtues animate and vitalize specific spaces within the geometry of this network, both editorial spaces and intratextual spaces. For instance, what start as epistemological virtues (the ability of the edition to be "clear" and to "explain") also become virtues of empowerment: those clear explanations serve and empower readers, who are construed as "active authors rather than simply... consumers." And the constitution of the various communities—contributors, editors, and readers—is understood by the social edition to be founded on affective virtues. As part of the editorial process, the editors discuss and negotiate varying values and priorities in collaboration with readers, via public social media, as well as a social media platform hosted by the edition's publisher.[7] The editorial process is described as a widely inclusive "conversation":

> With the firm foundation of documented encoding, all those working with the document can refer to, build on or adapt the project's foundation. The markup did not simply help the team keep track of the process; it also facilitated an ongoing scholarly conversation about the text. Readers can compare our transcriptions to the facsimiles included on each page of the Wikibooks edition and are free to contest (and even alter) our regularisations or corrections.[8]

The homologies between the collaborative work of editing the Devonshire Manuscript and the collaborative work of creating the manuscript itself in the first place redouble the emphasis on sociality; quoting Margaret Ezell's observation that the practice of manuscript compilation served to "cement social bonds" within women's literary circles, the authors note that, "by shifting our own editorial process into an environment representative of the inherent sociality of texts, *A Social Edition of the Devonshire Manuscript* hearkens back to the multi-author roots of the text itself."[9]

In noting and celebrating this shared emphasis on sociality, it is worth pausing over a few other elements of the resemblance that may nuance the picture. The authorship of the Devonshire manuscript exhibits not only the "inherent sociality" of all texts but also an intensified version of it: a coterie associated with the court of Queen Anne Boleyn, consisting of members of the nobility who were also in many cases closely related through familial as well as social ties. The manuscript enacts a directly interactive and collaborative process of authoring and annotation that goes far beyond the kinds of sociality marked through McGann's and McKenzie's attention to the roles of printers, publishers, illustrators, and other essential contributors to the production and circulation of texts. The elite nature of the group and its closed communicative circuit are thus close—we might almost say essential—adjuncts to its sociality. In drawing the analogy to the INKE editorial team, we can identify an analogous alignment of status (enacted through academic rather than class privilege and through professional rather than courtly ties) that similarly secures the boundaries and creates trust relationships on which the practices of social editing are founded. However, as their written accounts note, the team paid deliberate attention to tools and practices that could render those boundaries porous and expand those trust relationships to include a wider circuit of expertise and contribution. In building on this example and imagining the wider potential scope of "social editing," it would be important to consider what (possibly implicit or mystified) forms of connection and social uniformity may underpin the trust relationships that are assumed.

The Antisocial Edition

As I noted before, the INKE team situate their social edition within a history of digital humanities and a genealogy of the digital edition that begins with the "dynamic" nature of the electronic text and the "hypertextual" nature of interlinked digital archives, qualities marked by computing researchers in humanities computing as early as the 1980s in discussing digital editions and digital systems of publication and circulation.[10] If we were to draw a big diagram to illustrate the word "hypertext," it would certainly look very much like our social edition network: many nodes connected by arrows, all intercommunicating, buzzing with empowerment. But the social edition as the INKE team describe it is not the only way this narrative can play out, and to illustrate this I'd like to turn briefly to another, earlier experiment (perhaps chiefly a thought experiment) with "social" publishing: Theodor Holm Nelson's Project Xanadu. Begun in the 1960s and continuing even to this day, Xanadu was an attempt to create a platform for peer-to-peer publishing, annotation, and remixing of content. It is not a direct analogue of "scholarly editing," but a formation that in effect leapfrogs past the "social edition" in ostensibly the same direction: to eliminate what is hieratic and culturally prominent and exclusive, and to focus entirely on structures of communication and information exchange for use with works of literature and cultural knowledge.

In Xanadu, Nelson envisioned a distributed network to manage all writing, and a platform for reading, authoring, and comparison: "a new populist medium, a many-to-many publishing system, not centralized in editorial and publishing companies, but open to anyone." The result would be an enormously enhanced reading experience: "All different republications could in principle be viewed side-by-side by the user, thus leading to greater understanding of the material and of the points of view of the different documents, their authors and republishers."[11] He also envisioned a universal system of royalties and access fees. In his formal definition of the problem space, Nelson enumerates the functional requirements for such a system, including reliability, security against accident and malice, authentication and preservation of property rights, reuse, and affordable monetized exchange:

> It must be possible to create, access and manipulate this literature ... cheaply, reliably and securely from anywhere in the world. ... Documents must remain accessible indefinitely, safe from any kind of loss, damage, modification, censorship or removal except by the owner. ... It must be impossible to falsify ownership or track individual readers of any document. ... This system of literature ... must allow people to create virtual copies ("transclusions") of any existing collection of information in the system regardless of ownership; ... the system must guarantee that the owner of any information will be paid their chosen royalties on any portions of their documents, no matter how small, whenever and wherever they are used.[12]

In its proliferation of nodes with multiple interconnections, this vision shares some of its geometries with the social edition: creators, readers, annotators, and publishers are all highly pluralized and distributed. And it echoes the social edition's insistence on eliminating the institutional consolidation of power and capital in publishers and their control over production and dissemination. Xanadu's design anticipates modern social media platforms, but with a much more thoroughly distributed (imagined) architecture than WikiBooks or most of today's social media sites and tools. However, when we look at the edges instead of the nodes, we see some crucial differences. Foremost among these is a kind of "social distancing" instantiated and enforced through systems of formalized distrust: an emphasis on privacy, security, and authentication. In this respect, Xanadu anticipates systems like blockchain, which the foundational white paper on Bitcoin observes is explicitly architected around "cryptographic proof instead of trust, allowing any two willing parties to transact directly with each other without the need for a trusted third party."[13] As we noted above, the functional requirements for Xanadu include a significant threat model that anticipates risks of "loss, damage, modification, censorship or removal," as well as falsification of ownership and surveillance and tracking of readers. This threat model in turn is predicated on an economic model that pays careful attention to ownership, monetization, and exchange, and on the ability to set a formal value on information. Indeed, it is precisely the networked circulation posited by the massively distributed architecture of Xanadu that supports this formal valuation, by imagining a marketplace of sufficient scale to achieve competition among producers and accessibility by purchasers, very much in the manner of a platform like Etsy. Nelson's vision of Xanadu intensifies this effect further through its emphasis on interconnection and recombination of documents, through something called "transcopyright": through a system of micropayments, authors would be able to remix each other's work transparently while money flowed from place to place as needed to reflect these tiny transfers of value.

Xanadu's virtues are emphatically epistemological. They make for "greater understanding of the material and of the points of view of the different documents, their authors and republishers"—in other words, a fully transparent knowledge network in which each node's perspective can be known to all the others.[14] Xanadu thus anticipates the open access movement's goal of universally transparent access, but without many of the nuances we now recognize as essential, issues like restricting access to culturally sensitive materials, establishing community self-determination, and respecting local information-sharing practices.[15] In particular, the Xanadu system emphasizes the fungibility of both documents and people as entities to be managed within a system that accords uniform levels of agency under a uniform system of value. And it relies on this fungibility as a substitute for a more complex system of negotiated meaning that would require the agents (readers, authors, remixers, transcluders) to do the things the INKE team highlights as goals of their work: "facilitate knowledge transfer"; "engage in conversation."

Xanadu is based on a leveled free-market economics of "transparency" in which obvious concentrations of capital have been removed, or at least mystified; publishing companies have been eliminated and costs are instead set by individual content creators and transmitters, but economic barriers are still evident. Individual micropublishers, authors, and readers still need access to a presumed universal information network, and technical support for that network is assumed but not explicitly accounted for. The linked flows of information and money underscore the way Xanadu also seeks to establish documents as essentially fungible, their value established in monetary terms by the overall market of readers, rather than in terms of cultural or community value. Its sociality is thus reduced to a flattened, partial, and somewhat naive or disingenuous "everyone": a social geometry that achieves its flat and egalitarian structure through its omissions. There is knowledge at each node, but all forms of cultural authority have been evacuated, even those that would recognize communities' differential authority over materials in which they are directly concerned. We might characterize Xanadu as a kind of "post-social" edition: the virtues it most significantly *omits* are those of affect and sociality.

The Social Edition Revisited

The social edition as described by INKE alerts us to the importance of affective virtues in establishing an editorial scenario in which meaning can be negotiated, but it does not fully illustrate how those virtues could operate or how far we might be able to take its version of sociality. It establishes a space that is still animated by academic scholarship and agency, even while it shares and diversifies that agency, and sets it up on a platform somewhat separate from the academy. The INKE team acknowledges their goal of "blending traditional scholarly editing practices and standards with comparatively recent digital social media environments," and in that blending (particularly evidenced by the word "standards"), we may understand a reluctance to let go of the primary epistemological virtues of the "edition" as traditionally conceived: the way it establishes a position of authority that grounds its work of "explaining," even if that authority is now shared. Recent research on graph approaches to digital scholarly editing show a similar understanding of editions as "knowledge sites" where authority is pluralized and distributed within a bounded academic space.[16] Technologies like stand-off annotation, application programming interfaces (APIs), and registry services decentralize the edition and create conditions for "editions" to be reconceptualized as a distributed system of edition-knowledge. The design of these technological foundations retains concepts like provenance, permanence, and authority, resituating them at the system level.

But the graph model does open the door for more radical reimaginings, since the boundaries of the edition (which in the INKE model are still determined by the editorial team) are informational rather than organizational. Although there may still be reluctance to alter the basic epistemological orientation of the edition, at a structural level that change has already been put on the table. The field of critical archival studies has been pushing on precisely this reluctance in arguing that we need to remake the relationships through which cultural meaning is negotiated, along affective rather than purely epistemological lines. Critical archival studies thus offer us something like the limit case of the social edition. It proposes that documents are innumerable, that all documents have value in deeply situational ways, and that value is conferred by the community rather than by adherence to established professional protocols or metrics of prestige.

If applied to editorial practice, these propositions would have significant impact on the social geometry of the edition in several distinct and important ways. The first of these concerns the acknowledgement, sharing, and dispersal of agency. While acknowledging the real current force of institutional power and authority in establishing and authenticating cultural value, critical archival studies urge that this power be demystified and displaced to make space for community decision-making and ownership.[17] Importantly, as part of this shift, professional expertise must also be decentered. As Michelle Caswell argues, a principle of "archival pluralism" would entail

> acknowledgement of and engagement with ... multiple coexisting archival realities—that is, fundamentally differing but equally valid ways of being and knowing—most commonly made manifest in the archival realm by (sometimes) irreconcilably divergent—but still credible—ways of defining, transmitting, and interpreting evidence and memory.[18]

These principles put pressure on the status of the archivist—the professional training, institutional authority, and epistemological positioning (for instance, presumed neutrality) that underpin that role.

In an even more profound reconsideration of agency, a survey of archival-studies literature by Caswell, Jessica Tai, Jimmy Zavala, Joyce Gabiola, and Gracen Brilmyer draws together myriad sources showing how agency and authority can and must be radically pluralized and dispersed, to include not only "members of the communities documented and represented by marginalized identity-based community archives,"[19] but also documents, artifacts, and archival records, which are recast as agents through their enormous affective power, through their role as carriers of human memory and intention, and through their liberatory role in a human rights context in which they act as "agents of accountability":

> Building from a conception of records that highlights their power in inciting change in real-world and material ways, we can begin to conceive of the notion of records as agents imbued with an autonomous sense of purpose and will.[20]

This decentering and pluralization of agency also shifts the importance we attach to systems of information organization, including provenance,[21] metadata,[22] and information modeling.[23] Acknowledging that historical aggregations of documents may often be the result of violence, appropriation, or displacement, critical archival studies provides an understanding that organizational systems must not be implemented as further outgrowths of institutional power and violence (even under cover of terminology such as "professional standards" or "scholarly rigor" or "interoperability"), but must be animated by the many forms of agency that are understood to be ethically connected to the archive. With this acknowledgement, affective and social virtues of trust, mutual responsibility, and the "ethics of care" or "radical empathy" that Caswell and Marika Cifor propose as the foundations for an archival practice rooted in and oriented toward social justice[24] are established as the primary virtues of significance.

As a thought experiment, what would a social edition look like that operated with the *primary goal* of creating social connection and empowerment? Caswell and Cifor offer us a road map for thinking about this in their proposal to rethink four key archival relationships through an orientation toward radical empathy. The first relationship is between the archivist and the record creator: for purposes of our thought experiment, the relationship between the editor and the author and other participants involved in the production of the text. When the archivist or editor enters into a relationship of care with the creator, key decision-making processes are informed and guided by empathy. A simplistic version of this application of empathy would be to consider the author's intentions or wishes in developing editorial policy. From a perspective of radical empathy, this ethical consideration of the author's intentions differs from the use of "authorial intention" that has guided some traditions of editorial practice, in that it asks the editor to treat the author's wishes as a primary constraint on action, rather than as a form of information to be discovered and made visible. This might entail some significant revision to editorial practices currently considered routine, such as deciphering or unveiling deleted material, seeking or reconstructing materials that were destroyed or concealed by the author, presenting works outside of their original context, or choosing a format of publication (such as a printed book) at variance with the author's creative philosophy. A fuller exploration of this application of empathy to editorial practice would require us to imagine what it would mean to de-objectify the author and their work: to situate the author's work as something other than an object of study, and to orient the editorial enterprise as a whole toward goals other than scholarship as currently understood.

The idea of treating the author, and by extension their work, as an ethical agent echoes the urging of Caswell, Tai, and their coauthors that archival records and those represented within them be treated as agents,[25] and the second relationship Caswell and Cifor ask us to scrutinize is between the archivist and those represented within archival records: "The archivist has an affective responsibility to those about whom records are created, often unwittingly and unwillingly. Such stakeholders include Indigenous and colonial subjects counted, classified, studied, enslaved, traded as property."[26] From a perspective of radical empathy, the archival goal is to "recover and reassert the voices of record subjects in the archival process."[27] To apply this principle to the editorial ecology, we need to think about what the mandate to "recover and reassert ... voices" entails, as a way of restoring lost agency and presence in materials being edited. A useful example here is the editorial practice of the Early Caribbean Digital Archive (ECDA) in representing the narratives of enslaved people, originally embedded in white-authored documents, as separately authored works with their own metadata and distinct presence within the ECDA collection.[28] We also need to think imaginatively about who are the equivalent of the "record subjects," particularly in the case of literary and fictional works where those represented are in some sense nonexistent. The fictive entities themselves may have no analogous claim on the editor's affective consideration, but when understood as representations that draw from and have an impact upon actual persons and places they direct our attention towards entities that should have such a claim.

We are already seeing, as advocates of critical archival practice have also seen, some emerging complexities in applying these principles, such as in cases where a responsibility to the author is at odds with a responsibility to those represented. What about cases in which an author is an enslaver, a colonial administrator, an apologist for state-sponsored violence? To resolve these tensions we need to look to the deeper animating principles of social justice and community empowerment, and perhaps deeper still at principles of nonviolence and self-determination from which we can derive frameworks to help resolve these questions.

The last two relationships of importance here are the most challenging: between the archivist and users of the archive, and between the archivist and the community. Caswell and Cifor propose that "practising radical empathy with users means acknowledging the deep emotional ties users have to records. . . . We cannot ethically continue to conceive of our primary users as academic scholars."[29] Furthermore, archivists have "responsibilities towards unseen others," those who are not direct users of records but for whom the use of records has lasting consequences. "The archivist has an ethical obligation to empathize with all parties impacted by archival use—the communities for whom justice or impunity has lasting consequences, the community of people for whom representation—or silencing—matters."[30] To apply these obligations to the domain of scholarly editing, it may be apt to think about the pedagogical functions of the edition. By this I mean not the use of editions in the classroom, but rather the ways in which scholarly editions teach—or fail to teach—readers how to use the knowledge they offer, in the broadest sense. Scholarly editions (as we observed at the outset) typically imagine an audience of fellow scholars, in ways that strongly shape both *what* information is presented and *how* that information is presented. What would it mean to cease "conceiv[ing] of our primary users as academic scholars," in the sense that Caswell and Cifor propose? Not, that is, to cease serving academic scholars, but rather no longer to construe all users as having a purely *scholarly* relationship to information, one animated by an expert quest for knowledge? Radical empathy, in this context, might entail taking a much wider view of the kinds of impact that one's work might have, including the ethical consequences of that work: wider not only with respect to the kinds of people taken into account (students, the general public), but also wider with respect to the kinds of impacts we expect from an "edition." This may seem to stretch our sense of both the "edition" and the responsibilities one takes on in creating one, and this is worth remarking on, since it seems less surprising to encounter discussions of ethical responsibilities for members of the archival professions. Why does the role of the scholarly editor seem so much less laden with social responsibility? Is it because the academy is accustomed to construing archivists and librarians as service roles, as roles that are anchored in affective virtues, whereas the scholar's role is imagined as having primarily epistemological virtues?

If scholarly editors doubt that the works they might deal with themselves, as editors, would call for these kinds of ethical considerations—if the materials seem too distant in time, or too fictional, or too culturally inconsequential—I would suggest that this may be partly because we are not yet editing the most pressing documents. And here we may note that major funding programs including the National Endowment for the Humanities, the National Historical Publications and Records Commission, and the Mellon Foundation are slowly starting to aim their funding dollars toward broadening assumptions of what cultural heritage means and what materials should be the focus of attention. But I also wonder whether such doubt might ignore the ways in which editing works that are deemed canonical or hegemonic or mainstream might in fact have repercussions, even violent ones. These repercussions arise precisely in the denial (through an exclusive focus on epistemological virtues) of the violence of formations like hegemonic whiteness. If we edit a Renaissance sonnet in which a blazon presents a standard of white beauty without imagining how a Black child might encounter such a text in a high school English class, we have missed the point that Caswell and Cifor are potentially offering us.

Two notable digital projects, the ECDA and the Colored Conventions Project (CCP), are exploring important applications of these principles of editorial empathy. Both projects use practices like community transcription events and workshops that dramatically extend editorial agency and responsibility, and the ECDA has engaged participants in experiments in "critical fabulation" that ask readers to imagine empathetically the lives of enslaved people whose voices appear fleetingly in the embedded slave narratives recorded in the ECDA collection.[31] CCP presents a set of guiding principles for the project's work that resonate strongly with Caswell and Cifor's concept of radical empathy in the service of social justice goals; for example:

> Principle 1: "CCP seeks to enact collective organizing principles and values that were modeled by the Colored Conventions Movement."
>
> Principle 4: "Mirroring the Colored Conventions's focus on labor rights and Black economic health, our project seeks structures and support that honor the work members bring to the project through equitable compensation, acknowledgement, and attribution."
>
> Principle 5: "We seek to name Black people and communities as an affirmation of the Black humanity inherent in Black data/curation."[32]

Further, the CCP asks users of its data corpus to make a similar commitment.[33] These principles are challenging to follow, and I believe deliberately so: they require not only effort beyond what is typical, but effort that is specifically oriented toward an exercise of mindfulness, an attentiveness to the existence and humanity of other persons at every point and in every place: in documents, in data, in history, in working relationships, in editorial principles.

My original idea for this essay was a thought experiment: what would a "peer-to-peer" edition look like? I was fascinated by the idea of an edition platform based on something like GitHub: a shared repository of source documents, to which would be added at least one repository of representations of those documents, such as TEI-encoded transcriptions, or plain-text transcriptions with stand-off markup. There could be as many such repositories as were prompted by different approaches to the task of representation. Contributions of information could be made by copying a repository, making changes, offering those changes for incorporation back into the original repository. Debates over transcription or encoding strategies could be discovered through an analysis of differences between versions. I am sure somewhere in my mind was an echo of a presentation by Peter Robinson at the 2006 symposium "Digital Textual Studies: Past, Present and Future" (later included in a special issue of *Digital Humanities Quarterly*) in which he proposed a similar vision for a "new paradigm for scholarly editing":

> The lifeblood of this is going to be texts made freely available to everyone. I want to put the transcripts of Canterbury Tales manuscripts up out there on the web, for everyone. If this all works, I am very soon going to see those transcripts turning up all over the place, in all kinds of contexts, with all kinds of annotations, being used for all kinds of things I did not expect. I think this is wonderful.[34]

But in revisiting that piece, I found even this vision ends up leading back to a familiar geometry:

> The important exception is this: high-value, fully-published work which combines both exceptional scholarly effort with purposeful design and publication. An example of this is the Nestle-Aland text and apparatus: there are decades of work behind this, by the scholars in Münster, their partners, and their publisher. This is of such high value that, indeed, people are prepared to pay for this.[35]

The allure of Xanadu is all too real—and, as the contemporary allure of blockchain technologies reveals, it is evidence of a pervasive and enduring economic imaginary rooted in libertarianism and the disavowal of the social. The GitHub dream vision imagines not only a technology for brokering effortlessly shared information, but also an accompanying diminution or abdication of responsibility for dealing directly and empathetically with other human beings. As I've learned in the past two years, efforts like the Colored Conventions Project, whose constant attention to ethical and empathetic conduct is such an important model, take us much further in imagining what a genuinely "social" or community-oriented approach to editing could look like.

Notes

1. Patrick Sahle, "What Is a Digital Scholarly Edition?," in *Digital Scholarly Editing: Theories and Practices*, ed. Matthew J. Driscoll and Elena Pierazzo (Cambridge: OpenBook, 2016): 25–26 (emphasis mine), doi.org/10.11647/obp.0095.08.

2. Ray Siemens, Constance Crompton, Daniel Powell, Alyssa Arbuckle, Maggie Shirley, and Devonshire Manuscript Editorial Group, "Building a Social Edition of the Devonshire Manuscript," in Driscoll and Pierazzo, *Digital Scholarly Editing*, 137–60, at ¶1, doi.org/10.11647/obp.0095.08.

3. Siemens et al., "Building," ¶3.

4. Siemens et al., "Building," ¶12.

5. Siemens et al., ¶28.

6. Modern Language Association, "Considering the Scholarly Edition in the Digital Age: A White Paper of the Modern Language Association's Committee on Scholarly Editions," 2015, scholarlyeditions.mla.hcommons.org/cse-white-paper/.

7. Siemens et al., "Building," ¶22.

8. Siemens et al., ¶18.

9. Siemens et al., ¶12.

10. See, for instance, Jay David Bolter, *Writing Space: The Computer, Hypertext, and the History of Writing* (Hillsdale, N.J.: Lawrence Erlbaum Associates, 1990); Peter Shillingsburg, *Scholarly Editing in the Digital Age: Theory and Practice* (Ann Arbor: University of Michigan Press, 1996), 165.

11. Theodor Holm Nelson, "Transcopyright: Dealing with the Dilemma of Digital Copyright," *Educom Review* 32, no. 1 (1997), educause.edu/apps/er/review/reviewArticles/32132.html.

12. Theodor Holm Nelson, "What is Xanadu?," xanadu.com.au.

13. Satoshi Nakamoto, "Bitcoin: A Peer-to-Peer Electronic Cash System," bitcoin.org/bitcoin.pdf. I'm grateful to the editors of this volume for reminding me of this connection.

14. Nelson, "Transcopyright."

15. See, for instance, Siobhan Senier, "Digitizing Indigenous History: Trends and Challenges," *Journal of Victorian Culture* 19, no. 3 (2014): 396–402, doi.org/10.1080/13555502.2014.947188; Kimberly Christen, "Gone Digital: Aboriginal Remix and the Cultural Commons," *International Journal of Cultural Property* 12 (2005): 315–45, doi.org/10.1017/S0940739105050186.

16. See, for instance, Elena Spadini and Francesca Tomasi, "Introduction," in *Graph Data-Models and Semantic Web Technologies in Scholarly Digital Editing*, ed. Elena Spadini, Francesca Tomasi, and Georg Vogeler, Schriften des Instituts für Dokumentologie und Editorik 15 (Norderstedt: Books on Demand, 2021), kups.ub.uni-koeln.de/55227/1/Vogeler.pdf; Daniel L. Schwartz, Nathan P. Gibson and Katayoun Torabi, "Modeling a Born-Digital Factoid Prosopography using the TEI and Linked Data," *Journal of the Text Encoding Initiative*, Rolling Issue 2022, doi.org/10.4000/jtei.3979.

17. See, for instance, Michelle Caswell, "SAADA and the Community-Based Archives Model: What Is a Community-Based Archives Anyway?," SAADA (South Asian American Archive), 2012, saada.org/tides/article/20120418-704; Ricardo Punzalan and Michelle Caswell, "Critical Directions for Archival Approaches to Social Justice," *Library Quarterly: Information, Community, Policy* 86, no. 1 (2016): 25–42; Jessica Tai, Jimmy Zavala, Joyce Gabiola, Gracen Brilmyer, and Michelle Caswell, "Summoning the Ghosts: Records as Agents in Community Archives," *Journal of Contemporary Archival Studies* 6 (2019): article 18, https://elischolar.library.yale.edu/jcas/vol6/iss1/18.

18. Michelle Caswell, "On Archival Pluralism: What religious pluralism (and its critics) can teach us about archives," *Archival Science* 13 (2013): 277, doi.org/10.1007/s10502-012-9197-y.

19. Jessica Tai et al., "Summoning," 1.

20. Tai et al., 6.

21. See Punzalan and Caswell, "Critical Directions."

22. See Kimberly Christen, "Indigenous Knowledge Systems and Mukutu CMS," in *The Design for Diversity Learning Toolkit*, Northeastern University, 2018, des4div.library.northeastern.edu/indigenous-knowledge-systems-and-mukurtu-cms/.

23. See Timothy B. Powell and Larry P. Aitken, "Encoding Culture: Building a Digital Archive Based on Traditional Ojibwe Teachings," in *The American Literary Scholar in the Digital Age*, ed. Amy E. Earhart and Andrew Jewell (Ann Arbor: University of Michigan Press, 2011): 250–74, doi.org/10.3998/etlc.9362034.0001.001.

24. Michelle Caswell and Marika Cifor, "From Human Rights to Feminist Ethics: Radical Empathy in the Archives," *Archivaria* 81 (2016): 23, escholarship.org/uc/item/0mb9568h.

25. Tai et al., "Summoning."

26. Caswell and Cifor, "From Human Rights," 36.

27. Caswell and Cifor, 36.

28. Early Caribbean Digital Archive, "Early Caribbean Slave Narratives," ecda.northeastern.edu/home/about-exhibits/early-caribbean-slave-narratives-exhibit/. This work is grounded in project co-director Nicole Aljoe's foundational research in *Creole Testimonies: Slave Narratives from the British West Indies, 1709–1838* (New York: Palgrave Macmillan, 2012).

29. Caswell and Cifor, "From Human Rights," 37–38.

30. Caswell and Cifor, 38–39.

31. This phrase "critical fabulation" is drawn from Saidiya Hartman, "Venus in Two Acts," *Small Axe* 12, no. 2 (2008): 1–14.

32. Colored Conventions Project, "Colored Convention Project Principles," coloredconventions.org/about/principles/.

33. Colored Conventions Project, "Digital Records: Corpus," omeka.coloredconventions.org/ccp-corpus.

34. Peter Robinson, "The Ends of Editing," *Digital Humanities Quarterly* 3, no. 3 (2009): ¶35, digitalhumanities.org/dhq/vol/3/3/000051/000051.html

35. Robinson, "The Ends of Editing," ¶38.

CHAPTER 3

Creative Ecologies
The Complete-Works Edition in a Digital Paradigm

DIRK VAN HULLE

The complete-works edition (CWE) is a vital part of scholarship in the humanities. In literary studies of modern texts, however, CWEs are almost self-evidently conceived of as print editions, even in the digital age. As a result, the traditional model of a CWE is strongly conditioned by the affordances but also the limitations of the print medium. To challenge this dominant model, we need to work on a new, inclusive CWE model that uses cutting-edge digital technology and enables a new form of reading: reading across versions. In this endeavor, digital technology allows us, on the one hand, to preserve (rather than reduce) the full complexity of a literary oeuvre's production history and, on the other hand, to empower readers by providing them with the tools to navigate this complexity and make sure they do not get lost in the multitude of texts.

To fully fathom the challenge, it is useful to make a brief excursion into the realm of fine arts. When the National Gallery in London exhibits Georges Seurat's *Bathers at Asnières*, it does so by presenting it among several of its preparatory studies and sketches. When the Louvre in Paris decided to present Leonardo da Vinci's works on the occasion of the five-hundredth anniversary of his death, they explicitly chose to display his works among his sketches, his notebooks, and X-ray photographs of his paintings, showing all the *pentimenti*, literally all the "repented" or superseded aspects that have been hidden by subsequent layers of painting. These sketches, notes, and *pentimenti* are also appreciated by nonexpert audiences, as they recognize quite naturally that a work of art remains connected to the way it was made, and that knowing something about this genesis may contribute to one's appreciation of the painting.

What seems self-evident in the study of paintings is much less generally accepted in literature. This attitude is to a large extent conditioned by the print medium. To conceive of alternatives to this print paradigm, we can start with a thought experiment that imagines a change of mindset, a different way of conceiving of a writer's complete works, not unlike the approach adopted in fine arts. The difference between a print paradigm and a digital paradigm is fundamental and goes to the heart of the key questions: what is a work of art? And what, then, is an oeuvre (the author's "complete works")? Due to the codex format, the print paradigm tends to foreground a single-text approach to scholarly editing. If there are textual *pentimenti*, they are often relegated to a critical apparatus where the textual variants are listed. There is usually no space for facsimiles of manuscripts, sketches, notes, or doodles. These textual *pentimenti* are left out of the CWE. But the question is: How "complete" is a CWE without them?

By including these invaluable yet oft-neglected traces of creativity in a new digital CWE model, we can add a temporal dimension to the traditional setup of a CWE and present a writer's complete works not just as a set of finished products, but also as a process—an "oeuvre in motion," marked by a continuous dialectic between completion and incompletion. This implies the conceptualization of an author's "complete works" as a creative ecology.

The Oeuvre-in-Motion as a Creative Ecology

As mentioned above, the print medium has had a significant impact on the conceptualization of the CWE, and a digital paradigm diverges from the print paradigm in at least four important ways: 1) It challenges the single-text logic, which has dominated the print model for decades; 2) it provides an inclusive approach to the author's canon in the sense that it opens it up to include all the traces of its genesis and presents the completed works as an "oeuvre in motion"; 3) it withstands the tendency to compartmentalise that comes inevitably with the print model's need to separate the works into volumes; and 4) it offers an alternative form of reading: in addition to the syntagmatic axis of following the text's narrative sequence, it also enables users to read across versions, along the paradigmatic axis of comparing lexical alternatives (i.e., how the phrasing of a passage changed from one stage to the next).

The first divergence challenges the single-text logic. The print medium has prompted editors to present authors' "complete works" as a sort of wastewater treatment plant, separating the "pure" text from impurities, which are treated in the backwater of the critical apparatus. This purity discourse marks, for instance, the influential Greg-Bowers tradition of copy-text editing. Fredson Bowers presented the goal of textual criticism as follows: "The recovery of the initial *purity* of an author's text and of any revision (insofar as this is possible from the preserved documents), and the preservation of this *purity* despite the usual *corrupting* process of reprint transmission, is the aim of textual criticism."[1] One of Bowers's critics, the Swiss textual scholar Hans Zeller, found fault with the eclectic copy-text method because it "contaminatingly synchronises that which occurred diachronically,"[2] but he still employed a similar discourse of purity in his criticism. In the past few decades, this purity discourse has been questioned and criticized in editorial theory, but in editorial practice it has turned out to be difficult to find adequate alternatives.[3]

Besides safeguarding so-called textual purity, the CWE has always been an instrument in the processes of canonization. The traditional single-text edition in print format tends to reinforce two forms of canonization. It often helps establish an author's fame and status as belonging to the best writers of their period in literary history. At the same time, the CWE also plays a role in establishing an author's own canon, the set of works that are recognized as being genuinely by this author. This latter canon usually serves as the endpoint of the CWE: the reading notes, manuscripts, typescripts, proofs, and so on are mentioned only insofar as they have resulted in the published telos. This teleological approach certainly has its merits, but it raises questions both about the *completeness* of a CWE and about what constitutes the *work* or *works*.

The second divergence is an inclusive approach to the author's canon in that it opens up the canon and presents it as an "oeuvre in motion." As for the *completeness* of a "complete works" edition, it is often unclear what belongs to the writer's canon and what does not. Sometimes a complete works edition includes works that were not published during the author's lifetime. Archival research often unearths more, sometimes unknown unpublished works, which raises the question: Should they be included in a CWE? Even if the answer is yes, the obvious practical problem would be that it is impossible to publish a revised print CWE each time a new draft is discovered. Besides, writers sometimes keep notebooks that contain ideas and loose jottings that did not necessarily lead to any particular work. Some notes turned out to be dead ends, while others ended up in *multiple* works. The writer's manuscripts and other relevant materials (such as letters, notebooks, and diaries) have been dubbed the "grey canon" by S. E. Gontarski.[4] But even this revaluation suggests a hierarchy between the "real" canon and the "grey" canon. Items from this grey canon are traditionally regarded (and treated) as mere satellites orbiting around the central planet of the canon of the published works.

The third divergence counteracts the tendency to compartmentalize the oeuvre into a sum of works, contained in separate volumes. Perhaps even more fundamental than the issue of completeness is the question of what is meant by *works*. CWEs usually have a rationale that is quite explicit about such things as the choice of copy-text, but often less explicit about their organization. For CWEs in print, there seems to be an implicit consensus about the conceptual and material division between the reading texts and the critical apparatus. While the reading texts are the product of textual criticism, the apparatus is often regarded and treated as its by-product. This is the result of an ingrained teleological conceptualization of a CWE, which is to a large extent conditioned by the print medium. The first decades of scholarly editing in the digital age have seen quite a few interesting new, pioneering editorial enterprises, but seldom involving "complete works." In terms of scope, at least two tendencies mark the development of digital scholarly editions and digital archives at this moment. As to digital editions—probably because the development of a digital scholarly edition is a time-consuming task and funding opportunities are usually precarious and/or for the short term—many editing projects *limit their scope* to a single work, such as Virginia Woolf's *To the Lighthouse* (woolfonline.com), Henry David Thoreau's *Walden* (digitalthoreau.org), Johann Wolfgang Goethe's *Faust* (faustedition.net), or to a selection from the author's oeuvre, such as *Arthur Schnitzler digital* (arthur-schnitzler.de). The more comprehensive initiatives are usually conceived as digital "archives," which aim for completeness but are usually not designed to highlight the connections between the documents they host (e.g., Jonathan Swift Archive; Thomas Gray Archive; Shelley-Godwin Archive; Charles W. Chesnutt Archive; Walt Whitman Archive; Beckett Digital Manuscript Project; Charles Harpur Critical Archive; James Joyce Digital Archive). In other words, while most digital editions privilege a teleological approach and have a limited scope, the archive model is usually more complete but offers few *connections* between the documents.

These *connections* or *relations* between different documents are key elements in what distinguishes a digital edition from a digital archive. Similarly, relations also to a large extent distinguish a digital CWE from a print CWE. Due to limited space and the codex format, a printed CWE often necessarily presents a literary oeuvre as a set of individual works, bottled up in separate volumes. As a result, the writer's complete works appear as a sum of parts. By means of introductions and annotations, the editor usually has to remedy this by explaining that the oeuvre also constitutes a *Gestalt,* a whole that is more than the sum of its parts.

And that brings us to the fourth divergence: A *Gestalt* is not only greater than but also *different* from the sum of its parts. As Caroll Pratt writes in the introduction to Wolfgang Köhler's *The Task of Gestalt Psychology,* it is a common error to leave out the word "different" and simply define a *Gestalt* as "the whole is more than the sum of the parts."[5] This definition mistakenly ignores that a *relationship between* the parts is itself something that is not present in the individual parts themselves.[6] While a digital *archive* lays out all the parts, a digital *edition* assembles them by establishing the connections. When we treat the oeuvre as a *Gestalt,* this also raises the question of whether the work of art is a clear-cut "figure" (a finished product), or rather the dialectics between "figure" and "ground" (in the visual example of Edgar Rubin's famous drawing: between the vase and the two faces). Up till now, the editorial theory and practice of producing a CWE have considered the work of art to be the finished product (in the metaphor, say, the figure of a vase), which implies that the manuscripts and other traces of the production process are merely a background. But, even if that is the case, it is important that these traces of the writing process are recognized as such: as a ground whose contours give shape to the figure. Modern authors are often well aware of the function of the ground against which this figure came to the fore, and many of them therefore voluntarily place those traces of the creative process at their readers' disposal. Schnitzler, for instance, suggested that some of his unfinished "failures" would, in the future, be just as, or even more, interesting to his readers than the "successful" finished products. If these products are successful, they apparently hit a nerve among their audiences; they seem to "work." The rationale behind a genetic CWE model is that, in order to find out why a particular literary oeuvre "works," it is crucial to know how it was made.

A digital genetic CWE enables users to read across versions. The challenge is to reconceptualize the CWE in such a way that the literary oeuvre is presented in all its complexity: something that is both greater than and different from its parts because of the *relations* between them. Precisely because of this complexity, the challenge is to provide readers with the tools to navigate the labyrinth of documents, to discover the relations between them and find the genetic paths.

Deep Hermeneutics:
Combining Digital Editing and Genetic Criticism

To realize this, it may be beneficial to combine insights from *digital scholarly editing* and *genetic criticism*. The digital format allows for greater flexibility and scope; genetic criticism introduces draft material into the edition.

Digital scholarly editions, according to Patrick Sahle, are "guided by a digital paradigm in their theory, method and practice."[7] This "digital paradigm" is characterized by the use of multimedia, hypertextuality, modularized structures, fluid publication, and collaborative editing.[8] According to Hans Walter Gabler, this implies that "manuscript editing in the digital medium constitutes a fundamental extension of the modes of scholarly editing."[9] For this "fundamental extension," John Bryant's "fluid text" theory has laid an important foundation. Bryant duly notes that most texts exist in various versions, but "the problem of access" is a major reason why "fluid texts have not been analyzed much as fluid texts."[10] Although Bryant's theory stretches the boundaries of the fluid text beyond the author's life and includes all forms of adaptation and cultural appropriation, which is broader than what the suggested CWE model encompasses, it indicates a mentality switch that is largely conditioned by the technological advances in digital humanities, toward the text as a process rather than a (static and finished) product.

Genetic criticism challenges a single-text paradigm that, to a large extent, reflects a product-oriented logic similar to the one that characterized structuralism, dominated—according to Pierre-Marc de Biasi—by "a synchronic obsession with form."[11] This "synchronic" focus relates to the syntagmatic dimension of the CWE (the edited reading text, following the narrative sequence). Since the second half of the 1960s, genetic criticism supplements this with a "diachronic" axis, thus adding a paradigmatic dimension to the syntagmatic one. Genetic editions such as the FaustEdition give shape to this paradigmatic dimension, but only for one work or for a limited set of works. My suggestion is to combine the syntagmatic and paradigmatic axes for an author's entire oeuvre. The rationale is that, when both the syntagmatic and paradigmatic dimensions are mapped for the complete oeuvre, the edition fully enables readers to perform *inter*textual and *intra*textual research *across versions*.

Intertextuality is defined by Michael Riffaterre as "the *reader's experience* of links" between different works.[12] This also includes the genetically informed reader. A writer's manuscripts often contain allusions and references to external source texts that may be gradually obscured or undone in the subsequent drafts. If the CWE is conceived and presented as a creative ecology, it provides readers with an edition that enables the detection of this kind of invisible intertextuality, allowing them to discover layers of meaning that would otherwise remain inaccessible.

Intratextuality can be defined as a set of "links established by a reader between at least two texts written by the same author."[13] Writers often allude to their previous works, creating an intratextual network of references. For this kind of intratextual research *across versions,* readers require access not only to the "complete works," but to all the manuscripts as well. A CWE can thus enable readers to discover the manuscripts' hermeneutic potential. This kind of *deep hermeneutics* across versions is useful, not only for scholars. It is also beneficial to a wider readership, even high-school students, as it appeals to a younger, computer-savvy generation's strongly developed visual and digital literacy. The rationale is that manuscripts are not just texts; their digital facsimiles are digital images, containing deletions, additions, drawings, and doodles. Thanks to the online presence of this type of modern manuscript material, it becomes increasingly possible for these students' earliest encounters with literature to be a visual one, sparking a new generation's interest in literature in a novel way.

If a CWE really aims to be complete, it would ideally present the entirety of the author's writings, not just the polished end result of the published works, separated from the textual "impurities." These writings include marginalia in the books the author read, notes in separate copybooks, drafts, typescripts, sketches, doodles, self-translations, or corrected page proofs. This raises several questions: How can we present a writer's oeuvre as a *creative ecology*, a web of intertextual and intratextual relations, and thus open up new insights and give readers the opportunity to discover new avenues for interpretation? What is the role of the editor in such an undertaking? How does the production of a CWE according to a new paradigm impact the editor's role as it changes from being the executor of the author's will who "purifies" the texts to become a maker of connections, providing readers with tools to navigate the complete works? And how can we enable the macroanalysis of authors' complete oeuvres *across versions*?

Modeling the Edition: Four Axes

This is a suggestion to model the CWE in such a way that the reader/researcher can navigate the proliferation of relevant documents and analyses that such an endeavor generates. A good model, according to Willard McCarty, can be fruitful in two ways: "either by fulfilling our expectations, and so strengthening its theoretical basis, or by violating them, and so bringing that basis into question."[14] The envisioned model is of the latter type, as it challenges the status quo of the print paradigm. It operates along four axes:

1. *Teleology and Dysteleology*: Readers are enabled to approach the materials both in a teleological and in a nonteleological way. The teleological approach starts from the published works and organizes the edition accordingly (for instance by numbering the sentences of an anchor text or base text in order to enable a synoptic sentence view; or by providing a collation engine). The dysteleological approach organizes the edition according to the logic of the continuous process of writing, not just the chronology of *publication*.[15] This approach

regards the work less as *œuvre* than as *travail*—the hard work that goes into writing, that does not necessarily make it into publication, and that proceeds without necessarily having a clear goal. Some of the digital tools that support this approach are (1) the organization of the genetic edition using the notebook as a pivot, (2) the search engine, which searches across works and across versions, not only for text, but also for visual elements such as *doodles*,[16] (3) the author's digitized library insofar as it is still extant or their virtual library insofar as it can be reconstructed on the basis of the author's reading notes, and (4) three levels of chronology: small (on the word level, by means of genetic paths and collation),[17] medium (on the level of individual works, by means of genetic maps), and large (on the level of the oeuvre, by means of a manuscript chronology).

2. *Digital Archive and Digital Edition*: The difference between a digital archive and a digital edition is not marked by a clear-cut border, but it is a matter of degree.[18] One editorial project can serve both as an archive and as an edition, depending on the way the reader wishes to use the materials. This continuum between digital archive and digital edition is the second of the four axes. The decisive criterion that distinguishes a digital edition from a digital archive is the editor's role in establishing *connections* between the various versions and works. Instead of generating a single, critically edited reading text, the editorial team maps the genetic "paths" through the genetic dossier by indicating how a particular note derives from a particular source text and feeds into a particular draft. This involves discovering and making links, on the one hand, between exogenesis, endogenesis, and epigenesis, and on the other hand, between the microgenesis and the macrogenesis.

3. *Endogenesis, Exogenesis, and Epigenesis*: In addition to "endogenesis" and "exogenesis," denoting respectively the "inside" (the drafts and successive revised versions) and the "outside" (the author's interaction with external source texts that have left traces in the genetic dossier) of the writing process, the edition can also take account of the "epigenesis" (the continuation of the genesis after publication), acknowledging that at any point there is the possibility that exogenetic material colors the endogenesis and epigenesis.

4. *Macrogenesis, Microgenesis, and Nanogenesis*: The model enables the study of both the macrogenesis (the genesis of the oeuvre in its entirety across multiple versions) and the microgenesis (the processing of a particular exogenetic source

text; the revision history of one specific textual instance across endogenetic and/or epigenetic versions; the revisions within one single version). Moreover, in the case of born-digital works, especially if writers make use of keystroke-logging software, it is even possible to examine the genesis on the level of the nanogenesis (the genesis on the level of individual characters). The increase of born-digital works was initially believed to imply the end of genetic criticism.[19] In the meantime, studies of digital writing processes examining various file formats and media types,[20] making use of digital forensics[21] or of keystroke logging software,[22] show that, on the contrary, the genesis of born-digital works can open up areas of research (on the level of the single character or keystroke) that were beyond reach in analogue genetic criticism.

Creative Ecologies: The Writer's Desk

Against the backdrop of the preceding paragraphs, especially with regard to issues such as textual versus documentary orientation, teleological versus dysteleological approaches, and the digital archive-edition-continuum, one of the promising futures of digital scholarly editing is a sustained attempt to think in terms of *creative ecologies* instead of dichotomies. Opening up the genesis to the level of the oeuvre as a whole has consequences for genetic criticism as well. In de Biasi's seminal typology of the genetic documentation, for instance, the implied focus is on the *avant-texte* of separate works in relative isolation from the rest of the oeuvre.[23] Genetic criticism has traditionally focused on the unit of one publication, one work as a structural principle, for the same reasons digital scholarly editing has: the complexity of the material. But I think that both disciplines have reached enough critical mass and maturity to start thinking more in terms of the digital CWE. It is good to expand the notion of the genetic dossier. Instead of working with the notion of the *avant-texte*, instead of focusing on the genesis of one individual work, it would be useful to focus on the genesis of the oeuvre as a whole and work with the notion of the *sous-oeuvre*, in a slightly more specific sense than Thomas C. Connolly's understanding of the term[24] as the marginalized parts of a work that are traditionally eclipsed.

It would be beneficial, therefore, to open up the canon to include all the notes and drafts, sketches, and even books in the author's personal library, if it is still preserved. Writers often have several book projects underway concurrently. If we want to pay extra attention to forms of concurrent writing or *creative concurrence* in genetic criticism,[25] this implies that we reconstruct the everyday reality of how a work, in all its draft versions, interacted with the other works that populated the author's writing desk at any given moment.

To illustrate how intermingled the geneses of an author's individual works can be, it suffices to glance at Samuel Beckett's writing desk in the late 1970s.[26] The situation can be summarized as follows: Beckett was already working on a longer piece of prose called *Company* when he received a commission. In 1977, the actor David Warrilow asked him to write "a monologue on death."[27] Beckett replied on October 1 with the line "My birth was my death,"[28] and the very next day, under the preliminary title "Gone," he already started developing the theme: "My birth was my death"[29] is the opening sentence of the first draft that was to become a play called *A Piece of Monologue*. In other words, as soon as one is born, one starts dying. In the top left corner of this manuscript, Beckett wrote the rather mysterious note, "all 3rd"; and indeed in the next version (the first typescript, UoR MS 2069), the narrative voice suddenly changes from a first-person to a third-person narrator. As a result, the opening line becomes more ambiguous, for the sentence "Birth was his death" leaves open the possibility that the protagonist's birth meant the death of someone else. This ambiguity is even more pronounced in the published version of *A Piece of Monologue*: "Birth was the death of him." There is an autobiographical dimension to this ambiguity. Since Beckett was born on Good Friday 1906, the death of "him" was also Jesus Christ's suffering on the cross.

The transition from the manuscript to the typescript is quite a jump, and one wonders whether there have not been any intermediary versions that give us a sense of how and why Beckett made the change from first to third person narration in this play. Around the same time, on a piece of paper, Beckett was drafting a French poem ("*fleuves et océans*") that is dated "Ussy Toussaint 77" (November 1, 1977). The next day, on November 2, he wrote to Jocelyn Herbert that he was writing several pieces simultaneously. The manuscripts indicate that, on November 1, he was working on at least three literary projects in three different genres at the same time: the prose piece *Company*, the play *A Piece of Monologue*, and the poem "*fleuves et océans*."

On the one hand, the commissioned play had a thematic impact on the content of the poem, which opens with a pun on the standard expression "ils l'ont laissé pour mort" ("they left him for dead"): "fleuves et océans / l'ont laissé pour vivant." Like in the opening sentence of *A Piece of Monologue*, being alive (*vivant*) is presented as a process of dying. The creative concurrence becomes material in this case, because the poem is drafted on one side of a scrap of paper, the other side of which is covered with notes for *A Piece of Monologue*.[30] It is not entirely clear which of the two sides was written first, and it cannot be excluded that, vice versa, the poem also had an impact on the play. The loose jottings at the back of the poem's draft also thematize death: "Less dying to be done"; "Less to die. To die from. To die with. Ever less"; "Not much left to die" and "Dead & gone / Dying & going." Toward the end of the scrap of paper, the jottings become more concrete and start reading like stage settings for *A Piece of Monologue*, such as the following idea for the opening stage directions:

Fade up. 10". "Birth." 10". "Birth was his death. Etc."

The line "Birth was his death" corresponds with the first typescript of *A Piece of Monologue*, which suggests that there is a synergy between the third person narrative in this version of the play and the third person in the poem "fleuves et océans / l'ont laissé pour vivant." And the note is also the initial idea for a stage direction, so it can be considered as a first draft of the stage direction that was typed out for the first time in the second typescript (UoR MS 2070).

All the while, however, the manuscript of the prose text *Company* was still on Beckett's desk as well. The concurrence between the drafts of *Company* and *A Piece of Monologue* even became a form of confluence at some point.[31] After having been working on both projects concurrently for about eight months, Beckett tried on May 17, 1978, to insert an excerpt from *A Piece of Monologue* into *Company*, resulting in yet another change of the personal pronoun: birth was neither "my death" nor "his death," but "the death of *you*."[32] Soon, however, he decided that this merger did not work after all, and he cancelled the insertion in the *Company* manuscript with a large St. Andrew's cross (MS UoR 1822, 25r). After this brief attempt to merge the play and the prose piece, the three concurrent projects were published separately. Still, the creative concurrence remains noticeable in the themes of life as a form of dying and "his" birth being both the death of the protagonist and that of Christ.

Intratextuality across Versions

In addition to this creative *concurrence,* the oeuvre-in-motion is also marked by *recurrence.* In the stage directions of *A Piece of Monologue,* there is a word that recurs frequently throughout the play. The first word of the stage directions in the published version is "Faint." It has all kinds of variants in the previous versions, such as "Faintest" or "Infinitely faint." And the word recurs in various forms throughout the text. In and of itself, this word is rather inconspicuous. It is indeed faint, also in the sense that it does not strike anyone as particularly strong. It is a word that rather tries to efface itself, which makes it so suitable for this play, consisting of only one speaker onstage and next to him a standard lamp of the "same height" with a "skull-sized white globe, faintly lit." The plan on the scrap of paper indicated that, at the end of the play, the light was to fade out: "End: fade out general light. Hold on globe. Fade out globe." (UoR MS 2460). And in the published version, the light of the globe is said to be "unutterably faint." There are more than a dozen occurrences of the word "faint" in the play:

> *Faint* diffuse light. Speaker stands well off centre downstage audience left....
> Two metres to his left, same level, same height, standard lamp, skull-sized white globe, *faintly* lit....
> Till *faint* light from standard lamp. Wick turned low. And now. This night. Up at nightfall. Every nightfall. *Faint* light in room....
> Room once full of sounds. *Faint* sounds....
> Fewer and *fainter* as time wore on....
> *Faint* light in room. Unutterably *faint.* ...
> *Faint* cry in his ear. Mouth agape....
> Turns away at last and gropes through *faint* unaccountable light to unseen lamp....
> Nothing *faintly* stirring....
> Nothing stirring. *Faintly* stirring....
> On all sides nowhere. Unutterably *faint.* The globe alone. Alone gone.[33]

At first sight, its function seems mainly to translate the cycle of birth and death to the visual metaphor of the globe, the switching on and off of the mind in the skull. But *faint* also applies to sounds. There is both a visual and an auditory dimension to this word. And sometimes it refers to a combination of both senses, as in "faintly stirring." Beckett seems to convey a sense of synaesthesia by means of this word. This synaesthetic dimension may not be particularly striking if this play is analyzed as a separate unit, even if one has access to the entire genetic dossier. But when one opens up the genetic dossier to include the entire *sous-oeuvre*, the entire Beckett canon, including all the manuscripts—the entire genetic underground so to speak—the genetically informed reader may discover something else. In the *avant-texte* of another work by Beckett, called *Stirrings Still* (1989), there is an interesting moment in the genesis relating to the word *faint*. Among the drafts of this work, Beckett connected this word to a specific quotation.[34] The quotation reads, *per lungo silenzio fioco,* followed by Beckett's own translation, marked by an open variant: "faint / hoarse from long silence." The passage derives from Dante's *Inferno,* canto I, where Virgil appears for the first time as Dante's guide. He appears *fioco*, which can be either *faint* (in visual terms) or *hoarse, weak,* or *feeble* (in auditory terms). Because Virgil has not spoken for centuries, the auditory interpretation would make sense, were it not that, at that moment in the text, Virgil has not yet spoken to Dante, so his voice cannot appear "hoarse." Beckett made this observation in the 1920s in one of his student notebooks, when he studied Italian literature. More than fifty years later, he was apparently still preoccupied by this dilemma. This opens up a whole new intratextual dimension: since the word *faint* clearly had a very specific intertextual, Dantean meaning for Beckett, the next step is to see how this word functions in all of Beckett's works and to what degree it has a similarly Dantean resonance over the course of his career.

In conclusion, it is beneficial to any genetic research project to place a work in the context of the oeuvre as a whole, including the *sous-oeuvre,* to stay with the underground metaphor. Our notion of the oeuvre is often colored by the print paradigm. This print paradigm has conditioned us to focus on single-reading texts and to compartmentalize the oeuvre in separate volumes. One could compare it to a railway system in a big city like London: every volume corresponds to a railway station, and every railway station is a separate unit, an endpoint. The challenge for genetic critics is to create a metro system that connects these termini by discovering the underground connections among them. In the example of the word *faint* in *Stirrings Still*, archival research shows that there is an underground connection to something Beckett read fifty years earlier, Dante's *Divina Commedia*, and that this in turn connects to various instances of the word *faint* in several of Beckett's other works. By taking account of this wider range of the oeuvre as a whole, we may be able to discover more of these underground connections. For that is the strength of a CWE: thanks to making the connections, it presents the oeuvre not just as a set of works, but as a *Gestalt*, as something that is not just *more than* the sum of its parts, but also *different from* the sum of its parts.

Notes

1. Fredson Bowers, "Textual Criticism," in *The Aims and Methods of Scholarship in Modern Languages and Literatures*, ed. James Thorpe (New York: Modern Language Association, 1970), 30 (emphasis added).

2. Hans Zeller, "Structure and Genesis in Editing: On German and Anglo-American Textual Editing," in *Contemporary German Editorial Theory*, ed. Hans Walter Gabler, George Bornstein, and Gillian Borland Pierce (Ann Arbor: University of Michigan Press, 1995), 106.

3. See, for instance John Bryant, *The Fluid Text: A Theory of Revision and Editing for Book and Screen* (Ann Arbor: University of Michigan Press, 2002); Paul Eggert, *The Work and the Reader in Literary Studies: Scholarly Editing and Book History* (Cambridge: Cambridge University Press, 2019); Hans Walter Gabler, *Text Genetics in Literary Modernism and Other Essays* (Cambridge: Open Book, 2018); Jerome McGann, *A New Republic of Letters: Memory and Scholarship in the Age of Digital Reproduction* (Cambridge, Mass.: Harvard University Press, 2014); D. F. McKenzie, *Bibliography and the Sociology of Texts* (Cambridge: Cambridge University Press, 1999); Elena Pierazzo, *Digital Scholarly Editing: Theories, Models and Methods* (Farnham, UK: Ashgate, 2015); Peter Shillingsburg, *Textuality and Knowledge* (University Park, Pa.: Penn State University Press, 2017).

4. S. E. Gontarski, "Greying the Canon: Beckett in Performance," in *Beckett after Beckett*, ed. S. E. Gontarski and Anthony Uhlmann (Gainesville: University Press of Florida, 2005), 141–57.

5. Caroll C. Pratt, Introduction to Wolfgang Köhler's *The Task of Gestalt Psychology* (Princeton, N.J.: Princeton University Press, 1960), 9.

6. Pratt, 10.

7. Patrick Sahle, "What Is a Scholarly Digital Edition?," in *Digital Scholarly Editing: Theories and Practices*, ed. Elena Pierazzo and Matthew Driscoll (Cambridge: Open Book, 2016), 28.

8. Sahle, 18–19.

9. Gabler, *Text Genetics*, 133.

10. Bryant, *Fluid Text*, 9.

11. Pierre-Marc de Biasi, "Toward a Science of Literature: Manuscript Analysis and the Genesis of the Work," in *Genetic Criticism: Texts and Avant-textes*, ed. Jed Deppman, Daniel Ferrer, and Michael Groden (Philadelphia: University of Pennsylvania Press, 2004), 41.

12. Michael Riffaterre, "La Trace de l'intertexte," *Pensée* 215 (1980): 4–18 (emphasis added).

13. Kareen Martel, "Les notions d'intertextualité et d'intratextualité dans les théories de la reception," *Protée* 33, no. 1 (Spring 2015): 93–102.

14. Willard McCarty, "Knowing . . . : Modeling in Literary Studies," in *A Companion to Digital Literary Studies*, ed. Ray Siemens and Susan Schreibman (Oxford: Wiley-Blackwell, 2013), 395.

15. Dirk Van Hulle, "Sheherazade's Notebook: Editing Textual Dysteleology and Autographic Modernism," *Modernist Cultures* 15, no. 1 (2020): 12–28.

16. To make them searchable, the Beckett Digital Manuscripts Project categorizes the doodles according to a typology, divided into four main categories: objects, organisms, shapes, and symbols, each of which is subdivided into subcategories. Thus, the category "organisms" contains the subcategory "humanoid." By selecting this subcategory, the reader is presented with all the humanoid doodles in the author's manuscripts. The encoding also facilitates other searches such as the systematic search for dates, gaps (blank spaces in manuscripts), calculations and intertextual references. The latter category partially links up with the author's personal library.

17. For suggestions on integrating automatic collation in a digital edition, see Ronald Haentjens Dekker, Dirk van Hulle, Gregor Middell, Vincent Neyt, and Joris van Zundert, "Computer-Supported Collation of Modern Manuscripts: CollateX and the Beckett Digital Manuscript Project," *Digital Scholarship in the Humanities* 30, no. 3 (2015): 452–70, doi.org/10.1093/llc/fqu007; Dirk Van Hulle, Elli Bleeker, Bram Buitendijk, Ronald Haentjens Dekker, and Vincent Neyt, "Layers of Variation: A Computational Approach to Collating Texts with Revisions," *DHQ: digital humanities quarterly* 16, no. 1 (2022): 1–29. On "genetic paths," see Paolo D'Iorio, "Nietzsche on New Paths: The HyperNietzsche Project and Open Scholarship on the Web," in *Friedrich Nietzsche: Edizioni e interpretazioni*, ed. Maria Christina Fornari (Pisa: ETS, 2006): 474–96.

18. Paul Eggert, "The Archival Impulse and the Editorial Impulse," *Variants* 14 (2019): 3–22.

19. Marita Mathijsen, "Genetic Textual Editing: The End of an Era," in *Was Ist Textkritik? Zur Geschichte und Relevanz eines Zentralbegriffs der Editionswissenschaft*,

ed. Gertraud Mitterauer, Werner Maria Bauer, and Sabine Hofer, Beihefte zu Editio 28 (Tübingen: Niemeyer, 2009), 233–40.

20. Bénédicte Vauthier, "Genetic Criticism Put to the Test by Digital Technology: Sounding out the (Mainly) Digital Genetic File of El Dorado," *Variants* 12–13 (2016): 163–86; Melinda Vásári, "Securing the Literary Evidence. Some Perspectives on Digital Forensics," in *Philology in the Making: Analog/Digital Cultures of Scholarly Writing and Reading*, ed. Pál Kelemen and Nicolas Pethes (Bielefeld: Transcript, 2019), 287–309.

21. Thorsten Ries, "The Rationale of the Born-Digital Dossier Génétique: Digital Forensics and the Writing Process, with Examples from the Thomas Kling Archive," *Digital Scholarship in the Humanities* 33, no. 2 (2018): 391–424.

22. Lamyk Bekius, "The Reconstruction of the Author's Movement through the Text, or How to Encode Keystroke Logged Writing Processes in TEI-XML," *Variants* 15–16 (2021): 3–43.

23. Dirk Van Hulle, *Genetic Criticism: Tracing Creativity in Literature* (Oxford: Oxford University Press, 2022), 120.

24. Thomas C. Connolly, *Paul Celan's Unfinished Poetics: Readings in the Sous-Œuvre* (Cambridge: Legenda, 2018).

25. Dirk Van Hulle, "Creative Concurrence: Gearing Genetic Criticism for the Sociology of Writing," *Variants* 15–16 (2021): 45–62.

26. This case study was partly developed for the colloquium "Imperfect Itineraries: Literature and Literary Research in the Archives," March 4, 2022, Université de Lorraine-Nancy, and used as an example in the above-mentioned article in Variants 15–16.

27. Samuel Beckett, *The Letters of Samuel Beckett (1966–1989)*, ed. George Craig, Martha Dow Fehsenfeld, Dan Gunn, and Lois More Overbeck, vol. 4 (Cambridge: Cambridge University Press, 2016), 471n1.

28. Beckett, 471n1.

29. University of Reading, UoR MS 2068, fol. 01r.

30. UoR MS 2460, m18, fols. 01r–v; Dirk Van Hulle, "Beckett's Art of the Commonplace: The 'Sottisier' Notebook and Mirlitonnades Drafts," *Journal of Beckett Studies* 28, no. 1 (2019): 67–89.

31. See Matthijs Engelberts, *Défis du récit scénique: formes et enjeux du mode narratif dans le théâtre de Beckett et Duras* (Geneva: Librarie Droz, 2001).

32. Samuel Beckett, *Company / Compagnie: A Digital Genetic Edition*, ed. Georgina Nugent-Folan and Vincent Neyt (Brussels: University of Antwerp, 2024), BDMP9, EM, fol. 25r (emphasis added), beckettdigitalarchive.org.

33. Samuel Beckett, *Krapp's Last Tape and Other Shorter Plays* (London: Faber and Faber, 2009), 115–21.

34. Samuel Beckett, *Stirrings Still / Soubresauts* and *Comment dire / What is the Word: A Digital Genetic Edition*, ed. Dirk Van Hulle and Vincent Neyt, (Brussels: University Press Antwerp, 2011), beckettdigitalarchive.org.

CHAPTER 4

Charles W. Chesnutt and the Generous Edition

Collations, Annotations, and Genetic Histories

STEPHANIE P. BROWNER

Introduction

This essay makes two claims. First, although we have teaching editions of Black writers, there is an urgent need for scholarly editions. Second, these editions must be "generous," undergirded by an ethos that has emerged from the groundswell of work in Black bibliography, an ethos that foregrounds relationality, contexts, communities, and forebears, and rich in robust collations, annotations, and genetic histories.[1] We are in a new era of Black studies, one not unlike the 1960s, when scholarship took major strides in bringing forward fresh histories and theories. Generous scholarly editions, print and digital, should not shy away from making a contribution to this new era. All editions are marked by their moment. To claim otherwise is disingenuous, to shirk the responsibility the moment demands, and to seek refuge in a false claim to neutrality and disinterest.

Seven years ago, having surveyed the field of scholarly editions of U.S. writers, Oxford University Press concluded there was a need, and presumably a market, for a multivolume scholarly print edition of the writings of African American writer Charles W. Chesnutt (1858–1932). Chesnutt's short stories and novels have been at the center of groundbreaking scholarship on race for decades, and yet there are no scholarly editions of his fiction, not even of single works, much less his entire oeuvre. Oxford was prepared to take on the costs of publication and distribution, and the National Endowment for the Humanities (NEH) awarded a Scholarly Editions Grant to the first two volumes: *The Complete Short Stories* (ed. Stephanie Browner, Sarah Wagner-McCoy, and Richard Yarborough). Those two volumes and a third—*The Journals and Memoranda* (ed. Tess Chakkalakal and Mark Sussman)—are nearing completion. A prospectus for a fourth, Chesnutt's first published and now widely taught novel *The House Behind the Cedars*, is in development, and others will follow.

At the same time, The Charles W. Chesnutt Archive, launched as an undergraduate-course project twenty-five years ago, is growing and securing funding. Thanks to an NEH grant, it is now a well-structured TEI-conformant (Text Encoding Initiative) site, with faceted search capabilities. It offers all of Chesnutt's published works, and a manuscript wing has been developed that already includes the hand-corrected galley proofs of four of his book-length works. Encoding of the galley proofs required innovation, since the current TEI (P5) standard offers no guidelines for how to tag proofreading marks. This work has been documented, presented at the Association for Documentary Editing, and made publicly available.[2] Current work is focused on Chesnutt's correspondence. Expected to take six to seven years, the project will digitize, transcribe, and annotate all of Chesnutt's correspondence, incoming as well as outgoing. When this work is completed, scholars and readers will have access to more than eighteen hundred letters, a remarkably expansive epistolary world. Importantly, the stability and future of the site are accounted for since it is housed at the Center for Digital Research in the Humanities at the University of Nebraska and is fully integrated into the center's backup and preservation plans.[3]

Scholars involved in both projects have examined the case for editing Chesnutt simultaneously for print volumes and the digital medium.[4] The latter may seem to be the medium of the future, but concurrent projects are common, and print's advantages remain significant. A university press's interest and ability to provide financial support for production, distribution, and marketing is valuable, and the ongoing vitality of print editions is evident in the many multivolume print editions currently in process. Just to name U.S. writers, these include editions for Henry James, Mark Twain, Willa Cather, Charles Brockden Brown, Frederick Douglass, and Harriet Beecher Stowe, with Cambridge University Press, University of California Press, University of

Nebraska Press, Bucknell University Press, Yale University Press, and Oxford University Press, respectively. In this context, then, the question that initially seemed important to wrestle with fades, which is whether it's foolhardy to edit for both print and digital formats, and a more important question emerges: what are the specific demands that come with editing a Black writer?

Chesnutt did not become a major literary figure for study at majority-white institutions until the 1970s, and his introduction into the majority-white scholarly world was often burdened with misguided assumptions about discovery: the works had been forgotten and were just now gaining the attention they deserved. There was also early on an emphasis on his achievement in publishing in white and Northeastern venues such as *Atlantic Monthly*, and his standing was often attested to by reference to him as the first Black writer to appear in those pages.

But Chesnutt was never out of view for the Black community, including scholars, leaders, and writers, who honored him while he was alive and nurtured his legacy after his death. Late in his life, Chesnutt was asked to contribute to *The Crisis*'s influential symposium on "The Negro in Art." In 1928, Harlem Renaissance writer, activist, and lawyer James Weldon Johnson nominated Chesnutt for the NAACP's highest award: the Spingarn Medal. After his death, Chesnutt earned attention from a wide range of Black scholars. His books were advertised steadily in *The Crisis,* Carter G. Woodson's *Journal of Black History* promoted his fiction as essential to Black education, and in 1941 W. E. B. Du Bois's *Phylon* published a scholarly article on Chesnutt. In the 1950s, Arna Bontemps brought many of Chesnutt's papers to Fisk University for care and preservation, and his daughter Helen Chesnutt published a biography of her father with the University of North Carolina Press. In the 1950s, his second novel, a thinly veiled account of the 1898 Wilmington coup and massacre, was important to the young playwright Lorraine Hansberry. She dedicated seven years, before her early death, to dramatizing the novel, and the margins of her copy include references to the Black historians she was reading at the time. In the late 1960s, as the Civil Rights Movement and the founding of Black studies programs increased demand for books by Black writers, Chesnutt's published works were reprinted in facsimile editions. But it was Black scholar Sylvia Lyons Render who undertook the archival and editorial labor to publish, with Howard University Press, the fifty-five stories that had appeared only in magazines or newspapers or had never been published.

The publication history and context of Chesnutt's first story similarly bespeaks an ethics of community and care. A short story for children, "Frisk's First Rat" (1875) appeared in the *Fayetteville Educator,* a weekly newspaper central to the Black Fayetteville community. Founded by two men, one who came up through the Howard School, which Chesnutt also attended, and one who later served as a delegate to the Republican National Convention, the newspaper was unabashed in its attention to issues important to the community, both local and national. It published railroad timetables and accident reports, news of church events, and updates on civil rights activism, including extensive coverage of the battle for the 1875 Civil Rights Act. When it passed, the editors proclaimed, "We are at last a free people." To the bill's detractors, the editors retorted, "We assure our friends who have been so badly frightened by the bill that their parlors, their daughters, &c are just as safe now as ever." The newspaper's "Religious Department" was written by Chesnutt's teacher and mentor, Robert Harris, and when the newspaper published three "Compositions by pupils in the Howard School" about Eli Whitney, two were by Chesnutt's brothers, fourteen and thirteen years old at the time. Providing a glimpse into the curriculum at the Howard School, which had been built by the Freedmen's Bureau on land Chesnutt's father and six other Black men purchased, all three essays underscore the relationship between the efficiency gained with the cotton gin and an increase in the slave trade.

The range of voices in the *Fayetteville Educator* reflects the "diversification of voices, function, and conceptions of authority" that Eric Gardner found in his study of early San Francisco Black newspapers. The Fayetteville weekly was, like the Black Ohio newspapers Jewon Woo studies, both an "outlet for specific editorial voices" and "a document for active communal life."[5] It was embedded in a community and contributed to that community's well-being. A generous edition, then, would not only determine the best text for "Frisk's First Rat"; it would also give some sense of this publishing context. We have, in the past, used words like "authoritative" or "definitive" for scholarly editions, and these aptly captured the ethos of the times. Generous editions should be no less disciplined, careful, complete, and committed to the highest standards. But they might also be defined as open, generative, and importantly, embedded in and shaped by a larger community of scholars and readers. The success of such endeavors as The Colored Conventions Project and the Black Bibliography Project, in building and sustaining collaboration and in putting community at the center, have much to teach us. The rest of this essay will tease out what an ethos of generous editing might mean for three standard features of scholarly editions: collations, annotations, and genetic histories.[6]

Collations

In his 1997 essay "Editing 'Minority' Texts," William Andrews suggested that the usual "lists of textual variants, emendations, line-end hyphenations, and the rest of the panoply of textual description" were unnecessary.[7] Editions with robust textual apparatuses take time, and we needed African American texts to teach right then. But now, twenty-five years later, we have teaching editions of many Black writers, but few with collations.

Computer-assisted collation began in the 1960s, and by 1990 there were more than a dozen somewhat useful software programs. And yet, in 1994, as he contemplated collating eighty-three manuscripts of *The Canterbury Tales*, Chaucer scholar Peter W. Robinson discovered that few scholarly editions in the last few years had used computer collation. Nor did he find any existing programs to serve his needs as a medieval textual scholar. Thus, he wrote his own program and imagined a not-too-distant future when "the traditional editor could disappear altogether" and digital editions would include collation software that allowed readers to navigate for themselves the selection of texts for collation, the type of analysis, and the format of the results.[8] In the early 2000s, Jerome McGann similarly imagined such a future, and he and his colleagues at NINES (Nineteenth-century Scholarship Online) created Juxta, an online collation tool. Although Juxta is no longer available, there are other online nonproprietary collation tools (e.g., LERA and Variance Viewer). There are also collation tools embedded in programs such as TUSTEP, Classical Text Editor, Versioning Machine, Oxygen XML Editor, and CollateX. A 2020 review of machine collation programs finds much to like, but also concludes with concerns, most importantly that programs tend to embed assumptions about what can be ignored (spelling, white space, punctuation, handwriting, font, layout, etc.) and what is of interest.[9]

Automized collation must have clarity, from the start, about the goals of the edition, the interests of readers, and importantly, what is the smallest unit of comparison. For Chesnutt, whose works include nuanced visual rendering of dialect, collation must attend to such details as the placement of apostrophes and the presence or absence of a space before or after the apostrophe. Recognizing that much is learned in the process of doing hand collations, and reluctant to spend the time testing existing applications or designing our own, the editors of the print editions of the short stories elected to do manual collation. We did, however, enter every variant, tagged for type and location, into a bespoke program (in the language C) that facilitates analysis. The program's results, displayed in a spreadsheet, were particularly useful when there were hundreds of variants across as many as ten witnesses and when fine-grained analysis was important.[10]

One fundamental value of collation, of course, comes before collating even begins. It lies in the exhaustive search for all extant witnesses. For Chesnutt, this yielded a wealth of new information. Chesnutt began his career by publishing stories through syndication. We knew his stories had appeared in a few major city newspapers—the *Boston Evening Transcript,* the *Chicago Daily Inter-Ocean,* and the *Boston Daily Globe*. But intensive searches across diverse digital databases revealed that his stories appeared in many more city newspapers than previously thought (Atlanta, Louisville, Denver, San Francisco, and Portland [Oregon], to name only a few) and in small-town newspapers from coast to coast. Some stories have been found in thirty to forty venues, a number that will almost surely grow as more newspapers are digitized. We have also learned that stories Chesnutt sold to weekly magazines were later reprinted by daily newspapers, that one story presumed unpublished was in fact published, and that another was abridged and republished several years later, both in a story magazine and in newspapers. A conservative estimate suggests a total readership of between fifty and one hundred thousand for some of these works.[11]

We also found that collating syndicated stories not only returned us to the work of the prolific and influential editor Fredson Bowers in productive ways, but also challenged us to consider that attention to and reporting of every detail is integral to a truly generous edition. In wrestling with Stephen Crane's syndicated stories, for which there are no extant master copies or manuscripts (as is also the case with Chesnutt), Bowers suggested that editors consider "treating the accidentals of the revised text on the same critical basis as its substantives." But, as G. Thomas Tanselle pointed out in "Editing without a Copy-Text," Bowers did not follow his own advice. Although Bowers included accidentals and substantives in his emendation lists for the Crane stories, only substantive variants appear in the historical collation.[12] This leaves accidental variants in equally authoritative witnesses unrecorded. For Chesnutt, this would be a serious misstep. Although the indeterminacy of the source for each of the hundreds of variants across the multiple witnesses of Chesnutt's syndicated stories cannot be resolved, a collation of all accidental and substantive variants allows readers to ask, if not definitively answer, a host of questions that would be foreclosed by a less generous approach, such as collations that do not record accidental variants. With Chesnutt, as it turns out, much information lies in these seemingly small and insignificant changes and a truly complete collation allows us to consider how compositors and editors engaged Chesnutt's style, word choice, syntax, spelling, and punctuation.

While collation often yields small kernels of information that only sometimes provoke larger insights, at times the results are quite dramatic. Such is the case with the 1889 short story "The Conjurer's Revenge." Chesnutt was at the tail end of two years of intensive short story publishing, and it is the only story he published in the *Overland Monthly*, a San Francisco literary magazine. Founded in 1868 with Bret Harte as its first editor and stories by Mark Twain in its first issues, *The Overland Monthly* had a commitment to Pacific-region writers and culture. Chesnutt's story stands out as one of only a few each year that were not about the West. Ten years later the story appeared in his collection *The Conjure Woman*. This is the text that is reprinted and used by teachers and scholars, with the differences unremarked.

"The Conjurer's Revenge," like all the stories in the 1899 collection, is a frame tale, featuring a white northern couple, John and Annie, who have moved south for her health and bought land, which they are developing. In each story, they listen to a conjure tale from slave times as told by Julius, who had been squatting on the land but now works for the couple. In preparing three other previously published stories for the 1899 collection, Chesnutt focused on revising the frame tale, eliminating explanatory passages no longer needed in every story. And at first glance this may seem to be the case with "The Conjurer's Revenge," since changes to the frame tale include a cut of 461 words that reduces Annie's contribution to the dialogue.

But far more of Chesnutt's revisions are focused on Julius. In fact, over 80 percent of changes between the 1889 and 1899 texts are to the tale Julius tells, or to the words he speaks in the frame tale. Some of the changes foreground Julius's attention to his listeners, and several have Julius giving more cues to facilitate understanding of the story. But the preponderance of variants reveals Chesnutt's meticulous attention to Julius's words and syntax, and to rendering his speech visually. Sometimes Chesnutt changes a word from standard English to dialect speech (*was* to *wuz*, or *him* to *'im*); sometimes from dialect back to standard English (as in *yer* to *you*); and sometimes from one dialect version to another. Many changes add or delete apostrophes and add or delete single letters or space on either side of the apostrophe.

For more than a century, writers and scholars have meditated on the intertwined oral and print traditions of African American literature. In *The Souls of Black Folk,* Du Bois prefaced every chapter with bars of gospel songs; and his last chapter, "Of Songs of Sorrow," begins by invoking the sound of the renowned Fisk Jubilee Singers. The role of music, sound, speech, and oral culture are integral to Henry Louis Gates Jr.'s *The Signifying Monkey* and Paul Gilroy's *The Black Atlantic,* to name only two of many major works that have probed the relationship between orality and print. Dialect fiction, however, remains a knotty issue, and some of Chesnutt's most complex stories—popular in his day and widely taught now—put visual dialect at the center.

There is little consensus on Chesnutt's use of dialect. Eric Sundquist argues that, in Chesnutt's dialect, there is a "subtle, self-conscious examination of his relation to both the White plantation tradition and to those Black writers who may have pandered to the public taste." Paul Petrie has suggested that Chesnutt exploited "plantation-dialect regionalism's capacity for cultural mediation while ridding it of its white racist values." Seeing dialect as a trickster's mask, Houston Baker argues that Julius speaks with "conjuring efficaciousness" because he is fully aware that the sounds of his speech are "dear to the hearts of his White boss." Critic and novelist John Edgar Wideman suggests

Chesnutt's use of dialect reveals that the speech of the northern white man and the southern Black man are equally marked, and that the "obvious kind of power" of the former is "balanced by an unexpected force wielded by the supposed powerless." Several scholars, noting Chesnutt's remarkable stenography skills (he could record more than two hundred words per minute), have argued that Chesnutt's exacting depictions of orthographical features bespeak a desire to preserve a regional dialect that was disappearing. In *The Sonic Color Line,* Jennifer Lynn Stoever reads Chesnutt's dialect as writerly performances akin to the Fisk Jubilee singers performing spirituals for white audiences. In both instances the performances are not mere minstrelsy, but also transformational for the performer.[13]

Increasingly, scholarship and public debate have challenged us to think critically about speech, performance, language, race, and power, and new forms of social justice praxis recommend attention to who speaks, in what language or dialect, and in what settings. Not surprisingly, scholars have sought in Chesnutt's journals, letters, and essays, as well as the stories themselves, evidence of his own thinking about dialect, and certainly some readers find it troubling, particularly that Julius's speech is rendered with what seems to be "comic orthography" meant to capture "lazy, slovenly pronunciation."[14] Thus, in this context, meticulous attention to Chesnutt's revisions to Julius's speech at every level, from word choice and syntax to how it looks on the page, is critical. Even a cursory study of Chesnutt's manuscripts reveals that he wrote dialect easily. Handwritten revisions of dialect passages are squeezed in between typed lines and pour down the margins in a hand that seems not to pause as Chesnutt uses spaces, apostrophes, dropped letters, and colloquialisms, sometimes revising as he goes.

To date, we have had no "great deal of organized and digested information," in Paul Eggert's description of scholarly editions, of Chesnutt at work drafting and revising dialect, a language central to some of his fiction.[15] And while his use of dialect may seem to dabble in stereotypes, the speed of composition suggests intimacy and familiarity, and the hundreds of tiny revisions bespeak a kind of care, even loving attention, to the words, phrasings, sound, rhythms of a Black North Carolina storyteller, and to the visual play on the page of Julius's voice, wit, and intelligence. We often assume Chesnutt wrote primarily for a white audience. But that is not the full story. He worked hard to get his books into the hands of Black readers, and he read his stories aloud to Black audiences, at schools, churches, and public events in the North and South. In 1899, a few months after he would have made these revisions to "The Conjurer's Revenge," Chesnutt read two dialect stories at the Fifteenth Street Presbyterian Church in Washington, D.C. Elite and storied, led by abolitionists, orators, and activists, the church was pastored, in 1899, by the nationally esteemed Reverend Francis J. Grimké. Almost surely the pews were full, and without a doubt Chesnutt would have known the church's history. In 1865 the church was led by Rev. Henry Highland Garnett, the first African American to speak in the U.S. House Chamber; in 1870 it established the nation's first public Black high school; before the Civil War, the congregation included White House seamstress Elizabeth Keckley, who led church's Contraband Relief Association; and after the war Sojourner Truth helped the church raise money for the Colored Soldiers Aid Society. Presumably Chesnutt and Reverend Grimké spoke before and after the reading. *The Colored American* covered the event, observing that, while Chesnutt's talent for handling "the dialect of the North Carolina darky with rare skill is well known to the many readers of his books," the reading "demonstrated in a manner most entertaining, that he can speak as well as write dialect." The review concludes: "There was not a dull moment in the two hours, . . . and at the conclusion of the programme he received the hearty applause and individual congratulations of his auditors"[16] How did Chesnutt render Julius's words, his accent, the rhythms of his speech? How did the congregants hear him? Was there delight and pleasure and love in Chesnutt's voice when he read Julius's lines? Collation that attends to every detail of Chesnutt's rendering of dialect—as he wrote it by hand, typed it, and revised it—is surely editorial work that honors and matches the care Chesnutt himself gave to dialect writing. Put differently, if an edition is to serve the myriad questions raised by Chesnutt's use of dialect, it must make all relevant evidence available.

The question of how to present collations is not simple, and it is here that we might want to apply the notion of generous editing not only to a single edition, but to the decision to undertake concurrent editing in print and digital formats, something we initially worried was a luxury. The print edition of Chesnutt's short stories will use the familiar variants lists, while the digital archive offers high quality scans, and thus each offers distinct advantages. The variants list in a print edition is sometimes dismissed as ungainly, but it is a form that, as Richard Bucci has argued, "focuses attention efficiently on the changes."[17] For "The Conjurer's Revenge," the variants list is almost five hundred lines, four hundred of which draw our attention to the details of every instance of Chesnutt's careful rendering and revising of Julius's speech. The list also reveals patterns: which words get tweaked most often, for example, or when he makes a change in one version and then undoes it in the next. The variant list offers, to use Eggert's observation about scholarly editions in general, "a great deal of organized and digested information," and thus it completes the collation task many scholars may not be prepared to undertake. By contrast, although the Charles W. Chesnutt Archive does not yet offer a collation tool or any completed collations, it does offer scans and transcriptions of all three versions of "The Conjurer's Revenge." The images of the galleys, something the print cannot offer (due to costs), are particularly interesting: they allow the reader to see Chesnutt's hand as he makes the corrections in blue pencil.

Annotations

The ethos in Black bibliography that calls attention to relationality, contexts, community, and forebears has contributed to an important reframing of how we understand post-Reconstruction America. Four decades ago, Eric Foner's description of post-Reconstruction society as the "racial nadir" of the nation's history accomplished important work. It demolished any lingering purchase of the Dunning School's assertion that the "Redemption" and the end of Reconstruction were necessary to the South's economic recovery. But, for all that Foner's oft-quoted phrase does to bring into view disenfranchisement and legally sanctioned violence, work also done by such terms as "slavery by another name" or "neoslavery," it misses that this was also a period, as Foner himself documented, of bold interventions in racial politics and discourse. During these years, Black institutions were forged and strengthened, including schools, newspapers, political organizations, families, and churches.

Chesnutt was active across all these areas.[18] During the early years of fiction writing, he worked briefly as a reporter for Dow, Jones, and Company, a

Wall Street news agency in New York City, and then in the legal department at the Nickel Plate Railroad Company in Cleveland, Ohio, where he read law for two years with the company's senior counsel, Judge Samuel E. Williamson. He was one of the top court stenographers in Cleveland for over forty years, and his office often served as a gathering place for out-of-town lawyers. The national NAACP consulted him about political nominees they were considering endorsing, and Chesnutt attended NAACP events on the East Coast, chaired panels at NAACP conferences, and hosted events in Cleveland. He corresponded about law and politics for decades with white and Black leaders, and led a lively social and cultural life with his wife. Two of his brothers built a successful photography business in Cleveland, and one daughter, after earning a B.A. at Smith College, taught Latin at Cleveland's Central High School, where Langston Hughes was among her students. Another daughter taught briefly at Tuskegee Institute, which deepened Chesnutt's personal ties to Booker T. Washington, even as he disagreed passionately with him on voting rights. His son-in-law was a librarian at Case Western Reserve, and later head librarian at Howard University.

In a generous edition, whether print or digital, of his fiction or his letters, how do annotations help these relationships and communities, contexts and networks come into view? One common case for annotations is access. In his introduction to a 2017 edition of Martin Delaney's *Blake; or, The Huts of America*, McGann observes that the annotations in the 1970 Beacon Press edition "fall far short of what a reader of the book, whether a general reader or a scholar, needs."[19] The goal of this new edition, he explains, is to "improve readers' access" to Delaney's work. Improving access is laudable, and often adduced as a reason for annotations, but the argument can have a whiff of paternalism: the reader needs help or the text needs to be explained. This paternalism can be particularly troubling when the texts are by non-white writers. Some editors, by contrast, pride themselves on minimal annotations. Fredson Bowers' 1970 University of Virginia Press edition of Stephen Crane's *Tales of War* offers a particularly austere version of this approach. It is as minimalist with annotations as it is maximalist with collation. It has no annotations at all. The message is clear: the text's worthiness of our attention goes without saying, and the reader is assumed to be as capable of scholarly research as the editors.

The minimalist approach is appealing. Justifying an interest in Chesnutt would be patronizing, and it is best to assume readers are fully capable of research, much facilitated now by the internet. Moreover, paratext can be problematic. Annotations and introductions, unattached to an explicit argument or interpretation, and embedded in a scholarly edition, can seem to have a neutrality and thus authority to frame or define the text. But there are also problems with the minimalist approach. In its efforts to avoid interpretive intrusion, it enshrines the single text, as though texts exist outside contexts, networks, and contingencies of all kinds. The unencumbered text may be an example of the modularity in both computing and the humanities that Tara McPherson warned in 2012 can lead to an avoidance of relationality and complexity.[20]

So, if we want to embrace an ethos of generous editing, we might consider Anne Fernald's 2015 Cambridge edition of *Mrs. Dalloway* as a model. Running almost as long as the novel (130 pages for the 175-page novel), the explanatory notes (and these do not include textual notes) offer a kaleidoscopic map of the work's contexts, of Mrs. Dalloway's London, and of Woolf's life and writings.[21] Might robust annotations for Chesnutt's short stories and correspondence do the same thing for Chesnutt's writings and life and for Chesnutt's America? And what dangers might attend a practice of generous annotating?

In a 1906 letter to Chesnutt, Washington mentions that, during his upcoming visit to Cleveland he will stay at the Hotel Hollenden. A minimal note would identify the Hollenden Hotel as a luxury hotel in downtown Cleveland. A more generous note might add that, although Washington stayed there several times, in general Black guests were not welcome. An even more generous note might include information about the barbershop at the hotel. As both Chesnutt and Washington would have known, the hotel had a large and renowned barbershop, owned by a Black man. One year younger than Chesnutt, George A. Myers was influential in Republican politics at the city, state, and national levels. His shop had more than twenty employees—barbers, manicurists, porters, podiatrists—and it was a gathering spot for social and political elites. He served as a delegate to several Republican National Conventions, and his involvement led to offers of political appointments. He accepted none, but was instrumental in getting appointments for other Black men. In 1923 the hotel management decided that, when Myers retired and sold his business, all the Black barbers would be replaced by White ones.

A note with this much detail might raise concerns about editorial intrusion, about directing the reader with a heavy hand or using small details (Washington's hotel choice) as an excuse for providing a history of interest to the editors, or their political agenda, beyond what is needed for reading this 1906 letter. Indeed, our annotation does not include all these details. But noting Myers's business in the hotel was warranted, we concluded. Barbering was an important occupation for Black people, and in a 1930 speech "Advice for Businessmen," Chesnutt lamented the loss of this employment sector for African Americans. In that speech he also honored Myers as the "last outstanding example of success in this line in Cleveland."[22] Chesnutt also put a Black barber working in a Northern luxury barbershop at the center of one of his later stories. "The Doll," published in 1912 in *The Crisis*, the NAACP's monthly magazine, centers on a moral quandary: the barber finds himself shaving the white Southern man who murdered his father decades earlier, and must weigh his desire for justice and the consequences for his own family. Although a reference to the Hollenden Hotel in a letter seems to warrant a note that includes Myers, does the short story also need such a note? The fictional barber is the owner of the shop, which is in a hotel, and it is the "handsomest barber shop in the city," with "many colored barbers, in immaculate white jackets" and "frequented by gentlemen who could afford to pay liberally for superior service."[23] The ethos of a generous edition, as opposed to the minimalist approach, would suggest a note, perhaps at the end of the sentence that introduces the barber and describes his shop. We take seriously the dangers of annotations that make connections better left to readers, but are willing to risk the dangers of annotations that annoy today or later come to seem unnecessary and outdated. Ideally, a generous edition offers, unobtrusively, relevant information anchored to and arising from words, phrases, and references in the text, and in doing so helps bring Chesnutt's world, networks, and community more fully and richly into view.

Genetic Editing

The distinct affordances of print and digital editions are particularly evident in genetic editing. Indeed, many would argue that the digital environment can do justice to complex genetic histories in a way that print cannot. And while that may be true, the preparation of a print edition of a genetically complex work has much to teach us.

Extensive archives for Black writers before the Harlem Renaissance are uncommon, and the Chesnutt manuscript archive is one of the most voluminous. It includes several thousands of pages, mostly typescript and hand-corrected. Although scholars have turned to this remarkable archive to publish the works unpublished in Chesnutt's lifetime (six novels, one play, and sixteen stories), there are no in-depth studies of the genetic histories of any of the works for which we have more than one version, which include twelve published stories and sixteen unpublished stories. Most notably, the more than five hundred pages of hand-revised typescripts for one of his most often taught and studied novels, *The House Behind the Cedars,* have garnered scant attention.

Since its publication in 1900, this iconic novel about racial passing has spoken to the nation's race conscience. In the 1920s it was republished in serial form by *The Chicago Defender,* the largest-circulation Black newspaper at the time. The Black filmmaker Oscar Micheaux twice turned it into a movie featuring major Black stars and running in Black theaters across the country: as a silent film in 1927 and as a talkie in 1932. In the late 1960s, as the American literary canon was reformed, reprints began to appear, and now, in addition to trade editions, the novel has appeared both in a Modern Library anthology dedicated to Chesnutt and alone in the Modern Library Classics series. There is no scholarly edition of the novel, however, and few know that the work began not as a novel about passing, but as a short story about a Black community and a light-skinned, mixed-race woman who makes a bad marriage at her mother's prodding.

Chesnutt was at the height of his story-writing career when he wrote "Rena Walden," the title he used for this story, and he wanted it to appear in a leading magazine. He had published more than thirty stories in the previous two years in *Family Fiction, Puck,* the *Atlantic Monthly,* and newspapers around the country. He shared three drafts with George Washington Cable, with whom he had recently established a friendship, and he had the more established Cable forward the story to Richard Watson Gilder at *The Century.*

When Gilder's response came, Chesnutt chafed. Gilder called the characters "amorphous," to which Chesnutt retorted, in a draft letter to Cable, "I suspect that my way of looking at things is 'amorphous' not in the sense of being unnatural but unusual." To many whites, he noted, mixed-race people are an "insult to nature, a kind of monster." Chesnutt omitted these observations from the letter he sent to Cable, but he was undeterred by a reading he found so misguided. Four weeks later he submitted it to the *Atlantic Monthly*, telling Cable, "I mean to have it published." When the *Atlantic Monthly* declined, he proposed to its parent company, the book publisher Houghton Mifflin, a collection of stories to be called "Rena Walden and Other Stories," noting that he was willing to leave out or include other stories, "always excepting the longer one, 'Rena Walden.'" But Houghton Mifflin declined the collection proposal as well. Chesnutt's publishing pace slowed after this, although in 1895, he reported to Gilder: "After five years' study of life and literature, I have recast the story of 'Rena Walden.' . . . It is now a novelette of about 25,000–28,000 words."[24] Four years later, Chesnutt had further expanded "Rena Walden," and in 1900 Houghton Mifflin published *The House Behind the Cedars,* a novel about passing. The story was now, ten years later, fundamentally transformed and four times its original length.

Print is often valued for offering clean reading texts, which John Bryant has described as a "smooth" reading experience.[25] Thus, at the moment, we plan to provide a clear text of both the earliest extant manuscript—the 1890 short story—and the 1900 published text. The edition will also include a complete collation across the five manuscript witnesses (two of which are almost complete and three quite fragmentary). In part, a smooth reading experience of a text that is radically different from and, at the same time, fascinatingly similar to a well-known novel will help this early version come to life aesthetically. A clear reading text will allow and even encourage reading the 1890 story in relation not only to the novel Chesnutt published ten years later but also to the stories he was publishing during these years. Reproducing only the first version also accords with its distinct status. While the other drafts deepen our understanding of Chesnutt and his writing process, there is no evidence that he understood any of these four as ready to be shared or submitted for publication. They are appropriately understood as drafts. The 1890 story, by contrast, was a work he wanted to publish and sent out for review.

Producing a clean reading text of the first version will require resolving several difficulties, including how to treat the handwritten revisions on nearly three-quarters of the fifty-five typescript pages and how to handle eight missing pages. Regarding the first, we have opted not to incorporate the revisions, an unconventional decision, since changes in the author's hand are evidence of a later, perhaps more considered, intention. But it is the story Chesnutt submitted in 1890 that is of interest, and revisions made in 1890 cannot be distinguished from revisions made in 1895 when he returned to the manuscript. The missing eight pages pose a greater challenge to presenting a smooth and satisfying aesthetic reading experience. There are passages in later drafts that correspond to the missing pages, but they are much longer and the result would be a textual hodge-podge. Thus, a blank space of some ten or fifteen lines will indicate the missing pages, and the introduction will describe what later versions of the text suggest might have been on the missing pages in the 1890 version. The print edition may also include, space and cost permitting, a diplomatic transcription of the 1890 draft in addition to the reading text. This would capture Chesnutt's revisions, most probably made years later as he began to reconceive the story as a novella. This would allow readers to begin to wrestle with the contours of the text's development over time and might go far in capturing the tempestuous sites of revision that are common across Chesnutt's typescripts and in revealing the dialogic nature of his writing process.

In *The Work of Revision,* Hannah Sullivan suggests that genetic complexity, for modernists, is the result of an interest in fractured temporality and unsettled origins.[26] Following her lead, what might be gleaned from the genetic complexity of one of the most iconic works on race? What to make of the fact that it started as a short story with no white characters? Of Chesnutt's incessant revising? Is this a text that will not settle into one single form? Is Chesnutt grappling with a protean idea that might take many forms, searching for how to formulate his anti-essentialist understanding of race? Does this documentary record reveal a restlessness that arises when a Black writer, a light-skinned man who had two white grandfathers and could pass but did not, poked and prodded at the nation's insistence that race was fixed, indelible, eternal, even as evidence to the contrary was in plain view to all? Gilder found the characters amorphous, perhaps because they made visible what he could not see, or did not want to see, or certainly did not want to print. Do Chesnutt's typescripts allow a glimpse into the work of making visible, at the height of Jim Crow, the fundamentally amorphous nature of race? How might a generous print scholarly edition spur and support a new era of scholarship on a novel that has been speaking to and troubling the discourse on race for more than a hundred years?

We expect to ask similar questions of the digital edition we hope to build in the not-too-distant future. A digital approach to a genetic edition of *The House Behind the Cedars* will have to consider some of the most basic challenges that all digital editions confront, including financial support for technical expertise and the specifics of TEI encoding, presentation, and interface. But there is little doubt that this productive editing approach, one that has been primarily used for white authors, should be brought to bear on the works of Black writers. Chesnutt is among only a handful of Black fiction writers working before the Harlem Renaissance for whom we have such an extensive manuscript archive, but there are similarly rich archives for many twentieth-century Black writers, and there is no doubt that the future of digital scholarly editing must include attention to these materials. Indeed, given the absence of scholarly editing of Chesnutt to date and the different methods, affordances, institutional support, and final product between print and digital editions, there is little reason to worry about too much editorial attention to a novel that has been at the center of groundbreaking scholarship on race for the last three decades, but whose textual history is barely known.

The essays in this book come out of a symposium at the University of Nebraska that used the Walt Whitman Archive as the centerpiece for wide-ranging discussions of the future of digital scholarly editing. Inevitably, there were meditations on Whitman the poet, and also reflections on the decades of work necessary to create a digital archive that honors the expansiveness of the poet and his world. Might we also, in this spirit, and in the spirit that has motivated two decades of critically important work in Black bibliography, imagine generous editions, and in particular a multivolume print edition of Chesnutt and a digital archive, attentive to Chesnutt's expansive world? Chesnutt, too, cannot be contained between his hat and his boots.

Notes

1. No list can do justice to the last twenty years, nor to the steady hundred and fifty years, of important work in Black bibliography, print culture, book history, and editing, but these examples provide a sense of the range and the ethos: Jacqueline Goldsby and Meredith McGill, "What is 'Black' about Black Bibliography?," *The Papers of the Bibliographical Society of America* 116, no. 2 (2022): 161–89; Brigitte Fielder and Jonathan Senchyne, eds., *Against a Sharp White Background: Infrastructures of African American Print* (Madison: University of Wisconsin Press, 2019); P. Gabrielle Foreman, Jim Casey, and, Sarah Lynn Patterson, eds. *The Colored Conventions Movement: Black Organizing in the Nineteenth Century* (Chapel Hill: University of North Carolina Press, 2021); *The Colored Conventions* (coloredconventions.org); and *The Black Bibliography Project* (blackbibliog.org).

2. Brett Barney and Ashlyn Stewart, "Encoding Chesnutt's Galley Proofs," Association for Documenting Editing Conference, July 20, 2021.

3. The University of Nebraska–Lincoln team, with support from UNL's Center for Digital Research in the Humanities, includes researchers Antje Anderson, Samantha Gilmore, Ashlyn Stewart, Chaun Ballard, and Bianca Swift.

4. Stephanie P. Browner and Kenneth M. Price, "The Case for Hybrid Editing," *International Journal of Digital Humanities* 1, no. 2 (2019): 165–78.

5. Eric Gardner, "Early African American Print Culture and the American West," in *Early African American Print Culture,* ed. Lara Langer Cohen and Jordan Alexander Stein (Philadelphia: University of Pennsylvania Press, 2012), 75–92; Jewon Woo, "The *Colored Citizen*: Collaborative Editorship in Progress," *American Periodicals* 30, no. 2 (2020): 110.

6. Although this chapter will not take it up, digital scholars have begun to address the fact that the most common interface for accessing archives—the search function—is remarkably ungenerous, offering only the narrowest of openings into what are often vast collections (digital and physical). See Mitchell Whitelaw, "Generous Interfaces for Digital Cultural Collections,"*Digital Humanities Quarterly* 9, no. 1 (2015), digitalhumanities.org/dhq/vol/9/1/000205/000205.html.

7. William L. Andrews, "Editing 'Minority' Texts," in *The Margins of the Text,* ed. D. C. Greetham (Ann Arbor: University of Michigan Press, 1997), 47.

8. Peter M.W. Robinson,"Collation, Textual Criticism, Publication, and the Computer," *Text* 7 (1994): 82, jstor.org/stable/30227694.

9. Torsten Roeder, "Juxta Web Services, LERA, and Variance Viewer: Web based collation tools for TEI," *RIDE* 11 (January 2020), ride.i-d-e.de/issues/issue-11/web-based-collation-tools/.

10. The Chesnutt collations have been expertly done by Antje Anderson, editorial assistant at the Charles W. Chesnutt Archive, University of Nebraska–Lincoln, and professor emerita in English literature at Hastings College. The program was written by Mark Bauer, professor of practice in chemical and computer engineering at University of Nebraska–Lincoln.

11. Estimates can be made by using such sources as *N. W. Ayer & Son's American Newspaper Annual*, which provides circulation numbers by year for newspapers across the Unites States. Circulation for the *Chicago Inter Ocean*, which published eight of Chesnutt's eleven syndicated stories, was over one hundred thousand during these years. The *Cleveland News and Herald*, which published five syndicated stories, had a circulation of thirty-five thousand. For other efforts to estimate the extent of Chesnutt's readership, see John M. Freiermuth, "An Updated Bibliography of Charles Chesnutt's Syndicated Newspaper Publications," *American Literary Realism* 42, no. 3 (2010): 278–80; Charles Johanningsmeier, "Introduction," *American Literary Realism* 42, no. 3 (2010): 189–91; Charles Johanningsmeier, "Realism, Naturalism, and American Public Libraries, 1880–1914," *American Literary Realism* 48, no. 1 (2015): 1–24.

12. Frederic Bowers, "Multiple Authority: New Problems and Concepts of Copy-Text" (1972), repr. in *Essays in Bibliography, Text, and Editing* (Charlottesville, Va.: Bibliographical Society of the University of Virginia, 1975), 462; G. Thomas Tanselle, "Editing without a Copy-Text," *Studies in Bibliography* 47 (1994): 1–22.

13. Eric J. Sundquist, *To Wake the Nations: Race in the Making of American Literature* (Cambridge, Mass.: Harvard University Press, 1998), 35; Paul R. Petrie, "Charles W. Chesnutt, *The Conjure Woman*, and the Racial Limits of Literary Mediation," *Studies in American Fiction* 27, no. 2 (1999): 187; Houston Baker Jr., *Modernism and the Harlem Renaissance* (Chicago: University of Chicago Press, 1990), 44; John Edgar Wideman, "Charles Chesnutt and the WPA Narratives: The Oral and Literate Roots of Afro-American Literature," in *The Slave's Narrative*, ed. Charles T. Davis and Henry Louis Gates (Oxford: Oxford University Press, 1991), 60; Jennifer Lynn Stoever, *The Sonic Color Line: Race and the Cultural Politics of Listening* (New York: New York University Press, 2016), 166–77.

14. John Edgar Wideman, "Charles Chesnutt and the WPA Narratives: The Oral and the Literature Roots of Afro-American Literature," in *The Slave's Narrative*, ed. Charles T. Davis and Henry Louis Gates Jr. (Oxford: Oxford University Press, 1985), 60.

15. Paul Eggert, "Why Critical Editing Matters: Responsible Texts and Australian Reviewers," *English Studies in Canada* 27, no. 1–2 (2001): 197.

16. "Readings by Mr. Chesnutt Author of 'Conjure Woman' Entertains a Large Audience," *Colored American*, December 2, 1899, 5; republished in *Cleveland Gazette*, December 2, 1899, 2.

17. Richard Bucci, "Tanselle's 'Editing without a Copy-Text': Genesis, Issues, Prospects," *Studies in Bibliography* 56 (2003–2004): 36.

18. Notably, Barbara McCaskill and Caroline Gebhard, among others, have turned to Chesnutt's 1931 essay "Post-Bellum—Pre-Harlem" to rename the period that has long been called "Jim Crow" (*Post-Bellum, Pre-Harlem: African American Literature and Culture, 1877–1919* [New York: New York University Press, 2006]).

19. Jerome McGann, "Editor's Note," in *Blake; or, The Huts of America* (Cambridge, Mass.: Harvard University Press, 2017), xxxvi.

20. Tara McPherson, "Why are the Digital Humanities So White?: or Thinking the Histories of Race and Computation," in *Debates in the Digital Humanities,* ed. Matthew Gold (Minneapolis: University of Minnesota Press, 2012): 139–60.

21. Anne E. Fernald, "Explanatory Notes," in *Mrs. Dalloway* (Cambridge: Cambridge University Press, 2015), 175–311.

22. Charles Chesnutt, *Essays and Speeches,* ed. Joseph R. McElrath Jr., Robert C. Leitz III, and Jesse S. Crisler (Stanford, Calif.: Stanford University Press, 1999), 532.

23. Charles W. Chesnutt, "The Doll," *The Crisis,* 1912, 248, at The Charles W. Chesnutt Archive, accessed October 05, 2022, chesnuttarchive.org/item/ccda.works00036.

24. See Joseph R. McElrath Jr. and Robert C. Leitz III, eds., *To Be An Author: Letters of Charles W. Chesnutt, 1889–1905* (Princeton, N.J: Princeton University Press, 1997), 67n2, for the letter from Richard Watson Gilder to George Washington Cable, May 28, 1890; see 68n5 for the draft Chesnutt letter to George Washington Cable; see 69 for the letter from Chesnutt to Cable, July 25, 1890; see 76 for the letter from Chesnutt to Houghton, Mifflin & Co., September 8, 1891; see 83 for the letter from Chesnutt to Cable, April 11, 1895.

25. John Bryant, "Editing Melville in Manuscript," *Leviathan* 21, no. 2 (2019): 116.

26. Hannah Sullivan, *The Work of Revision* (Cambridge, Mass.: Harvard University Press, 2013).

CHAPTER 5

Computational Literary Studies and Scholarly Editing

FOTIS JANNIDIS

Introduction

In the last ten years or so, trends that in some cases had been decades in the making have combined into a perfect storm. The digitization efforts of libraries, archives, and other institutions, which have been ongoing since the 1980s, have made it very easy today to access large quantities of literary texts. The development of methods for quantitative analysis of literary texts, which in the case of stylometry goes back to the 1960s, has opened up more to computational linguistics and natural language processing (NLP), and it can integrate new methods from there into research programs. And lastly, computational linguistics and NLP have achieved a whole new quality of semantic and structural processing of texts after decades of preliminary work using machine learning, especially through the "deep learning" revolution.

Computational Literary Studies (CLS) came into being in this constellation. CLS methods are something quite old in the sense that they would be inconceivable without the attempts to build literary research on clearly conceived corpora and to clearly define and survey the features of interest, such as those developed in formalism and structuralism. Nor are they conceivable without the relatively broad tradition within what later became known as the digital humanities of extracting textual, stylistic, metrical, rhetorical, and other textual features and using them for questions of authorship attribution or period or genre description. Nevertheless, they are at the same time something entirely new, because many of the working tools that have been in use for about ten years require an extensive collection of texts, such as in topic modeling, and this requirement is increasing, for example in the pretraining of language models for domain adaptation. Typical work processes in the field of CLS start from a literary research question, develop a conceptual modeling of a relevant literary research phenomenon, and derive one (of several possible) operationalizations from it. In most cases, this involves the quantitative examination of a textual property. To do this, the phenomenon in question is annotated in a corpus, and then a model, like a neural network, is trained with this data, which allows this text property to be extracted automatically from a large collection of texts. Now you can count the frequencies of a textual property and, if you are lucky, you can answer the question raised by it.

Today, CLS has established itself as a new, small research field. As of recently, there are two journals that publish relevant results, and two conferences in which exclusively or predominantly CLS results are negotiated. In addition, there are a number of monographs and collections of essays. There are professors who have made CLS their central research topic, monographs, and anthologies: in short, everything that exists when a new subject establishes itself.

But what about the relationship to the other major pillar of the digital humanities (DH), digital editions? At the DH conference, the two fields run side by side in independent tracks. There doesn't seem to be much exchange, if only because the intricacies of a digital edition are a closed book for many in CLS, while the sophisticated techniques of CLS, whether involving statistics or NLP, are not accessible to most editors. One can say that, on the one hand, we have elaborately annotated data and, on the other hand, the methodological knowledge of how to analyze complex literary data. What is missing is a model of how to bring these two sides together.[1] The aim of this chapter is to discuss such a model—others are certainly equally plausible—and to demonstrate its feasibility with a practical example. The actual results are less interesting in this context of discussion of an exemplary study, since the main aim here is to present a model of textual analysis that relates these two fields to each other.[2]

In order to be able to discuss modeling questions in concrete terms, I will use the example of the *Faust* edition, for two reasons: because I was involved in the creation of the edition and because it is a verse drama, which, as we will see, makes many things easier.[3] The *Faust* edition is a hybrid edition, available both in print and digitally. In fact, only a small part has been printed, while digitally there is a much larger part that includes everything that has been printed. This is the historical-critical edition of the drama *Faust* by Johann Wolfgang Goethe, probably the most famous German-language drama. The edition comprises three parts: the constituted text, an archive, and a part on the genesis of the work. The constituted text contains the 12,111 verses and the variants for each of these verses. The archive contains all handwritten and printed witnesses in facsimile images and transcriptions. One of the special features of this edition is that, following the demands of the German editorial-theory tradition, it attempts to distinguish between findings and interpretation, and hence there are two transcriptions: a documentary transcription and a text-genetic one. From the display of variants in the constituted text, one can jump to the corresponding manuscripts or prints. Under "genesis" there are visualizations that break down the process of the text's creation, which took over fifty years, and also the distribution of witnesses across the verses of the drama, which is quite uneven, as Goethe repeatedly destroyed manuscripts in the first decades of his work. The edition lives as a website where the texts can be read, browsed, and searched. It is also accessible on Github, where one can download not only the software used to create the edition, but also the XML-encoded texts (github.com/faustedition). In principle, anyone can build their own *Faust* editions in this way, but above all, interested parties can re-use the edition for their own purposes. An open license (CC by-nc-sa) is intended to promote this re-use.

Computational Literary Studies

CLS has developed rapidly in the last ten years or so, and this is reflected not least in the extensive inventory of methods that can now be drawn on. The most established methods are probably topic modeling, sentiment analysis, stylometry, and the analysis of co-occurring and semantically related words.[4] For the first time, digital content-based text analysis has been given a real working basis through the possibilities of topic modeling and other semantically rich representations. Topic modeling can be applied to any text collection and determines the distributions of topics in documents and the distributions of words in the topics (across all documents). These "topics" are in fact not necessarily topics. Rather, words that frequently occur together in a given passage length are identified as belonging to a topic. Often the fact that words are thematically related causes this co-occurrence, but so can other factors, such as that they are part of a particular rhetorical strategy, or that they are misspelled in a similar way (OCR errors), or come from the same nontextual language. Three other methods have also established themselves as fruitful approaches to "distant reading" in recent years: sentiment analysis, stylometry, and word-field analysis.

Sentiment analysis, in its simplest version, examines the polarity of texts—whether they tend to feature positive or negative emotions overall. Developed to capture the polarity of shorter texts, sentiment analysis was quickly picked up in the CLS field as an indicator of the positivity or negativity of a given text passage. This resulted in attempts to describe plot as a polarity curve over the course of a text. In recent years, this method has been supplemented by a more complex representation of the text: not only polarity, but also emotions are mostly described today. Often based on models of five or eight basic emotions, the dominant emotions in shorter texts or their courses in longer texts are described. We will discuss an example of this approach in more detail below.

Stylometry, which has a long history in the form of authorship attribution, has established itself as a standard application in CLS through some important algorithmic developments and their implementation in the form of easily accessible software. For many practitioners, this is their first contact with the research field.

The analysis of co-occurring and semantically related terms, which can be understood as a kind of word field analysis, is behind one of the more impressive results in CLS. Ted Underwood shows in his book that an early finding of Heuser and LeKhac, that a specific group of highly correlated words linked to the seed word *hard* shows a steady increase between 1800 and 1880, is really indicative of a long-term trend in English and American literary history starting around 1750 and ending 1950.[5] This new field is developing methods quickly. The sophistication of its methods has increased dramatically in the last decade, quite in parallel to the explosion of methods in computational linguistics. On the other hand, many aspects have yet to mature, like standards for metadata and data exchange, for example, or standards for the evaluation for new methods by using reference tasks. Not least, the multilingualism of the field poses a challenge to the development of shared methods.

Modeling the Edition

The basic idea of this chapter is rather simple: to model one of the main features of digital editions in such a way that it can be related to the results of the computational analysis of its literary text. These results can include anything from one number to complex information structures like graphs containing relations, weights, and attributes. For the sake of simplicity, we will look mainly at one type of result: number per textual unit. Because our example is the edition of Goethe's *Faust,* which is written in verse, the verse is our textual unit. We will apply some sort of analysis to the text and the result will be a number (or some other numerical representation) for each verse. Then we will relate this information structure, the roughly twelve thousand verses of the play each annotated with a number, to our model of the same text as an edition. In the first section, we will describe the basic model, and in the second section we will talk about methods of selecting and filtering our data.

Digital editions fulfill a number of tasks in literary studies: they document which relevant witnesses exist for a particular work; they document the variants of origin or transmission, mostly relating to the first or last version of a work; they bring together all documents reflecting the origin or transmission, such as letters of authors from the time of creation; they comment on passages worth explaining; and more. In printed editions, these different tasks are signaled by typographic markings. The same is true of digital editions, but only a few are designed to make these different editorial features accessible in a machine-readable way. Actually, today, when it is obvious that the dual use of editions—read by humans and processed by machines—is their future, this duality should be reflected in their public presentation. But it is seldom done. This is not due to the digital tools; the TEI (Text Encoding Initiative) guidelines provide for corresponding information, but either it is not used in this way or the texts are not made available in the TEI encoding to readers, who are precisely also potential users. Only then will the division of labor that has otherwise been established in the field of CLS also be realized in the field of editions: Some annotate corpora for their specific questions, while others use them to develop new algorithms to answer the questions.

We focus here on the documentation of variants, which plays a role in almost all critical editions. We can think of a text as a sequence of text units. For each of these text units, there are no variants, or one or more variants. In the simplest case, then, we represent the data of the edition as a sequence of the number of variants. This is just one way to proceed. Many other approaches are feasible, depending on the text and the features of the edition. But this approach should be viable for most.

So far, we have treated all variants in the same way; we have made no distinction between the variants. Depending on the question, this can be the appropriate procedure, as when one does not have a clear idea of whether there is a connection between the type of variant and the phenomenon one is analyzing. Sometimes, on the other hand, one will want to exclude certain types of variants. How one classifies the variants also depends on the tradition in which one stands and the research question at hand. One could now proceed by taking a philological concept of variant type and operationalizing it for automatic recognition of these variants. For example, one could take the concept of orthographic variant and model it in such a way that it could be operationalized into an algorithm for identifying spelling variations automatically. For the sake of simplicity, I will present below two strategies that allow a rather vague concept of semantic similarity between variants to be implemented.

In both cases, I will simplify the research design considerably. We can think of the verse-drama *Faust* as a sequence of verses (between which there is some additional text in the form of act and scene details and stage directions, but we will ignore them in this paper). This is a one-dimensional model that contains a node for each verse, to which the verse number and the text of the verse are assigned. The variants now extend this model into the second dimension, as we can have zero, one, or more variants for each verse. Obviously, to each variant paradigm, we could apply subtle analyses, such as locating the biggest semantic differences. For our purposes, I simplify this by saying that, if there is at least one variant, I will look at only the first and last stages and ignore all the others. So what we are interested in below is the relationship of the first version of a verse to the last.

The first strategy is based on using the Levenshtein distance to calculate the distance between the two versions. "[The] Levenshtein distance between two words is the minimum number of single-character edits (insertions, deletions or substitutions) required to change one word into the other."[6] From "house" to "mouse," it is one edit, the replacement of *h* by *m*; similarly, it is one edit from "Faust" to "Faust!," the insertion of the exclamation mark. The Levenshtein distance makes it easy to count the changes in the text. However, it has the obvious disadvantage that the procedure is semantically blind. The distance from "Faust" to "Faust." is exactly the same as that from "bird" to "bard."

Now we can determine for each verse of a scene how great the semantic distance is between the first and the last version. If the distance is very small, then we are probably looking at one of the many orthographic variants in *Faust*. This allows us to distinguish relevant from nonrelevant variants, if we are primarily interested in the change in meaning of the text in the genesis.

As already mentioned, however, this approach is somewhat crude, since the Levenshtein distance counts only letter changes. With today's tools of artificial intelligence (AI) and NLP, we can implement a richer concept of semantic distance. In the following, I use "Sentence-BERT" to obtain a vector representation for each verse.[7] We can think of vectors as lines in a multi-dimensional space, starting from the origin and reaching a point defined by the numbers of the vector. Two different vectors are then two such lines, and we can represent the distance between these vectors as the cosine of the angle between them, as has long been common in computational text analysis (see Figure 5.1). The mathematical and algorithmic details, however, are not so important for our purposes. What is important is that, in this way, we have an instrument that allows us to convert the difference in meaning between two versions into a number that expresses the distance between the variants. Both methods allow us to identify the verses that have been particularly intensively edited, or to aggregate this verse-related information across the scenes so that we can see which scenes have been particularly heavily edited. Figure 5.2 shows those scenes. The basis here is the semantic distance between the variants as measured using Sentence-BERT. In fact, the results of the two methods correlate to a high degree.

Let us summarize: We can introduce the variants of an edition into textual analysis as a new and essential information structure. In the simplest case, this can be done on the basis of the (standardized) number of variants per textual unit, which, in the case of the Faust drama, is the verse. However, we can also filter the variants by type so that we look at only the variants relevant to our question, for example, by using the semantic distance between the first and the last variant as a weight. And of course we can also combine the number of variants and the semantic distance to create a relevant representation of the genesis of the text. This representation of the genesis is the starting point for further consideration.

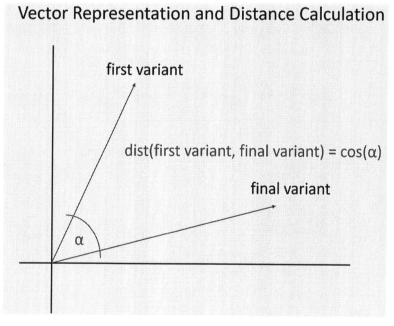

Figure 5.1. The geometry of meaning: this figure shows how text segments can be represented as vectors and the distance between vectors can be understood as semantic similarity.

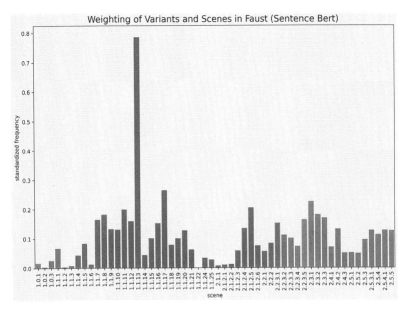

Figure 5.2. A bar chart showing scenes of *Faust* weighted based on semantic distance. Higher bars indicate more semantically diverse variants.

Modeling the Literary Text

The simplest way to model the literary text is to use its structure, something we have done already above, when we used the scenes to aggregate the frequency of variants per line. For a literary scholar, this is a natural way to think about a text, and usually it is quite useful. But nevertheless it is a design or modeling decision. The structuring elements of a text, its chapters, scenes, stanzas and the like, are important units during the production of texts and may therefore yield interesting results as models. But this is a choice on the part of the modeler, and as a choice in the context of research, it should be well founded in our research interests.

Other models arise when we do not start from the given text structure, but use another feature of the text, such as the character who speaks the text in a drama. Behind this could be the thesis that there are characters who have given the author cause for particularly numerous revisions. As usual, we use standardized values: the raw-count values alone cannot be used here

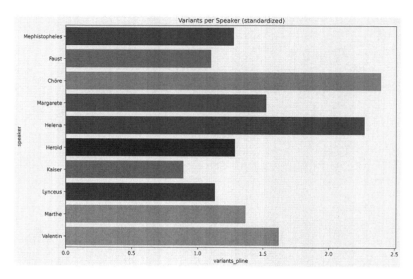

Figure 5.3. A bar chart showing textual variants per speaker in Goethe's *Faust*, standardized. Noticeable outliers with values above 2 include Helena and the choruses.

either, since the characters in *Faust*, for example, speak different numbers of verses, so we divide the number of variants of each character by the number of verses the character speaks, and thus obtain a value for the number of variants per verse (see Figure 5.3).

We can see that a value slightly above 1 is typical for most of the more important characters in the drama. There are only two very noticeable outliers upward with values above 2: Helena and (surprisingly) the choruses. The reason for this is the use of ancient verse measures, which Goethe was more uncertain about and had the classical philologist Friedrich Wilhelm Riemer check. This philological knowledge thus confirms the insight of the data analysis: these characters and their text have special properties.

How we model the text is, as I said, not predetermined, but entirely dependent on our research interest. If we want to test the thesis that the texts of female characters differ from those of male characters, we can structure our data accordingly. The same applies to other character features like age or social rank, or features of the fictional world (e.g., is the space in which the scene is set relevant?), or textual features, such as verses that have a certain rhyme scheme that differ from those that have a different one or none at all. The main effort here is to assign each text unit, in the case of *Faust* each of the approximately twelve thousand verses, to exactly one of the groups (e.g., "male") that constitute the structure (for example "gender").

As described above, the model of our edition is a sequence of verse numbers, and for each verse we have the number of variants. With the model of the text structure, we can create a second information structure: this also consists of the sequence of verse numbers, but now we assign information to each verse, such as the name or gender of the speaker or the number of stresses in the verse. This is the formal representation of our text structure, and this is the second pillar in our three-column model.

CLS Data Structure

The third information structure, the third pillar of our analytical model, consists of the data we create using a CLS-analysis procedure. Typically, such procedures make information explicit (and countable) that a human reader might also collect while reading, but mostly implicitly. In what follows, we present two such procedures, first the automatic analysis of emotions and then the analysis of rhyme. As indicated above, there are now a great many such analytical procedures available, as a result of the leaps and bounds in the development of NLP culminating in the recent pretrained large language models that power tools like ChatGPT.

The two information structures, the values collected via CLS procedures (such as the frequency of certain emotions) and what I called above a text model (such as the gender of characters), are put in relation in many CLS studies—this is not limited to editions. On the contrary, when one uses editions for this purpose, one mostly uses the reading text and ignores precisely the information that is special to an edition, like the variants, document descriptions, commentary, and so on. This may not be obvious because, in most CLS studies, many texts are analyzed and the text model is not so clearly visible as a model of a text.

So we have three information structures: (1) the variants of the edition, (2) the text model, and (3) the data collected via CLS. Above we saw that it can be fruitful to relate (1) and (2), for instance when we studied the frequency of variants aggregated by characters. As just mentioned, the relation between

(2), the textual model, and (3), the CLS data, is not particularly relevant to editions, so I will not discuss this relation further here. What interests us in the following is the relation between (1), the variants, and (3), the CLS data.

Emotions

As part of a longer running project, my research group, together with the group of Simone Winko in Göttingen, has developed a method for automatic detection of emotions in nineteenth-century poetry.[8] The project focuses on the transition from the poetry of realism to that of early modernism. As is common in supervised machine learning, we annotated the phenomenon under study in numerous texts and then trained a model to detect it automatically. For the annotation, we used an iterative process to define guidelines outlining which emotions to recognize, how to handle borderline cases and problems, and so on. In total, when the model was trained and applied to the *Faust* text, we had annotated 1278 poems, and most of them multiple times. The hierarchical annotation scheme consisted of forty emotions arranged in six groups: Love, Joy, Surprise/Agitation, Anger, Sadness, Fear. (The interannotator agreement, i.e., the agreement between different annotators of the same poem, is rd. 0.75 γ[9] at the level of the six group emotions). The quality of the model, in this case its capability to automatically recognize emotions, varies somewhat, depending on the number of relevant annotations (Table 5.1). This means that we had a not inconsiderable number of errors in the automatic assignment of emotional categories to a poem, but in most cases it worked.

If we now apply this model to the text of *Faust*, we find that: for about two thirds of the verses, there is no emotion; otherwise the emotions love and joy dominate; which are opposed by almost as many verses containing (in order of frequency) sadness, anger, and fear. If we compare these results with the distribution of emotions in poetry, we notice that love is noticeably more frequent in *Faust*, while sadness is clearly less frequent.

	Love	Joy	Agitation	Anger	Sadness	Fear
F1(macro)	0.77	0.73	0.62	0.71	0.74	0.79

Table 5.1. Performance scores for automatic detection of emotions in nineteenth-century poetry. F1 scores range from the lowest value, 0, to the highest value, 1.

In CLS, it is common to relate CLS values (3) to those of a textual model (2), such as in analyzing the gender of the characters speaking a particular part of the text. This would allow us to answer questions such as whether certain emotions are more common in texts that have female speakers. However, we want to focus here on the relationship between the variants and the CLS data. Since we now have two sets of numbers of the same length, and our research interest is to see whether there is a relationship between them—that is, whether the number of variants increases when a particular emotion or emotions as a whole increase—we can simply calculate a correlation between them. However, the result is negative: there is no significant correlation.

Rhyme

Our second experiment looks at a different text feature: rhyme. For each verse, we automatically collect the information of whether the verse is part of a

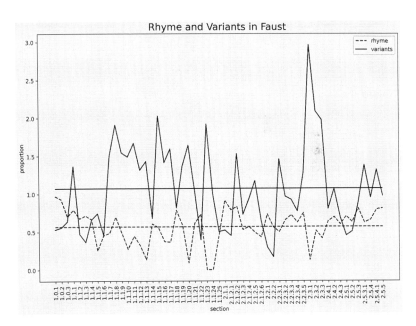

Figure 5.4. A line chart showing rhyme and variants aggregated to scenes in Goethe's *Faust*. In many cases, an increase in variants per scene is accompanied by a decrease in rhymes.

rhyme or not. For this, we use a tool, the Metricalizer, which, as tests have shown, is quite reliable at detecting rhyme.[10] In this way we generate a list in which each verse number is assigned either a 1 or a 0, depending on whether it is or is not a rhyme. For simplicity, we aggregate this information to scenes and standardize it. Strictly speaking, we then have a constellation in which we are using all three columns of our model. Figure 5.4 shows the result.

It is not easy to see, but in quite a number of cases, where we observe an increase in variants per scene, we can observe a decrease in rhymes such as from scene 1.1.11 to 1.1.12, from 1.1.23 to 1.1.24, and especially from 2.3.1 to 2.3.3. If the increase of values in variants is more often accompanied by the decrease of values in rhymes, then we can expect a negative correlation. This is also the case with a value of -0.56 (p-value < 0.0001). Regarded philologically, there are probably two independent factors at work here: in the first part, the specific history of the transmission of these short scenes, and in the second part, the fact that, in the encounter with Helena in the third act, the Greek verse measures were revised relatively frequently.

Two Cultures

The type of research proposed here poses particular challenges for those who would undertake it, as very different competencies must be present. To describe it ideally: on the scholarly editing side, deep historical knowledge is required (including the ability to read difficult hands and decipher complex manuscripts). On the side of CLS, it requires knowledge of methods and approaches with an emphasis on programming, machine learning, and statistics. The state of methodological development and digitization skill varies widely. In the field of scholarly editing there are a number of well-known and robust methods; but then, the digital turn is still happening for many practitioners. In the field of CLS, there are only a few methods that are really robust under all circumstances and that are always well understood in their dependencies; new methods are being developed in rapid succession and the new possibilities of digital tools are being tested very close to the cutting edge of development.

These differences are reinforced by different forms of knowledge and frames of thinking. Editors tend to think in terms of literary or historical studies, interpretively, or in a broad sense of the concept hermeneutically, whereas the representatives of CLS think in terms of applying their methods in the contexts of empirical work, as they have developed in the social sciences, for example. This concerns not least the handling of errors, or we might say the "error culture" of the two fields. In the field of scholarly editing, the ideal of the perfect text applies: errors are a stigma. At the same time, everyone knows that there are always mistakes. In the field of CLS, on the other hand, it is assumed that all methods are flawed; consequently, it is necessary to make empirically based statements about their error rates in order to judge the usefulness of tools, approaches, and algorithms. As errors cannot be avoided, they have to be measured and analyzed.

These differences make cooperation more difficult in practice. Above all, they mean that such cooperation takes time, so that those involved can get used to the respective customs and practices of the other side and adjust to them. In my experience, it is only when this happens, when deviation from the rules of one's own field is accepted not as a mistake but as a legitimate characteristic of the other field, that productive cooperation can begin. Through this cooperation, however, completely new insights can be gained, especially when the procedures presented here are applied across several texts, indeed across many editions.

Notes

My thanks to two members of my working group: Thorsten Vitt, who provided me with a version of the text of *Faust* formatted to make the analysis easy, and Leonard Konle, who applied the emotion detection.

1. Modeling has been recognized as one of the main activities in the digital humanities (DH); see for example Willard McCarty, *Humanities Computing* (London: Palgrave Macmillan, 2005). My understanding owes a lot to my conversations with Julia Flanders and is documented in our introductions to *The Shape of Data in Digital Humanities: Modeling Texts and Text-Based Resources*, ed. Julia Flanders and Fotis Jannidis (London: Routledge, 2018).

2. This essay owes much to a paper by Gerrit Brüning, which he presented in 2017 at a conference I organized, and which could only now appear. Brüning outlines, first theoretically and then in his 2021 supplement also practically, how one can classify variants and thereby possibly assign some of the variants to an intention of the author. To my knowledge, his contribution is the first to deal systematically with the question of how to utilize variants in editions quantitatively in order to answer questions in literary studies. See Gerrit Brüning, "Modellierung von Textgeschichte. Bedingungen

digitaler Analyse und Schlussfolgerungen für die Editorik," in *Digitale Literaturwissenschaft. DFG-Symposium 2017*, ed. Fotis Jannidis (Berlin: Metzler and Springer 2022): 307–37. The classification of variants is also discussed in Erik Ketzan and Christof Schöch, "Classifying and Contextualizing Edits in Variants with Coleto: Three Versions of Andy Weir's *The Martian*," *Digital Humanities Quarterly* 15, no. 4 (2021), digitalhumanities.org/dhq/vol/15/4/000579/000579.html.

3. Johann Wolfgang Goethe, *Faust, Historisch-kritische Edition*, ed. Anne Bohnenkamp, Silke Henke, and Fotis Jannidis, in collaboration with Gerrit Brüning, Katrin Henzel, Christoph Leijser, Gregor Middell, Dietmar Pravida, Thorsten Vitt, and Moritz Wissenbach, release candidate 1.2 (Frankfurt am Main / Weimar / Würzburg, 2023), faustedition.net/.

4. Most of these methods are explained in detail in one of these monographs that have helped to establish the field: Matthew L. Jockers, *Macroanalysis: Digital Methods and Literary History* (Chicago: University of Illinois Press, 2013); Andrew Piper, *Enumerations: Data and Literary Study* (Chicago: University of Chicago Press, 2018); Ted Underwood, *Distant Horizons: Digital Evidence and Literary Change* (Chicago: University of Chicago Press, 2019).

5. Ryan Heuser and Long Le-Khac, *A Quantitative Literary History of 2,958 Nineteenth-Century British Novels: The Semantic Cohort Method*, Stanford Literary Lab Pamphlet 4 (Stanford, Calif.: Stanford Literary Lab, 2012); Underwood, *Distant Horizons*.

6. See Vladimir I. Levenshtein, "Binary Codes Capable of Correcting Deletions, Insertions, and Reversals," *Soviet Physics Doklady* 10, no. 8 (1966): 707–10. This English translation and its Russian original are cited in the Wikipedia page for "Levenshtein Distance" (last modified 8/3/2023).

7. See Nils Reimers and Iryna Gurevych, "Sentence-BERT: Sentence Embeddings Using Siamese BERT-Networks," in *Proceedings of the 2019 Conference on Empirical Methods in Natural Language Processing, Association for Computational Linguistics* (2019), arxiv.org/abs/1908.10084.

8. See, e.g., Anton Ehrmanntraut, Thora Hagen, Fotis Jannidis, Leonard Konle, Merten Kröncke, and Simone Winko, "Modeling and Measuring Short Text Similarities. On the Multi-Dimensional Differences between German Poetry of Realism and Modernism," *Journal of Computational Literary Studies* 1, no. 1 (2022), doi.org/10.48694/jcls.116.

9. See Yann Mathet et al., "The Unified and Holistic Method Gamma (γ) for Inter-Annotator Agreement Measure and Alignment," *Computational Linguistics* 41, no. 3 (2015): 437–79, doi.org/10.1162/COLI_a_00227.

10. For the Metricalizer, see web.archive.org/web/20230308082231/https://metricalizer.de/en/. See also Klemens Bobenhausen, "The Metricalizer–Automated Metrical Markup of German Poetry," in *Current Trends in Metrical Analysis*, ed. Christoph Küper (Frankfurt am Main: Peter Lang, 2011): 119–31.

CHAPTER 6

The Walt Whitman Archive at a Quarter of a Century

ED FOLSOM

How else, as cofounders of the Walt Whitman Archive, should Ken Price and I begin to think about its first twenty-five years, but with allusions to and quotations from Whitman himself? It is of course tempting to edge toward the inevitable and say something like, "We celebrate ourselves," which in some sense we are doing by using our anniversary as an occasion to gather this distinguished group of scholars to think about the futures of digital humanities (DH) scholarship. "We celebrate ourselves and sing ourselves, / And what we assume you shall assume." But we all know there *is* no center around which multiple futures organize themselves. If we *were* to begin with the way we celebrate ourselves, we would need to underscore the etymology of "celebrate," just as Whitman encouraged us to do: never to use a word without knowing its etymology, what Emerson called its "fossil poem." *Celebrate* comes from roots meaning "to return to," "to frequent in great numbers," "to repeat often." And *that* is the twenty-five-plus-year process that we call the "Whitman Archive": it—whatever *it* is—has been and remains a process of returning to it again and again, day after day, and being surprised (just as Whitman was surprised by his absorptive democratic self that changed and grew with every new experience it engaged) by just how large and varied and diverse it can become as we return to it again and again and *re*-turn it. We all learn in the course of our lives to use a most appropriate phrase when we celebrate a recurring event, like an anniversary or a birthday: "Many happy returns!" Because more than a *thing*, the Whitman Archive is an *event*, a process that Ken and Matt Cohen and I and so many others keep returning to; it is *that* kind of celebration.

So I want to begin not with a quotation from Whitman, but instead with a quick backward glance to those days decades ago when the Whitman Archive people regularly hung out with the Emily Dickinson Electronic Archives folks as we created what we called "The Classroom Electric," a series of what we then thought, foolishly, would be permanently useful websites for teachers, websites that brought Dickinson and Whitman together in productive and illuminating ways. And it's also a look ahead in this gathering of scholars to Marta Werner's focus once again on Dickinson. My evocation of Dickinson is a very familiar little poem of hers, one that I've heard over the past couple of months used on at least three different occasions, and one that I never hear without thinking of the origins of the Whitman Archive:

> To make a prairie it takes a clover and one bee,
> One clover, and a bee.
> And revery.
> The revery alone will do,
> If bees are few.

One place I heard the poem read recently was at a gathering of some neighbors in Iowa City who were involved in a prairie restoration project, where the poem was offered as Dickinson's suggestion that *reverie* is a kind of delusional thinking that may in fact be crucial to get the process of prairie restoration started, when so many in the community don't think the project is worth doing or will never get done. But reverie can sustain the creators through uncertain times: you need to dream big, envision what could be, in order to get started. That is art. One ecological writer says about this poem that maybe it "is suggesting that we begin making something long before we know enough, and long before we pick up our tools."[1] We begin with reverie, and reverie can sustain us through a lot of tough times. But eventually we need that clover and bee.

Now, I don't want to assign roles to actual people here, because, in the course of the development of the Whitman Archive, countless people have been the clover, the bee, and the reverie. But when I hear this poem, I see Ken

Price, Charlie Green, and me in a little room at the College of William & Mary in Williamsburg, Virginia, Ken and I standing at Charlie's desk with a computer and a single screen. In that moment, the reverie I had brought to the project seemed to have found its single clover and single bee. It was a tiny prairie we were building then. And we needed the reverie to sustain us. And we sure as hell needed to know a lot more about what actually made a prairie. I was from Iowa, which was just then in the business of trying to restore tall-grass prairies all over the state, and little did we know then that Ken would soon enough be moving to Lincoln, on the edge of the tall-grass prairies as they turn to mixed grasses and rise to the plains. Dickinson, who had never seen an actual prairie, imagined her way to creating one: she knew the basic ingredients. Ken, Charlie, and I, who had never seen the making of an actual online archive, were trying to imagine our way toward something we at first named the "Walt Whitman Hypertext Archive." And while we wouldn't be making a prairie, we were soon *on* the prairie making an archive that had everything to do with leaves of grass.

All institutions have their origin tales, and the one most often told of the Whitman Archive is that I planted the idea in my 1992 essay in *Resources for American Literary Study,* later reprinted in the book *Prospects for the Study of American Literature.* Here is what I wrote back then, thirty years ago, in the era of the floppy disk. This was my reverie, which I began, characteristically, by complaining: I noted the disaster of the long-promised but endlessly delayed journalism volumes in the New York University Press *Collected Writings of Walt Whitman,* and I commented on the many difficulties of using the then-recently issued three-volume variorum of the printed editions of *Leaves of Grass* as part of the *Collected Writings* project. Then I said:

> One project awaiting some enterprising scholar (or group of scholars) with computer facility is a hypertext version of *Leaves of Grass* (and other Whitman books) that will allow computer access to the various editions by scanning color page-by-page photographs of the texts into a database, then allowing anyone to examine the physical attributes of the various editions on a computer screen: all scholars could then have all the editions (including *Drum-Taps, Specimen Days, Two Rivulets,* etc.) present in state-of-the-art computer realization, complete with cross-referencing, textual annotation, and publishing history.

Facsimiles of Whitman's manuscripts and corrected proof sheets could also be included, thus allowing scholars to call up each step in the evolution of Whitman's poems. Such hypertextual scholarship could revolutionize commentary on Whitman.[2]

Everything about that paragraph now is laughable, including the naïvete of my blithe assumptions about how easily "the computer" (maybe programmed by one "enterprising scholar") would make this imagined new variorum. I'm reminded that *reverie* has its own telling etymology and can be tracked to roots meaning "wild conduct," "raving," "delirium," "a fit of abstract musing." Only in the past year have we finally published on the Archive something that only *just* begins to approach what I have always thought of, in my digital delirium, as the "magic button" that would allow users to pop up on their screen all the original notes and drafts of any and all of Whitman's writings, along with his corrected proofs, his continual rewriting and rearranging and clustering and cutting and adding. Do you want to see "The Sleepers" take shape? Just click the magic button and watch the poem evolve from a random notebook jotting through multiple drafts that would split into several poems, including the 1855 poem that would shift even more and evolve into the final 1881 version that most readers today encounter. The Whitman Archive's amazing new 1855 *Leaves of Grass* variorum edition that Nikki Gray led the way on over the past few years *begins* to do (*now* 30 years later) for one edition of Whitman what I imagined some computer-savvy folks (a busy bee or two) could accomplish by 1995, or maybe 2000 at the latest.[3]

In fact, the true origin of the Walt Whitman Archive was not my raving essay, but Ken Price's response to it. If mine was the reverie, his was the actual clover and bee that turned an ill-formed dream of an archive into the small but quite real beginnings of the *Whitman Archive*. At William & Mary, Ken had formed or found a remarkable hive of grad students who understood "the computer" in ways Ken and I didn't, and in my case, still don't—people like Charles Green and Rob Nelson and Matt Cohen, all of whom convinced Ken that the Walt Whitman *Hypertext* Archive was a project worth starting. The Institute for Advanced Technology (fondly acronymed IATH) at the University of Virginia, with John Unsworth and Daniel Pitti, was the pioneering DH center, and Ken asked me to join him in a digital scholarly adventure that led to many long days at IATH, where much larger bees had much vaster fields of clover they tended. John and Daniel and Jerry McGann and others at IATH told us how and why we were hopelessly naïve about our project, to which Ken and I had generously pledged *five full years*. Now, nearly thirty years later, we feel we've finally begun, and have taken some baby steps toward my still-reveried magic button.

 I had wanted in this brief essay to give an institutional history of the Whitman Archive as it enters its second quarter-century, a backward glance, maybe a sentence or two for every year or so; looking back on it, its multiple projects and incarnations now seem to have sped by with that kind of deceptive velocity. It is, in fact, difficult to offer an "institutional history," because it's hard to think of the Whitman Archive as an "institution": there's very little brick and mortar involved, much as we've all envisioned and even joked about a Whitman Archive building, if not a Whitman Archive campus. What we *are* physically, alas, is contained in small offices in Lincoln and Iowa City. But, as with all institutions, it's the *people* who form the history, and it is stunning to me to realize that the people who have worked on the Whitman Archive now number nearly two hundred in our first quarter-century. While Ken Price and I have been there from the beginning, and Matt Cohen virtually from the beginning, the Whitman Archive would not exist without the dedication, imagination, and work of so many who have now gone on with their own careers and have left day-to-day Whitman Archive activity, but whose work is inseparable from the archive, in fact whose work defines it: from Charles Green to Elizabeth Lorang to Nicole Gray. It's a mistake to begin naming names, both because there are so many and because it would not be illuminating unless you happen to know these truly remarkable and talented folks. At any given time, about twenty-five people (graduate students, professors, tech specialists, and, more importantly, *colleagues and collaborators*) are devoting some major portion of their working life to the archive. The cast of collaborators shifts, but the work goes on, made possible by our other radiating fields of collaborators: the National Endowment for the Humanities, the National Archives and Records Administration, the Institute of Museum and Library Services, the Department of Education, the University of Nebraska–Lincoln, and the University of Iowa. Without their financial support, the Whitman Archive would not be possible and would have died soon after it was begun. There are a lot of bees tending to the clover now, even on days when reveries are few.

I'd like to add just a couple more words about collaboration and collaborators, since that is really the history of the Whitman Archive. My prediction is that what we call "digital humanities" will someday be thought of simply as "collaborative humanities," because DH is by definition the building of teams. It's not the end of individual scholarship, but the end of *hermetic* scholarship: collaborative humanities is about everyone's individual work (one clover, and a bee, and reverie) feeding into the context of a vaster and vaster collaborative network (the making of a prairie). And the Whitman Archive team is still learning just how broad and exciting and unexpected that collaboration can be, as we now have worked with IATH at the University of Virginia and with the amazing Center for Digital Research in the Humanities at Nebraska, whose staff have become the technical architects of what we have discovered is an ever-evolving "product," or perhaps more accurately, not a product at all but a "process." Iowa's Digital Scholarship and Publishing Studio has become a collaborator as well, and the list keeps growing, right out to our thousands of visitors/users/readers who come to the Whitman Archive for reasons we often could not fathom, but who join us as co-creators each time they point out a problem, a typo, a dead link, or a wrong identification, each time someone tracing their family genealogy comes upon a letter Whitman wrote to one of their great-grandparents or a great-grandparent wrote to Whitman, and those surprise collaborators provide us with details about that correspondent that we never would have found ourselves.

So it's really no history I can offer here, rather just a very brief fictional story, with its own mythical beginnings, its wildly growing cast of characters, and its ever-changing face on your computer screens. When I wrote about the archive in *PMLA* back in 2007[4]—in the era of the CD-ROM—analyzing database as a new genre, one particularly fit for Whitman, who developed a kind of database poetry, where his catalogs enacted a sort of data ingestion, one of the respondents to my essay, Meredith McGill, worried that we were creating a site that was too poetry-centric.[5] "Yes, it looks that way," I replied to her, "but just give us a few years." "Check back in 2023," I might have said if I were confident enough, "where you'll find Whitman's fiction in a superbly detailed edition, his journalism in ever-expanding and expanded forms, his notebooks and manuscripts, his poetry in translation, and a vast array of criticism." There's no *product* to this collaborative endeavor we've all set out on, just an ever-changing cast with an ever-growing list of new things to edit and to describe and to figure out. Thanks, Walt, for being so large: you've now got a collaborative community continuing to discover and reveal your multitudes.

I am still amazed at every time I glance at one page of manuscript notes Whitman made just a couple of years before his large 1860 edition of *Leaves of Grass* appeared (Figure 6.1). Whitman himself seemed to know 150 years ago that there was just emerging "A New Way & The True Way of Treating ... History, Geography, Ethnology, Astronomy," just about any area of knowledge, by creating "long lists of dates, terms, summary paragraphic statements, &c," and that "New Way" was via the collection of "*data,* all-comprehensive, and to be pursued as far and to as full information as any one will": *that* open presentation of more and more data will be "the best way of inditing [composing] history," of composing without reducing the subject, whatever it is, that always slips the boundaries of any narrative we could write about that subject.

As is often the case, Whitman was prescient here. He sensed that the explosion of information around him (in his case, fueled by innumerable developments in industrial printing technology) was producing "so many books" that getting them all "in any history" was now hopeless, so humans would have to develop some system of coded shorthand, "long lists" of *data* that would be "all-comprehensive" and would contain "as full information as any one will" and will offer "the best way of inditing history for the common reader." History (and all other types of human knowledge) would have to be composed in a very different way as a result of the massive proliferation of information. From now on, increasing data would give us the tools for *inditing* history as well as for *indicting* all the previous histories that had been written. Since any history is a narrative built on necessarily selective data, histories that absorb more and more data will become rolling indictments of the partial stories we've heard before.

Whitman, of course, had no concept of *data* as we think of it today, the coded materials that form the electronic databases that all literary scholars

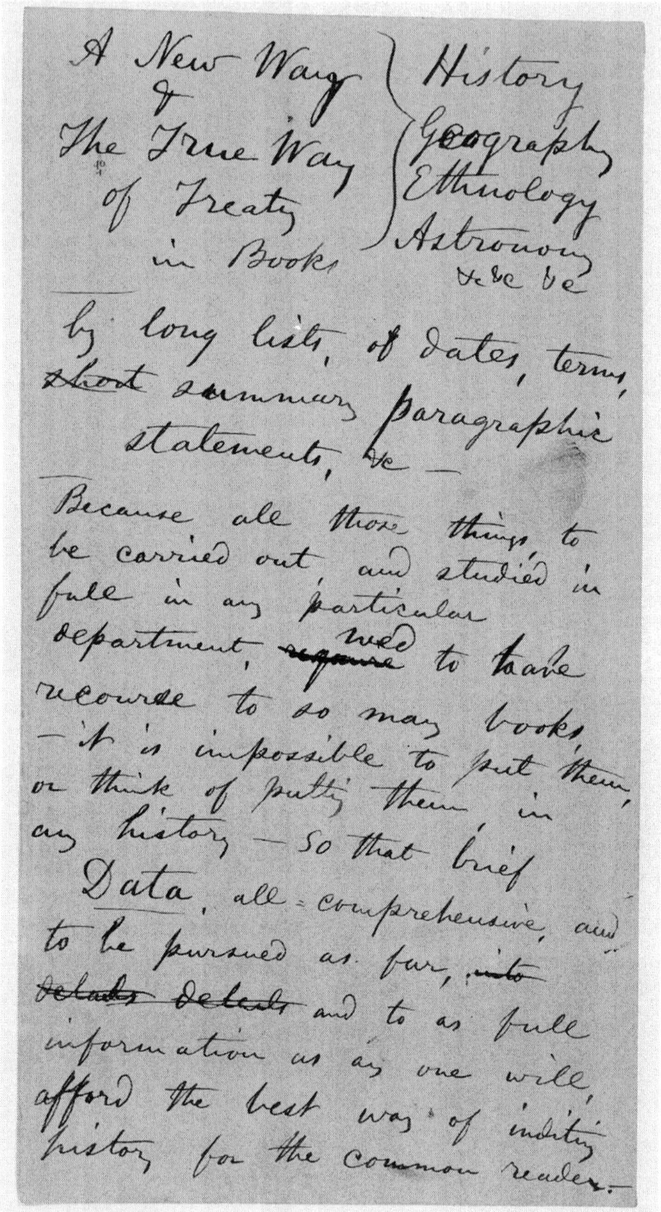

Figure 6.1. Walt Whitman's notes about the use of *data* in "inditing history for the common reader." Courtesy of the Berg Collection, New York Public Library.

now routinely use. But his notion of data was certainly already edging toward that modern notion. In the 1864 Webster's *Dictionary of the English Language*, *data* is defined simply as "something given or admitted; a ground of inference or deduction" (from the Latin for "to give"). Whitman, though, was already pushing the word toward a definition that would become incorporated into dictionaries only around the turn of the century: "Facts, esp. numerical facts, collected together for reference or information" (as the *Oxford English Dictionary* defines a usage traced to 1899). The more computer-nuanced definitions did not begin to emerge until the 1950s and 1960s.

It's probably no surprise that Whitman, who often built his radically innovative poetry on a cataloging technique that gained its force by piling on detail after detail, was an advocate for a new data-driven history. "Song of Myself," after all, can be read in one sense as a database of impressions of nineteenth-century America, data "all-comprehensive, and to be pursued as far, and to as full information as any one will." For Whitman, the world itself was a kind of pre-electronic database, and his notebooks and notes are full of lists of particulars—sights and sounds and names and activities—that he dutifully enters into the record. Anyone who has read one of Whitman's cascading poetic catalogs knows this: those catalogs are always indicators of an endless database, a suggestion of a process that could continue for the duration of a lifetime, a mere hint of the massiveness of the database of our sights and hearings and touches, each of which could be entered as a separate line of the ever-expanding poem. It's why Whitman loved photography and saw it as the new democratic art. It was the first technology, we can now see, that suggested what today we think of as *database*: what most struck early commentators about photography was its relentless appetite for details, for every speck that appeared in the field of vision. Many hated photography for precisely that reason; it insisted on flaws and extraneous matter that a painter would have edited out of the scene in order to create beauty. But beauty, Whitman said, *democratic* beauty, was *fullness*, not exclusion, and required an eye for completeness, not a discriminating eye. Photography was teaching us to see the world as a database, a vast and *indiscriminate* accumulation of givens.

So the Whitman Archive: our attempt at an all-comprehensive set of data that suggests this author we call "Walt Whitman" is not containable, but is always escaping us. "Missing me one place search another," he tells us at the end of "Song of Myself," in a line that could serve as a kind of stripped-down instruction for using the Whitman Archive. Whitman's key metaphor, leaves of grass, was always meant to generate in the reader *not* a manicured and well-kept lawn of identical blades of grass, but rather the tall-grass prairie that he celebrates again and again in poems like "The Prairie Grass Dividing": that vast sea of diverse grasses, with their rhizomatic roots creating a tangle of relationships impossible to sort out, interconnected in a fertile database waiting for unseen connections to be discovered. It's a prairie waiting for the reverie of you, whoever you are.

Notes

1. Steve Glass, "Emily Dickinson Offers Advice on Prairie Restoration in 'To Make a Prairie,'" *WingraSprings,* November 12, 2017, wingrasprings.wordpress.com.

2. Ed Folsom, "Prospects for the Study of Walt Whitman," *Resources in American Literary Study* 20 (1994): 140–41. This essay was revised as "Prospects for the Study of Walt Whitman," in *Prospects for American Literary Study,* ed. Richard Kopley (New York: New York University Press, 1997), 133–54.

3. See the *Leaves of Grass* (1855) Variorum, whitmanarchive.org.

4. Ed Folsom, "Database as Genre: The Epic Transformation of Archives," in "Remapping Genre," ed. Wai Chee Dimock, special issue, *PMLA* 122 (October 2007): 1571–79. This essay is the focus of a forum, with responses by Jerome McGann, Jonathan Freedman, N. Katherine Hayles, Peter Stallybrass, and Meredith McGill (1580–608), and my reply (1608–12).

5. Meredith McGill, "Remediating Whitman," *PMLA* 122 (October 2007): 1592–96; my reply to McGill is on 1611.

PART II

THE CONVERGENCE OF DIGITAL ARCHIVING AND SCHOLARLY EDITING

CHAPTER 7

Digital Archival Ethics

Representation, Access, and Care in Digital Environments

K.J. RAWSON

In line with the purpose of *People, Practice, Power: Digital Humanities Outside the Center*, edited by Anne B. McGrail, Ángel David Nieves, and Siobhan Senier, my aim here is to "foreground the *human* side of digital humanities (DH) infrastructure."[1] As the editors of that volume explain, the contributors to the collection "insist on rethinking infrastructure in *human* terms, which is perhaps one of the more radical things DH can do."[2] For my work in digital archives, this shift is a radical reorientation to archival infrastructures in that it diminishes the centrality of historical objects, database design and functionality, and even metadata, and instead elevates the importance of the people who are in and around historical objects in our collections, who are behind the database design and functionality, and who create and are impacted by the metadata.

Drawing on a feminist "ethics of care," particularly as theorized by archives scholars Michelle Caswell and Marika Cifor, this essay will focus on the affective responsibilities that DH practitioners assume when curating digital content in online archival environments. More specifically, I am interested in applying a feminist ethics of care approach to the Digital Transgender Archive (DTA), a project that I founded and continue to direct. Released in 2016, the DTA is a freely available collection of primary-source materials and discovery resources related to trans and gender-nonconforming people throughout the world. Available at digitaltransgenderarchive.net, our digital collections are provided by over eighty archives where the corresponding analog objects are maintained. We currently have approximately 12,325 items documenting a wide range of people who transgressed gender norms prior to the year 2000.

Though impossible to capture fully here, the human infrastructure of the DTA is an expansive web of people who have been and continue to be part of the project's universe, including: subjects who are represented in the collections; record creators, memory holders, and other stewards of these histories; archivists, librarians, and other professional knowledge workers who collect, preserve, describe, and provide access to these collections; volunteers and staff, including undergraduate and graduate students, as well as a grant-supported digital archivist, who conduct research, process collections, and provide outreach to users; staff at granting agencies and grants officers who envision and fund opportunities for growth; the project's advisory board and other colleagues and administrators who provide direct and indirect support for the project; developers, designers, and other skilled professionals who shape the look, feel, and functionality of the site; users who visit the site and those who indirectly encounter our materials in other spaces; and myself, who has shepherded the project throughout its lifecycle so far. While a feminist ethics of care approach could extend to all of the above, this article will be particularly focused on people who are represented in our collections and those who are accessing our collections because these two constituencies often have the least voice and power in digital archives ecosystems.

I will begin this chapter with a brief discussion of feminist ethics of care as the theoretical framework that informs my approach here. Next, I will turn to how people can be represented in digital archival contexts and the ethical considerations that are embedded in the process of archival description. Finally, I will consider ethical access and the responsibilities that digital archives have for anticipating user needs and impacts. As I explore the feminist ethics of care in the DTA, I will share a series of questions that our project uses as we evaluate ethical representation and access in digital environments, which may be a concrete take-away for other practitioners. My hope is that this discussion of digital archival ethics will be beneficial to a wide range of DH projects, though it will certainly be most relevant for those involving primary-source databases and content curation made available to a broad audience online. Though I am presenting the DTA as a specific example to consider, I want to be clear from the outset that I do not mean to imply that we have it all figured out. On the contrary, this article is part of a series of publications and public talks in which I candidly share the processes we follow, often still in their formative stages, in order to be transparent and accountable and to solicit feedback and collaboration.[3] Throughout this chapter, I argue that, because ideological neutrality is not possible or desirable in digital archives contexts, it is the responsibility of digital archivists to carefully attend to ethical representation and access—specifically for the people who are most impacted by our work—even when doing so may seem insurmountably challenging.

Ethics of Care in Digital Archives

The ethics of care framing that undergirds this essay can be traced to, among others, Carol Gilligan's work in the late 1970s and early 1980s, specifically her well-known book *In a Different Voice*. Even when treated within the context of second-wave feminism, Gilligan's work has been criticized by some for essentializing women as caretakers. However, Gilligan's theorization of care continues to offer a poignant response to dominant masculinist worldviews that emphasize individual rights at the expense of the collective, as well as arguments that interdependence and care should be widely valued, irrespective of gender. As summarized by Bethany Nowviskie, an ethics of care offers two essential shifts: "The first is toward a humanistic appreciation of *context, interdependence, and vulnerability*—of fragile, earthly things and their interrelation. The second is away from the supposedly objective evaluation and judgment of the philosophical mainstream of ethics—that is, away from criticism—and toward personal, worldly *action and response*."[4] Applied to a digital archives context, a feminist ethics of care pushes beyond any singular focus on the contents and workings of particular digital archives, and instead asks us to consider broad humanistic contexts that are based on interdependence, affective connections, and real-word action.

Caswell and Cifor's widely cited article "From Human Rights to Feminist Ethics: Radical Empathy in the Archives" explains that, by taking an ethics of care approach in an archival context, "archivists are seen as caregivers, bound to records creators, subjects, users, and communities through a web of mutual affective responsibility."[5] They highlight the role of archivists as being central to the dynamic web of relationships among a number of different stakeholders who are integral to the archival process. This framing is a significant departure from typical archival practices that either focus on highly individualized rights or neglect to consider the rights of some stakeholders altogether. In a feminist ethics of care, archivists can approach their work as always in conversation with and connected to a series of others for whom they take on some affective responsibility. Caswell and Cifor further specify that archivists should consider their relationships with four groups—record creators, record subjects, record users, and broader communities—and all of these relationships should be "marked by radical empathy."[6] As they explain, "the notion of empathy we are positing assumes that subjects are embodied, that we are inextricably bound to each other through relationships, that we live in complex relations to each other infused with power differences and inequities, and that we care about each other's well-being."[7]

Elspeth Brown and Myrl Beam extend Caswell and Cifor's work to trans archival contexts by discussing the care work involved in conducting trans oral histories and making them accessible in digital environments. Closely echoing both Nowviskie's and Caswell and Cifor's use of ethics of care, Brown and Beam explain: "Trans care work in this context is a form of mutual aid, built over time through consensual interaction, affective labor, and resistance to hierarchy. This form of queer and trans care work values interdependency and queer kinship models in producing an ethics of care that does not rely on a definition of the normative family unit."[8] Here again, archival work informed by an ethics of care centrally values interdependency, relationships, and affective responsibilities. Brown and Beam continue: "Those engaged in writing metadata ... must enter into an affective bond with the narrators, their community, and their history. This archival work is a form of emotional justice, a praxis of trans care in relationship to the documentary evidence of the trans past." Drawing explicitly on Hil Malatino's concept of trans care in that passage, Brown and Beam theorize metadata creation as a critical moment of care work that is central to digital archiving.

In the context of the DTA, attention to care is particularly pressing in light of our contemporary moment in which trans people in the United States are facing unprecedented public attention and attacks while we continue our struggle for fundamental human rights. Within this landscape, Brown and Beam's description of trans archival work as "mutual aid" speaks to how desperately history is needed to support the ongoing work of trans activism. Malatino beautifully explains: "When the milieu you inhabit feels hostile, it's deeply comforting to turn to text and image from another time. I was desperate for representation, but more than that, I was desperate for some sense that other subjects had encountered and survived some of the transphobic, cissexist bullshit with which I was being repeatedly confronted. I needed resources for resilience. I wanted a roadmap for another way of being."[9] To borrow Malatino's phrasing, the DTA's work can thus be understood as providing contemporary trans people with critical "resources for resilience."

As we orient the DTA's work according to an ethics of care, what that means, in the simplest terms, is that we strive to center people rather than objects. This upends the "normative focus within archives," which is "the care of objects, rather than the care of people."[10] Though we have an expansive "web of mutual affective responsibility," to use Caswell and Cifor's phrase, for the purposes of this article, I will narrow my focus to two particular groups of people we extend care to: those who are represented in our collections and those who access our collections. In the next two sections, I will discuss our specific ethical considerations and our protocols for representation and access in the DTA.

Representing People with Care

How do we respectfully and accurately represent people in digital archival collections? Within the context of the DTA, this is a pressing question with high potential impacts. A number of the people on our site are still alive, and so we are accountable to them in a very present and literal way (i.e., it is not uncommon for us to be in direct conversation with people included in our collections). However, our commitments of care are certainly not limited to those individuals who are still alive. For the very reason that the DTA was created—to provide greater access to trans-related histories in the face of systemic exclusions and erasures—we are attuned to the exclusions and erasures that we can inadvertently perpetuate through our archival processes, including our descriptive practices. Mx. A. Matienzo argues: "Naming is fundamentally unavoidable in knowledge representation. As such, we need to make a decision whether we choose to name with an intention of justice, or with the pretense of neutrality and objectivity."[11] As a project driven by social-justice aims, we recognize and seek to navigate carefully our impactful role in the knowledge representation process.

Before we delve into some of the specific considerations of representing people in the DTA, it's helpful to put trans archival representation into a broader context of historical documentation of a minoritized group. Consider this simple visualization of historical information loss (Figure 7.1). Even if it were desirable, we could never fully document all of a person's lived experiences or a community's activities. As Figure 7.1 reminds us (though it is far from being to scale), there is a tremendous amount of information loss in each stage of the documentation process. Of the selected documentations of individual people's lives and community activities, only a miniscule percentage become archived, or stored for long term preservation and made available for researchers. In effect, then, each stage of the archival process functions as a representational layer that gets further removed from people's lived experiences, which illustrates that archival documentations are always already representations of the lives they are documenting.

I have belabored this point, which is generally taken for granted, because the information loss represented by the dotted lines is significantly greater for oppressed communities than for more privileged groups. As a result, we have a particular responsibility to attend to ethical representation because we have fewer materials representing fewer people, and thus they hold more power and impact. The earlier we reach back into history, particularly for pre-1950s periods, the more likely it is that the documentations that we

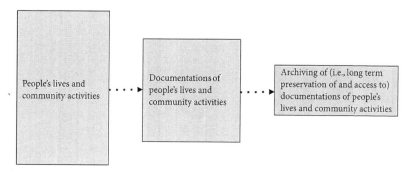

Figure 7.1. A diagram of information loss in the process of archival representation.

have available were produced by those in power in order to exoticize, ridicule, and shame those who refused to conform to gender norms (while cautioning others against such behaviors). The combination of these forces, such as the lack of materials overall and the rarity of finding materials created by those who transgressed gender norms, dramatically increases the importance and representational effects of the documentations we include on our site.

The DTA itself is a powerful representational layer in that our collecting scope, which states that we include documentations of any person who transgressed gender norms pre-2000, requires us to interpret the actions and activities of historical figures and highlights those activities as key features of a person's life. Though we are focused on *practices* of gender transgression rather than those who *identify* as trans (or other related terms), we strive to be careful in how to represent individual people so that the "transgender" framework of our project does not become deterministic over the individuals represented in our holdings. Not only is the term "transgender" anachronistic as an identity label prior to the late twentieth century, but our conceptions of sexuality, sex, and gender as separate identities is a recent phenomenon, and it remains highly culturally specific.

Given this broader context, we have developed an ethics review that involves a series of questions concerning representation (the subsequent section will share our questions concerning access). Though these questions are often unanswerable, we use them to slow down our archival process. Here, we take inspiration from Kimberly Christen and Jane Anderson's argument concerning decolonial Indigenous archival frameworks that slow archives can productively disrupt the "ongoing colonial logics of rapid access and endless circulation where Indigenous materials continue to be subject to the same colonial logics."[12] As with Christen and Anderson's approach, ours is an intentional strategy to infuse an ethics of care into our workflow and ensure that we are focusing on the people represented in the materials we are handling. We use the following questions to evaluate how we represent people ethically in digital archives, with some elaboration on each:

Should this person be included in our collections?
> Rather than evaluating specific objects for inclusion, we reorient our focus to the people being represented by those objects. We take this approach

because we recognize that the simple act of including a person on our site has the potential to shift the way they are remembered and represented elsewhere.

How will circulation and dissemination impact this person or their memory?
Once we determine that a person can be included in our collections, we then consider the potential impacts of inclusion. Is this individual alive, and if not, how recently did they pass? Does this person already have a public profile? Is this person already known to have transgressed gender norms or are we outing them in some way? Has this person already been interpreted to have a particular identity (e.g., someone claimed as a lesbian) that we would be challenging by including them in a transgender project? In answering these types of questions, there is no formula or rubric that we use to determine how to represent a person; instead, these questions slow down our process, inform our descriptive practices, and often suggest additional pathways for research or conversation.

Will any private information be shared?
While some forms of information such as social security numbers and home addresses need to remain private, most of our collections include information that some would consider private whereas others wouldn't. Ruha Benjamin argues: "The politics of knowledge ... is deeply entangled in a politics of the private and in who gets to lay claim to privacy and subjectivity."[13] It is certainly difficult to be in the position where only rarely can we directly communicate with those who are represented on our site in order to ensure that they retain their claim to privacy and subjectivity. In the absence of that opportunity, we try to follow any historical evidence that we can find that would help us understand how much privacy a person sought. On the one hand are figures like Lou Sullivan, who demonstrated clear commitment to sharing his story: he helped to establish the GLBT Historical Society, sought to publish his extensive diaries, and worked to ensure that all of his records were available to researchers. On the other hand, we encounter figures who marked their materials "private" or carefully presented their life stories to erase all of their trans-ness. In cases like Sullivan's, we have very little hesitation to include materials

documenting his life, even those that are highly private (though we do try to restrict the exposure of other people's private information within those materials). For those who have indicated a greater desire for privacy, we evaluate how much exposure they already have and the kinds of representations that are presented elsewhere. We are careful not to assume that all people want to be publicly out as trans or gender nonconforming, but we also do not want to default to a shame-based assumption that being out is undesirable. Benjamin goes on to argue: "For oppressed people, I think privacy is not only about protecting some things from view, but also about what is strategically exposed."[14] With that in mind, we strive to balance privacy with strategic visibility. Our policies page explains that we "redact last names on sensitive materials that were not designed or intended for public circulation," and we urge visitors to contact us "if any materials on this site violate personal privacy."[15]

Beyond copyright, what rights do the subject(s) and creator(s) of this resource have?
Copyright is an important consideration for any digital archival project, but it is only minimally helpful for evaluating ethical usage. For our project, evaluating official copyright can be useful in that it builds in a clear and intentional step where we determine who owns rights to content and we strive to contact them. Through this process, we often have an opportunity to discuss not only whether people want their materials to be included on the site, but how they want to be represented. Frequently, though, we are unable to contact either the creators or subjects of a resource and we are left to evaluate the materials on our own. Generally, we focus on how much creative content is involved, whether there are expectations of privacy that we might violate, what kind of audience a resource was created for, and what expectations the subjects and creators might have had for the circulation of this resource. As I will discuss at greater length in the subsequent section, we have also been following the lead of Indigenous archival initiatives that have challenged the cultural heritage sphere's over-reliance on state-granted intellectual property rights, which fail to properly value community creation practices or the various people who may have deep rights to objects that are legally unrecognized.[16]

Does this individual have an opportunity to represent and describe himself, herself, or themself?

A significant portion of our holdings are about, rather than by, people who transgress gender norms. As a result, it is common for individuals who are represented in our collections to be spoken about and spoken for, without having the opportunity to represent and describe themselves. Not only does this impact the ways that they are described with subject terms and free-text description, but our team is often left to interpret a person's life based on highly flawed and severely limited documentations. For example, we are often unaware of how particular figures felt about their given names—did they consider it a "deadname" (a given name, usually assigned at birth, that a person no longer uses and might be used to out or shame a person), or did they continue to embrace it for strategic or personal purposes? Since we do have some people who are represented on the site who ask us to include both their given name and their chosen name, we can find ourselves in a difficult position between respecting a person's presentation of themselves, which we always do, and being careful that we do not appear to endorse the use of deadnames for all trans people or in other contexts. With certain historical figures, we do opt to include full given names, even when that person's chosen name is available, because in those cases censoring a person's given name would effectively render that individual invisible and undiscoverable by the name by which they were publicly known. Despite our project's trans-affirming context, this practice has the problematic effect of perpetuating the transphobic documentations of a person's life, but we have yet to identify any less harmful options that do not further erase that person's existence.

What subject terms are available to describe this person, and which ones should be supplied?

Only after we have determined that certain materials will definitely be included in our collections and we have reviewed privacy, rights, and opportunities for self-representation, do we turn to questions of description. Within the first few months of processing materials for our database, we learned that it was incredibly difficult to describe trans-related historical materials using the subject terms that are available in broad vocabularies such as the Library of Congress Subject Headings. Instead, we turned to the Homosaurus (homosaurus.org), a thematically focused set of more than three thousand terms related to LGBTQ+ cultures that can be used in any cultural heritage institution in order to allow users to find materials related to those concepts. The Homosaurus was an immediate and transformative benefit to the DTA because it offered a degree of granularity to accurately and ethically describe people represented in our materials. Of course, archival description is rife with power differentials, and scholars and archivists can consult a rich corpus of scholarship on description.[17] Within the scope of the DTA, we attempt to favor community-based terminology versus terminology created by outsiders, though this is rarely straightforward given the complexities of language development and circulation.

These six questions, though certainly not comprehensive, are key considerations for our ethics of care approach to archival representation. Shared across all of these questions is a sustained focus on the people who are represented in the materials on our site. There also are many more trans-specific considerations when determining how to represent people ethically in archives (and other cultural heritage institutions) than I have detailed above.[18]

The DTA assumes affective responsibilities toward the people who we include in our holdings, though we certainly do not claim to represent those individuals flawlessly. Unfortunately, it is altogether too likely that we are inadvertently perpetuating harm in the ways that we have represented people in our collections, or even in having collected materials about them at all. Yet our valuation of people rather than objects and our attention to ethical representation offer important preliminary interventions in digital archives initiatives.

The Ethics of Access

This back-end evaluative process about how to include people ethically directly shapes the front-end access we provide on our site. Most digital archives, ours included, are created based on a commitment to increase access to historical resources. Yet this goal of increased access is often taken for granted as an unequivocal benefit. Recent conversations around the ethics of access have been led by Indigenous archivists and scholars (and settlers who work with Indigenous resources) who have revealed the persistent colonial logic of archival practices, including digital archival practices. For example, Ellen Cushman (Cherokee Nation Citizen) points out that "the more decontextualized, categorized, itemized, arranged, installed, and chronologically organized, the more damage archives do to the understandings, practices, and objects they hope to preserve."[19] In discussing two projects developed with Indigenous knowledge frameworks, the Mukurtu content management system and the Local Contexts initiative, Christen and Anderson advocate for a "shift to building an archival ecosystem that emphasizes connections and care and archival processes that do not treat access and ownership as blunt instruments, but instead, recognize that there are various modes and types of culturally specific circulation, exchange, stewardship, and sharing practices that frame the hard work of archival caring."[20] Not only do these approaches reveal the harmful legacies and ongoing colonizing effects of archives, particularly the glorification of open and undifferentiated access and the harm that has caused to Indigenous communities specifically, but they offer a powerful alternative model that centralizes relationships between people, connections to place, and culturally specific access practices.[21]

The DTA uses an ethics of care approach to be carefully attuned to the dynamic and transtemporal relationships between the people who are represented in our collections and those who are accessing the collections. More specifically, we strive to evaluate critically the impacts of access on both those who are represented in the collections and those who are accessing them. The access benefits for contemporary researchers who are using a digital archive are generally obvious: researchers can gain understanding, knowledge, and "resources for resilience," often leading to personal enrichment or professional gain.[22] However, there can also be moments when the needs of these two groups are not in alignment, such as when researchers seek all available primary sources and want them in pristine and untouched shape (for fullest access), on the one hand, and when subjects in our collections request that we restrict, redact, or otherwise edit sources to protect privacy or ensure appropriate access, on the other. While we understand the research benefits of having unfettered access, our first priority is to protect the interests of those who are represented in our collections, even when it curtails access. Part of our affective responsibility to subjects involves providing access that does not further harm. This commitment is particularly pressing in our current political landscape and given the instances we are aware of when people have used materials from the DTA for harmful effects. In other words, ethical access is an imperative if we are striving to have a just and equitable project that attends to the actual impacts it has on people, particularly trans and gender-nonconforming people.

Christen offers a helpful reframing of what most digital content providers mean by open access: "While openness may seem to be a neutral and homogenous term and standard for access, it is in fact a culturally determined and political act. Making digital content open to all, to do with what they will without question, is very rarely what proponents of open access mean. Access and openness are almost always more complicated, more nuanced, and conditional."[23] This has certainly been true for the DTA. While we recognize that our efforts to make trans-related materials more widely available to the public is itself a political act, we recognize that the ideology that undergirds the concept of open access is itself political and is always heavily conditional. To help elucidate the DTA's evaluative process concerning access, including our approach to the complicated impacts of access, I have included below a series of questions that we consider, along with a brief discussion of each.

Who will most benefit from access to this item?

While conversations about access often focus on researchers who are most likely to be working with archival collections, rarely is such access framed in terms of benefit. In theory, archives, specifically digital archives, provide a public service by collecting, preserving, and providing access to historical materials (private and restricted-access archives notwithstanding). But who are the actual researchers using these collections and, importantly, what do they gain by working with archival resources? In the case of the DTA, a significant proportion of our users of whom we are aware are academic researchers or public historians, both of whom stand to benefit from our collections, both in status and financially. When contextualized within the extensive history of cisgender researchers benefiting from studying trans people (often with considerable harm done to trans people), it becomes clear that the DTA can contribute to this problematic legacy if we rely too heavily on engagement by cisgender scholars as a central indicator of our project's impact. Instead, rather than defaulting our inclusion decisions to support credentialed, institutionally affiliated, and privileged (particularly white, cisgender) researchers, we consider first and foremost whether trans people and trans communities will benefit from accessing specific resources. We expand our understanding of benefit by striving to value personal enrichment over academic research potential, and connection with community over number of hits.

Who will pay the costs of access?

As the general public is becoming increasingly aware of the importance of data privacy, digital archives need to examine more closely the potential impacts that our work has in making information about people more widely available. Even when we are careful not to share information that obviously compromises privacy, we are contributing to a dynamic information landscape where it is increasingly possible to gather information on specific individuals from seemingly innocuous data points. Who is most likely to be targeted or harmed by such access? More broadly, just as the benefits of access are not equally distributed, the costs of access are also inequitably shared. For the DTA, in particular, following the trenchant critiques of trans visibility presented in the book *Trap Door* and in the film *Disclosure,* we are attentive to the ways increased trans visibility can inspire a violent backlash that often targets trans people of color, particularly trans women of color.[24] Beyond the individualized impacts of sharing more information about specific trans people, both alive and deceased, our project itself contributes to the increased cultural visibility of trans people that can elicit a violent response. Finally, and again following the leadership of Indigenous cultural heritage practitioners, we need to be aware of the harm that can be caused by unfettered access to certain materials and the harm that encounters with certain content will cause some users. In addition to our small but growing collections related to Two-Spirit and trans Indigenous people for whom access protocols can be highly important, we are also mindful of the broader harms of access that users of our site can experience when they encounter difficult objects in our collections.

Are users of all abilities able to access all resources?

In centering an ethics of care approach to access, we consider how users of varying abilities will be able to engage with our site and the contents of our collections. For example, we check our site for color contrast, alt text of images, form and tab labels, and other elements that support full access. As we upload items, we aim to provide machine-readable descriptions of content, such as text transcripts of audio resources, captions for videos, and descriptions of images; however, we are admittedly not always able to do so because of funding capacities, time limitations, or donor restrictions. This becomes particularly concerning if there is an entire subset of items (such as oral histories from a particular project) that are not accessible for users, in which case we will flag those items for enhanced description. We also consider access in terms of intellectual accessibility and we write our content with the intention of making it comprehensible to young teenage users (and we periodically get feedback from users in this age group to evaluate how successful we are).

Should there be limited access to certain items?

As part of our evaluation of the costs and benefits of access to our collections, we also consider whether differential access—meaning that only certain users are granted access to specific materials—is a necessary step to support ethical access. This approach is quite common in physical archives, where embargos, restrictions, and mandatory usage agreements are part of the everyday work of offering mediated access to archival collections, though these practices can certainly introduce problematic gatekeeping. In the digital archives realm, most content providers are either fully open or limited by paywalls to subscribers. Mukurtu, a content management system designed to share Indigenous digital heritage materials in "culturally relevant and ethically-minded ways," has added significant nuance to conversations about access to highlight who is best served by unfettered access and who may be most harmed.[25] The DTA has not yet formally implemented differential access (though the technical infrastructure is mostly in place to do so), largely because we do not have a decision-making body who would oversee this process. We are currently exploring traditional knowledge (TK) labels, available via the Local Contexts project, to determine whether they would support more ethical access to some items in our collections.[26] Beyond these database-hosted solutions, we do make de facto differential access decisions when we work with archivists to digitize collections that we do not make available on our site, though they are available to researchers upon request.

Should users give consent before viewing explicit content? If so, how?
Should users be warned about harmful content? If so, how?

These two questions cover similar ground and, taken together, demonstrate the range of curatorial options that we have developed to provide more care-oriented access for users. Within the context of the DTA, we classify items as explicit when they visually depict "violent, graphic, or racist content," and harmful when they include "references to or depictions of self harm, hate crimes, violence (sexual, physical, and systemic), and discriminatory or dehumanizing language and images, as well as material produced or circulated in exploitative contexts."[27] Though an unfortunately significant portion of our collections can be classified as harmful given the nature of trans history, we felt that it would better reflect our project's values and educational aims to frame harmful content overtly for our users. To do this, we developed a visible but minimally intrusive content warning statement that we add to item-level descriptive metadata so that users encounter it when they navigate to an item-level page. Our approach to explicit content involves a higher degree of mediation: in recognition of our users who are underage or who do not want to be confronted with unanticipated explicit content, we follow a feminist consent model where we add a popup warning that visitors must click through in order to see an item (and we use a stock thumbnail if there is explicit content in the thumbnail image). Beyond these approaches to harmful and explicit content, we have two additional and more intensive levels of mediation, as represented in Figure 7.2: redacting or blurring access to items, or not including them at all. We exercise these two

Figure 7.2. Four options for mediating explicit and harmful content, in order of the amount of curatorial power exercised.

options only in rare circumstances when the benefits of access do not outweigh the potential harms caused.

In *Race After Technology*, Benjamin defines the "new Jim Code" as "the employment of new technologies that reflect and reproduce existing inequities but that are promoted and perceived as more objective or progressive than the discriminatory systems of a previous era."[28] Digital archives, which have certainly been promoted as progressive tools for supporting more equitable access, can often be rightfully accused of reproducing inequities, often to the detriment of oppressed communities. While the platforms that underlie our work have tremendous potential, particularly for projects focused on oppressed communities redressing historical erasures, if we are not guided by people-centered ethical frameworks, our projects will only uphold and extend discriminatory systems.

Put another way, I would offer Sofia L. Leung and Jorge R. López-McKnight's poignant question to evaluate information environments: "What does it look like to NOT oppress another group of humans?"[29] This chapter can be read as an exploratory response to that question through a detailed discussion of the practices of the Digital Transgender Archive. The feminist ethics of care approach that I have advocated for here brings us to precisely the same outcome that Leung and López-McKnight offer: "When we accept everyone's humanity and realize our responsibility toward one another, what kind of futures can we build together? Any futures we construct must take into account the experiences of all peoples, not just the most vocal, privileged, and visible."[30] As with the Indigenous-focused projects that inspire our practices, we have sought to "include cultural, ethical, and historical checks at each step," which then "encourages collaboration, relies on historical specificity, and has ethical considerations embedded at every step."[31] We are still developing our processes and our practices are still evolving, which is to say that our work is always ongoing and we invite feedback, critique, and change.

Notes

1. Anne McGrail, Angel David Nieves, and Siobhan Senier, "Introduction," in *People, Practice, Power: Digital Humanities Outside the Center,* ed. Anne B. McGrail, Angel David Nieves, and Siobhan Senier (Minneapolis: University of Minnesota Press, 2021): viii.

2. McGrail, Nieves, and Senier, "Introduction," x.

3. See, for example: Eamon Schlotterback, Cailin Flannery Roles, and K.J. Rawson, "Investing in Project Maintenance: Auditing the Digital Transgender Archive," *Digital Humanities Quarterly* 16, no. 1 (2022), digitalhumanities.org/dhq/vol/16/1/000611/000611.html; Rawson, "The Rhetorical Power of Archival Description: Classifying Images of Gender Transgression." *Rhetoric Society Quarterly* 48, no. 4 (2018): 327–51.

4. Bethany Nowviskie, "Capacity through Care," in *Debates in the Digital Humanities 2019,* ed. Matthew K. Gold and Lauren F. Klein (Minneapolis: University of Minnesota Press, 2019): 425 (emphasis original).

5. Michelle Caswell and Marika Cifor, "From Human Rights to Feminist Ethics: Radical Empathy in the Archives," *Archivaria* 81 (2016): 24.

6. Caswell and Cifor, 25.

7. Caswell and Cifor, 31.

8. Elspeth H. Brown and Myrl Beam, "Toward an Ethos of Trans Care in Trans Oral History," *The Oral History Review* 49, no. 1 (2022): 34.

9. Hil Malatino, *Trans Care* (Minneapolis: University of Minnesota Press, 2020), 51.

10. Brown and Beam, "Toward an Ethos," 35.

11. Mx. A. Matienzo, "To Hell With Good Intentions: Linked Data, Community, and the Power to Name," keynote address, Library Information Technology Association Forum, Minneapolis, Minn., November 14, 2015.

12. Kimberly Christen and Jane Anderson, "Toward Slow Archives," *Archival Science* 19 (2019): 99.

13. Ruha Benjamin, *Race after Technology: Abolitionist Tools for the New Jim Code* (Cambridge: Polity, 2019), 127.

14. Benjamin, 127.

15. "Policies," Digital Transgender Archive, accessed September 26, 2022, digitaltransgenderarchive.net/about/policies.

16. Kimberly Christen, "Relationships Not Records: Digital Heritage and the Ethics of Sharing Indigenous Knowledge Online," in *Routledge Companion to Media Studies and Digital Humanities,* ed. Jentery Sayers (New York: Routledge, 2018): 403–12.

17. See two recent examples: Jessica Tai, "Cultural Humility as a Framework for Anti-Oppressive Archival Description," *Journal of Critical Library and Information Studies* 3, no. 2 (2021); and Dorothy Berry, "Descriptive Equity and Clarity Around

Blackface Minstrelsy in HTC Collections," accessed September 29, 2022, dorothy-berry.com/minstrel-description.

18. For a more extensive discussion of trans affirming metadata, see the Trans Metadata Collective, "Metadata Best Practices for Trans and Gender Diverse Resources," accessed September 29, 2022, zenodo.org/record/6686841#.YzX41OzMKFF.

19. Ellen Cushman, "Wampum, Sequoyah, and Story: Decolonizing the Digital Archive," *College English* 76, no. 2 (2013): 130.

20. Christen and Anderson, "Toward Slow Archives," 111 (emphasis original).

21. We are admittedly still in the early stages of reckoning with the DTA's colonizing logics and impacts. The DTA was awarded a grant from the Council on Library and Information Resources to support a three-year (2022–2025) trans BIPOC digitization initiative. One major part of that initiative is to develop resources and protocols specific to the Indigenous materials in our collections. This process is already suggesting major paradigm shifts that are dramatically reorienting our work.

22. Malatino, *Trans Care*, 51.

23. Christen, "Relationships," 406.

24. Reina Gossett, Eric A. Stanley, and Johanna Burton, *Trap Door: Trans Cultural Production and the Politics of Visibility*, ed. Reina Gossett, Eric A. Stanley, and Johanna Burton (Cambridge, Mass.: MIT Press, 2017); *Disclosure*, dir. Sam Feeder (Netflix Original Documentary, 2020), 100 min.

25. Mukurtu CMS, accessed September 29, 2022, mukurtu.org/.

26. Local Contexts, accessed September 29, 2022, localcontexts.org/.

27. For more details on how we make determinations about each of these categories, see our detailed "Policies" page, accessed September 26, 2022, digitaltransgenderarchive.net/about/policies.

28. Benjamin, *Race after Technology*, 5–6.

29. Sofia Y. Leung and Jorge R. López-McKnight, "Conclusion: Afterwor(l)ding Toward Imaginative Dimensions," in *Knowledge Justice: Disrupting Library and Information Studies through Critical Race Theory*, ed. Sofia Y. Leung and Jorge R. López-McKnight (Cambridge, Mass.: MIT Press, 2021), 318.

30. Leung and López-McKnight, 318.

31. Christen, "Relationships," 407.

CHAPTER 8

Categories of Freedom
Colored Conventions, End-Movement Discourse, and the Nineteenth-Century Black Protest Tradition

SARAH LYNN PATTERSON

The Colored Conventions movement (CCM; 1830–1900) was one of the longest running nineteenth-century protest systems created and led by Black people in the United States. Beginning with Black theologian Reverend Richard Allen's platform-building meeting in 1830, the near-annual continuation of political sessions across the nineteenth century sustained self-fashioned advocacy initiatives, allowing Black-led leadership bodies to create policies and disseminate ideas. With a focus on the nuances of the Black experience, these procedural events produced literary tracts to demand Black constituencies' access to basic citizenship rights as a response to mass disenfranchisement of free and yet enslaved Black people leading up to and beyond the American Civil War (1861–1865). And so, the movement's activity was chiefly recorded in printed pamphlets carrying iterations of the "Colored Convention" tagline on the title pages of Black writers' event proceedings. Scholars regard the convention minutes and related historical materials held in the digital archive ColoredConventions.org as the nucleus of research on the CCM platform similar to the ways Black writers' and activists' foundational contributions to the broader Black American protest tradition rely on the 2013 *Pamphlets of Protest: An Anthology of Early African American Protest Literature, 1790–1860*, the collections "North American Slave Narratives" and "The Church in the Southern Black Community" from the digital archive Documenting the American South, and the Schomburg Library of Nineteenth-Century Black Women Writers. The editing practices of the

Colored Convention Project's (CCP) at ColoredConventions.org reflect an intentional chronological arrangement of historical proceedings with integrated cultural materials and accompanying digital exhibits to build on the movement's own style, historical contexts, and major themes in ways that enable the analysis of end-movement discourse that this essay undertakes.

An analysis of the movement's conclusion during the years leading up to 1900 is best pursued via a turn to the concept of a nucleic core archive, part of the CCM's textual corpus. While ColoredConventions.org aligns the primary documents that Black delegations published with other cultural materials, this turn calls for a renewed focus on the creation of Black-centered protest spaces by way of delegations' self-published primary documents. An intensive examination of a single pamphlet of Black national minutes, *Proceedings of the National Conference of Colored Men of the United States, held in the State Capitol at Nashville, Tennessee, May 6, 7, 8 and 9, 1879*, reveals how Black writers packaged in one bound text of late-century digest literature the many aspects of social justice activism involved in facilitating Black meetings during the final decades of movement activity. Mediated by one of the largest Black delegations in CCM history, this literary work captures performances of racial solidarity and the facilitation of racial uplift plans while also demonstrating a late-movement convention body's ability to negotiate the transition from early movement to end-movement styles of Black delegate representation.

The 1879 delegation partly signaled the conclusion of the CCM by publishing a comparatively sophisticated pamphlet of proceedings, which houses delegate debates about the efficacy of tying its organizational work to the CCM. Most delegations' publishing committees that produced 1830s and 1840s convention pamphlets placed greater emphasis on printing resolutions that reflected its delegates' majority-rule decisions while summarizing or leaving out their in-person debates and the extended crowd reactions that contributed to these decisions. They granted limited textual space to mentions of newspapers that the convention body endorsed, or they published committee reports on endorsed newspapers. Publishing committees often printed high-ranking attending delegates' speeches rather than formal, single-authored argumentative essays by nonattending Black leaders. On the other hand, the 1879 pamphlet features an extended section of transcribed dialogue between multiple delegates with typography of the attending audience's sound effects during a major in-person debate about the delegation's tenuous relationship to the CCM. It features a full-page commercial advertisement for an existing newspaper edited by a standing delegate in addition to mentions of other newspapers the delegation supported. The pamphlet also features an uncommon appendix section, and its long-form essays from some nonattending Black leaders build on or refute arguments discussed during in-person proceedings in addition to addresses and committee reports that commonly appeared in antebellum minutes. This delegation departed from traditional styles of CCM leadership by foregrounding anti-CCM discussions and by positioning attending audiences as empowered constituents.

In this essay, I describe the ways trends associated with themes, types of evidence, and political values of single meetings like the 1879 convention can be linked to major eras in a benchmark social movement. Using labels to describe convention discourses—conservative, moderate, and radical—I define relationships between individual meetings that produced political literature to articulate the struggles for freedom that the movement exemplifies and the nature of Black leadership bodies' organizational contributions to the American Black protest tradition. By proposing a range of conservative to radical approaches to "Colored Convention" ideologies, I argue that the 1879 National Conference of Colored Men is a key case study for understanding turn-of-the-century changes in the platform. In concert with tabulations of the movement's broader protest ethos, this method of investigating end-movement discourse focuses on the utility of a high-quality hybrid document by oscillating between formalist and new-historicist approaches to Black literary studies in the context of a social movement framework. A formalist approach views a literary work as a universe of its own making, emphasizing the autonomy of a text in relation to objective rather than intertextual discourse between literary works and multiple languages.[1] The new-historicist approach that Stephen Jay Greenblatt heralded in the 1980s calls for an interpretation of a literary work in connection with the social, political, and economic conditions out of which it emerges.[2] This essay privileges a formalist framework as one kind of evidence, while sampling categories of freedom discourse drawn from the broader movement to show the concentration of ideologies that appear in the 1879 pamphlet.

This essay's turn to a hyperfocused, single-event analysis centered on the Black convention minutes does not dismiss the necessity of a broader survey of cultural materials for a history of nineteenth-century Black civil rights advocacy. Rather, this analysis acknowledges the techno-organizational advancements of end-movement delegations that are reflected in the 1879 pamphlet's numerous styles of public-oriented civic engagement. The cohort's representation of the Black protest tradition in the pamphlet employs rules of order, a list of elected or appointed delegate representatives, a list of delegate's pledged and paid contributions to cover expenses, resolution-based policies, demography, municipal and other statistics, single-author essays, advertisements, and the citation of newspaper literature, among other content. In contrast, early-movement minutes tended to lack such variety. Scholarship about Black-led advocacy during the antebellum era often draws from contemporaneous cultural materials to uncover discursive patterns pertaining to Black-centered racial uplift across genres in relation to individual meetings or thematically connected groups of meetings and across time, place, and intent. Apparent in the organization of documents represented by ColoredConventions.org, the CCM's start-up phase gained traction through a multimodal partnership between "Colored Convention" print proceedings and related literature. Information appearing in Black and white newspapers such as the *Frederick Douglass's Newspaper* by the orator, slave-narrative author, and editor, and *The Liberator* by the white abolitionist editor William Lloyd Garrison are key examples. Moreover, the movement depended on the activities of charitable and educational organizations and the activism of Black women with local and organizational ties to conventions at a time when Black women struggled to hold positions as delegates.[3]

The Social Justice Archive

This essay works against the grain of typical approaches to understanding a social-justice archive to better characterize the CCM's end by studying a single convention pamphlet. *Proceedings of the National Conference of Colored Men of the United States, Held in the State Capitol at Nashville, Tennessee, May 6, 7, 8 and 9, 1879* amasses most aspects of the movement franchise in one textual space while also recording an opening debate among Black leaders that calls for a departure from the namesake markers of the CCM enterprise. The Walt Whitman Archive's single-author focus locates transhistorical political engagement in a single generative figure with Whitman as a poet of many voices and a contemporary of the CCM. In contrast, the CCP's ColoredConventions.org harnesses Black cohorts' intra-action networks and methods to bring attention to the movement's multivocal structure and strengths in community-building. The site helps to democratize access to a history of nineteenth-century Black literary production previously dispersed, in part, between collections. These include the print anthologies *A Survey of the Negro Convention Movement, 1830–1861* (1953) and *Proceedings of the Black State Conventions, 1840–1865* (1979).[4]

Mirroring the Walt Whitman Archive's approach to making the author's "vast work freely and conveniently accessible to scholars, students, and general readers," the CCP's comprehensive method of digital representation temporally streamlines a variety of geocoded textual and visual materials, capturing a growing tally of hundreds of convention sessions, as well as the convention naming practices, leaders, and sites of activity. This approach to content organization democratizes a history of Black protest in conjunction with a distinct area of the nineteenth-century Black protest tradition. Original facsimile and crowd-sourced transcribed minutes constitute the core of the ColoredConventions.org archive. We supplement this core with event calls, newspaper articles, petitions and memorials, advertisements, photographic images, and ephemera, as well as narrative-based exhibits and educational curricula.

The CCP wields the tools of the twenty-first century, especially new media, to provide insight into African Americans' structurally collaborative platform, which, by 1880, "had to rely almost exclusively on the embryonic form of modern ethnic-group leadership—social-organization-type leadership" not only in Southern states, but also in the Northeast, the Midwest, and the far-West.[5] Leading up to the postbellum era, the average Black delegate worked through committee-based, unpaid positions to substantiate claims for "a redress of grievances" driven by racism.[6] An examination of the 1879 National Conference of Colored Men in Nashville reveals the nature of the CCM's transition from the antebellum to the postbellum era.

From Performance to Textual Reproduction: The 1879 National Conference Held in Nashville

The meeting minutes for the 1879 National Conference in Nashville read like a marquee event in the Colored Convention franchise. Sessions were stacked with high-ranking Black politicians such as the former interim governor of Louisiana Pinckney B. S. Pinchback, the son of a white planter and an enslaved woman. The former Alabama congressman James Thomas Rapier served as a secretary tasked with producing the postevent pamphlet of minutes. The resulting document's opening pages evidence the multimodal nature of CCM literary production, which includes original writing and content editing. According to the pamphlet's review of the first day of sessions, after a delegate's introductory eulogy, the celebrity troupe out of Fisk University, the six-member Jubilee Singers, performed the Christian spiritual "Steal Away to Jesus" in the central hall of the Tennessee State Capitol Building—"in splendid style" and "amid great applause." Instances of humorous banter between delegates make an early appearance in the minutes. Rather than superfluous interjections, these interactions capture nuanced relationship-building at the core of a national-level assembly, the success of which depended on collaboration between travelling community organizers. In a more serious vein,

> Rev. Allan Allensworth arose to a point of gallantry, stating that several gentlemen were sitting while ladies were standing. A change in position, as suggested by the delegate from Kentucky, was accordingly made.[7]

Another resolution presented in favor of protecting attending Black women further defines the unfurling nature of delegate representation, which was nonetheless heavily inscribed with masculine signifiers throughout the print proceedings: "*Resolved*, That the action of the railroad conductors, in forcibly ejecting the ladies of the Jubilee Singers from the ladies' car, merits our undivided condemnation."[8] From celebratory oratory to debates leading to the passage of event-level ordinances, this sampling from event culture embodies the delegation's performance of moral duty across topics. The rhetorical features of the products of collaborative writing at such Black meetings bring attention to delegations' joint authorial-editorial dexterity. The execution of the convention platform relied on the ability of delegates to tackle emergent issues as they unraveled in real-time with as much vigor and intentionality as the handling of entrenched topics such as emigration proposals that had a history of appearing as Colored Conventions agenda items since the movement's launch in 1830 (see Figure 8.1, showing positions on emigration taken at Colored Conventions).

The official political pamphlet of the 1879 national convention prompts special consideration as a representative text with which to consider the larger movement's categorical legibility. The forum takes place between the ultimate decline of the Freedmen's Bureau, which occurred by 1877, and the decline of the larger movement, which occurred by 1900. On the other hand, the 1879 *Proceedings of the National Conference of Colored Men* anticipates the forthcoming Great Migration of African Americans from the rural South to urban cities in the North, Midwest, and the West when an estimated six million Black people migrated between 1916 and 1970.[9] The delegation pursued a national-scale agenda, though the regional concerns of African Americans from the South, including emigration and a healthy lifestyle, dominate the argumentative suppositions behind many of the items appearing in *Proceedings of the National Conference of Colored Men*.

Emigration discourse in the 1879 literature completes a circular trajectory, from beginning to end, of the movement's investment in Black constituent concerns surrounding raced-based societal mistreatment. The emigration debates emerged because of a divisive post-Reconstruction political environment in the South. The 1879 meeting mirrored the exigency or high responsivity of early 1830s and 1840s convention delegations, which called meetings to debate about Black people's emigration out and away from cities or states with active race-based forced removal policies. These meetings primarily sought recourse for Northern free people, particularly Black constituencies with liminal, highly vulnerable social statuses. Black women, fugitives from slavery, lynching victims, and child victims of segregationist school policies are some examples of vulnerable groups. Records show that a proliferation of opinion, a deficit in time and pecuniary resources, and the unlikelihood that agenda items would succeed postevent strained the efficacy of convention work throughout the CCM's run.

Year	Place	Level	Topic	Position
1830	Philadelphia, PA	National	Canada and Emigration	The delegation supported emigration to Upper Canada, but not to Africa.
1832	Philadelphia, PA	National	Emigration to Canada	Delegates sought to buy lands collectively in Canada to create a large settlement of freed colored people.
1835	Philadelphia, PA	National	Emigration	Delegates opposed colonization as a promotional scheme because it was not republican in ideology, and because they should remain on American soil.
1851	Albany, NY	State	Emigration	Delegates strongly opposed any emigration scheme and the Fugitive Slave Act.
1852	Baltimore, MD	State	Emigration	Delegates issued recommendations for emigration to Liberia, Africa.
1854	Cleveland, OH	National	Emigration	Delegates pressed free Blacks to purchase land in Canada (West) to increase political rights and upward social mobility.
1879	Nashville, Tennessee	National	Southern Emigration	Delegates mostly supported emigration to Western states and territories due to inequality and intimidation.

Figure 8.1. Positions taken at Colored Conventions on the question of emigration, 1830–1879.

As a self-funded enterprise with mostly unpaid convention organizers at the helm, the 1879 National Conference of Colored Men at Nashville magnified the traditions of the movement, while its mediated (re)production in print reveals internal fissures along the boundaries of acceptable decorum and political direction in the post-Reconstruction era. Practical approaches to good health and to reducing poverty and mortality rates, for example, dampen the impact of arguments for increased emigration of Black communities away from the Southern states. Distinguishing features of the 1879 convention include a comparatively large, approximately 144-member, delegation and the sophisticated quality of the pamphlet's compilation of materials. Typographical notations in the minutes mark the exuberance of "uproarious" crowds attending the two-a-day meetings.[10] The appearance of typographical signifiers like "[Laughter.]" and "[Applause.]" contributes to the lively tone of the pamphlet's 115 bound pages.[11] An appendix of ten essays on race-based sociopolitical issues and four committee reports demonstrates the body's advancements in publication efficacy.

However, the need for budgets capable of covering the pecuniary demands of large-scale, multiday events also defined a style of charitable leadership in tune with CCM concepts of moral duty. The production of print proceedings reveals the financial strains of the delegate position, as well as opportunities for creative engagement among professional classes of its attendees. It would have cost the average reader twenty-five cents to purchase a copy of the proceedings. In the proceedings, the former Congressman James Rainey calls for a committee on "finance to collect funds for stationery, (and) printing" and to acquire two recording pages who would perform tasks upon assignment and handle parts of the publishing process alongside the committee on printing.[12] Rainey later raised $105.50 on the third day to cover such convention expenses.[13] But by the end of the event, the "net amount raised by the conference did not meet one-half of the expense of publishing the proceedings," as the compiler of the minutes, J. W. Cromwell, pointed out.[14] One result of the conference's limited budget is reflected in the finished pamphlet's appendix, with a list of delegate donations in increments of one dollar and fifty cents.[15] This partial list of delegates points to the unpaid position that each delegate occupies by describing their donations to the event. This concluding section of the minutes also includes the works of attendees and absentee participants who could not attend but shared a previously prepared essay. The New Jersey-based William Stewart's "The Necessity of a National Review Devoted to the Interests of the Negro-American" appears in the pamphlet as one of several papers read aloud during the proceedings. It presents a case for the public presses' powerful influence over the masses. For Stewart, weekly literary papers and magazines carry broad appeal as luxury items that help to shape an individual's character while also displaying the aesthetic capacities of American printed content. Differently, national reviews that host research-based essays and commentary are construed as far less popular with the average reader, though they offer a far more productive means to reshape the image of African Americans through an intentional engagement with their population-based concerns. Stewart's pitch for a periodical devoted to Black people's interests apart from political or religious sectarianism and with the purpose of dismantling nefarious public policy largely echoed the pamphlet in which his own essay was published. Moreover, this set of proceedings helps to explicate the budgetary strains created by large-scale events, as it also offers a means for understanding the generally fractured history of document production for the movement. By acknowledging budgets, printing costs, methods of distribution, and affiliated media entities, the organizational properties of the Colored Conventions platform become clearer.

Categorizing "Colored Conventions" in Movement Studies

With a firm temporal marker (1830–1900) and a body of known referential titles for movement events as a starting point, I raise greater taxonomical distinctions that require researchers to calibrate their studies with a more local focus. The use of organizational tropes that bring relational clarity to conventions according to activities, values, and material resources presents a legible set of categories characteristic of CCM freedom struggles. Scholars have relied on flexible designations to historicize and analyze the Colored Conventions archive. Derrick Spires has used the term "black hole" and Ivy Wilson has deployed the term "shadow" to deal with issues of invisibility and sparsity that characterize some African American figures, organizations, beliefs, and their associated political literature in an era offering both a warranted hope for full liberation and prevailing obstacles entrenched in most areas of society.[16] Examining the internal CCM dynamics provides a three-dimensional characterization of movement culture as both sharing a history with other American social movements and also embodying distinctive features. This method still recognizes the seventeenth and eighteenth centuries' American Great Awakening, the Religious Society of Friends, and other Puritan congregations, and the establishment of nineteenth-century Black Protestant denominations that help to contextualize the civic-oriented platform. Indeed, Black convention delegations embraced ceremonial rituals of piety such as prayer, religious song, and ministerial leaders; elements of the Black sermonic tradition also influence CCM literature.

The CCM tradition of observing the condition of Black constituencies serves as the primary analytical base by which the movement should be regarded as a secular social movement. As I have argued elsewhere, following the first decade of its founding, the movement became increasingly guided by a public-facing rather than a religious-facing construct of social organization.[17] A moral ethos toward delegates' duty to serve communities' needs best describes the methods of the constituent-based representation that other core convention rituals upheld. These rituals include debates, votes, resolutions, and petitioning; these democratic methods provide the core substance of convention documents. In his opening remarks, Pinchback promotes an aesthetics of political performance (or decorum) that is distinct from agents of early American Protestant discourses, including the fiery sermonic traditions of Jonathan Edwards's Great Awakening and a departure from Reverend Allen's ties to a single denomination, the African Methodist Episcopal Church.

The Decline of a Movement: Convention-Naming Practices

The pamphlet captures a debate over convention naming practices to ascertain delegate eligibility, which signals a decline in the movement's momentum. The discussion reviewed the basis of community representation and the purpose of a predominately Black-led political meeting. The movement's ongoing debates about delegate seniority and the right to convene movement-sponsored events reflect the heightened diversification of political identities among the pool of activists who claimed association with the ethos of the

CCM. President Pinchback yields the Speaker's stand of the "House of Delegates" to Mississippi delegate John R. Lynch, who orally represents a leadership decorum capable of quelling early unrest about two points.[18] They relate to "the aims, objects and purpose" of a "Conference" and a "Convention."[19] Lynch's first supposition is that the "Conference" should be recognized in the tradition of Colored Conventions, since the "mode of its formation was so familiar to the people of the country that we would meet with no opposition."[20] This position stands, even though the original organizers initially construed the event "not in the interest of any particular political party, especially not as Republicans, not as Democrats, but as free, independent American citizens" intending to present "to the country the grievances of the colored people."[21] The second supposition acquiesces to a "set of gentlemen, chosen by people in a meeting claiming to be delegates," who think the question of emigration demands "important proportions" of the meetings' primary foci.[22]

The 1879 body had hoped to distinguish itself from the "National (Colored) Convention" circuit's leadership by embracing the term "National Conference."[23] But the body was aware that others had "incurred the expense of both time and money" in selecting and sending delegates under the assumption that the forum would be a traditional national-level "Colored Convention" event that would welcome community-elected or -appointed delegates.[24] Nonetheless, the original organizing cohort accepted delegates who traveled to join the proceedings as fully empowered voting members despite the misunderstanding. Each side—originals and assumed members alike—acted on the assumptions of delegation formation that had operated at loosely related "Colored Convention" meetings since the 1830s. The terms "Colored Convention," "Convention of Free People of Colour," "Convention of Colored Citizens," "Convention of Colored Men," "Convention of Colored Freemen," "Convention of Colored People," and "Convention of the Colored Population" brought together mostly autonomously organized meetings under the movement's platform. Without one of these iterations of the "Colored Convention" tagline (members of the contemporaneous media who had reviewed the events and sought a succinct term to describe like-proceedings regularly used the term "Colored Convention"), organizations with all-Black and predominately Black leadership cohorts are nearly indistinguishable as one of

Categories of Freedom 133

the movement's ligaments. A sign of the franchise's declining cohesiveness is reflected in the instability of naming practices surrounding its events and its declining ability to remain relevant based on a shared use of derivatives of the platform's main title phrases.

STYLE IN THE 1879 PAMPHLET:
THE VOICE OF THE 1879 AUDIENCE IN TYPOGRAPHY

Convention decorum directly impacted the 1879 convention literature. At the breakout session of the four-day event, a battle between civic solemnity and charismatic advocacy rose as a leading organizational trope for pursuant discussions. Convention President Pinchback opened the inaugural day's proceedings with a lament. Instead of a welcoming, promiscuous crowd of biracial backers (colored and white citizens of all classes), his opening remarks described a "disturbing" disunity in reference to "those who have so persistently disturbed the proceedings."[25] Pinchback's appointed spokesperson, delegate Lynch, promoted a style of discourse "conducted as to reflect credit upon the race . . . (and) the country"[26]: "I . . . express the hope that all who feel an interest will calmly, deliberately and dispassionately consider the questions for which we have been convened."[27] A rebuttal comes from the Texas delegate B. F. Williams, a self-described "old man" whose stance was informed by his former residential status in Tennessee and "the prayers of our forefathers and mothers."[28] According to Williams, convention officers' interest in calm deliberation constitutes an unnecessarily competitive and authoritarian tone of foreboding. From Williams's position, "this Conference (is) more like a house of mourning" than a place to consider the troubles of represented communities.[29] Sounds of the attending audience incorporated throughout the exchange strongly suggest that the audience agreed with Williams.

The 1879 pamphlet highlights the audience's participation in the convention. The 1879 pamphlet allows the audience to participate in convention proceedings. The debate is recorded across 1.5 pages in the form of a dialogue between Pinchback, Williams, and an unnamed delegate, with the attending audience's sound-based reactions "from the galleries" and the recording secretary's commentary.[30] The following sequence of notations appears in the text as the debate on decorum unfolds. They are integrated into Williams's speaking lines in ways that suggest they are direct responses to his argument.

[Applause.] [Applause.] [Applause.] [Laughter.] [laughter.] [Laughter and applause.] [laughter,] [Renewed laughter.] (pointing his finger toward the person interrupting him.)[31] [uproarious laughter,] [Laughter and applause.] [Applause and laughter.] [Immense applause from the galleries, followed by uproarious and prolonged applause.][32]

From the lens of an audience's empowerment, this sequence may be read as an American realist redevelopment of the chorus in ancient Greek theater. This depiction of an extemporaneous performance reinvents a chorus that oscillates between "music-rhythms" and "speech-rhythms."[33] In Greek tragedies, background rhythms incorporate visually disembodied voices in the stage action to help direct the main action of a theater play. In this case, a typographical sequence directs a performance captured in print. If an audience's sound-rhythms typify audience direction, then the sequence politicizes crowd sounds that function as auditory support for joyous or clamorous proceedings rather than mournful engagement as delegates discuss serious topics on the debate floor. Alternatively, the sequence reflects nineteenth-century

Conservative	*Moderate*	*Radical*
1830 National Colored Convention	1869 Colored National Labor Convention, Washington, D.C.	1843 National Colored Convention, New York
1835 National Colored Convention		1848 National Colored Convention, Ohio
1840 New York State Colored Convention	1879 National Conference of Colored Men, Tennessee	
1843 Mid-Atlantic Temperance Colored Convention		
1854 Massachusetts State Council of Colored Citizens		

Figure 8.2. Political positions taken at Colored Conventions, 1830–1879.

abolitionists' recording techniques and journalist methods. As Nicole H. Gray argues, antebellum abolitionists relied on phonography, "or verbatim reports ... claiming to replicate extemporaneous speeches" in print "as a way of ensuring accurate representation."[34] Print circulation of these texts reanimated "the conditions of publicity (the attraction of attention) attendant upon the original events themselves."[35] Denoting recording techniques as a part of Black realist styles of event documentation, the 1879 pamphlet's writing cohort deploys early-century methods to convey to public readers greater authenticity as they report on real activities.

Figure 8.2 lists the types of discourse—conservative, moderate, and radical—employed at different years' Colored Conventions.[36]

Debates in the 1879 Convention Pamphlet: Migration, Health, and Housing

Migration proved to be a dominant topic at the 1879 meeting, drawing impassioned arguments that favored and opposed African Americans' "exodus" of out of the South.[37] Across the minutes, migration is hailed as a totem of conversations about Black people's upward socioeconomic mobility in the postwar era. By the second day of meetings, each delegate was asked to submit a written report on "the true condition of the masses, ... of their respective States with regard to labor and education," with the goal "that such statement govern the action of this Conference with respect to the subject of migration."[38] Many delegates viewed this charge as a call to action for delegates to organize the masses. Alternatively, some debates about a mass exodus denounced state governments in what constituted a public court of opinion. These debates demand improvements in race-based social relations and working conditions given the risk of the depletion of Black constituencies in the South. When taken together, the differences on this subject reflect an identity crisis among the delegation reflective of ongoing platform struggles and the convention's initial interest in the term "Conference."

Emigration debates in the minutes demonstrate delegates' ability to propose a variety of political strategies to confront national crises (see Figure 8.1). The delegate J. A. Braboy from Indiana informs white American "friends" that "a mass exodus of the race" will occur because of a dearth of biracial efforts for securing equal rights for all people in their roles as allies.[39] The delegate David Wilson of Huntsville argues that a petition from each represented state should be sent to Congress and the president to create a "new Canaan," a self-styled utopia in a western state wherein migrating populations could settle.[40] Wilson believed such a state could be founded on "Republican principles, to be governed by (the colored people), from governor down to the humblest officer, without fear or intimidation" and with full land ownership.[41] Braboy's and Wilson's positions raise the recurring centrality of imaginative realism and righteous indignation as motivators for grievance claims aired in the civic sphere on behalf of Black constituencies.

Positions on migration are reflected in resolutions and reports. Believing the south to be an important homestead, some delegates argue that, once rights and privileges such as fair wages are guaranteed, Black populations will remain. Other delegates tie the issue of fleeing populations to the "perfectly ... sincere" belief among white Americans of "colored inferiority and rightful subordination."[42] In the pamphlet, Black westerners like J. C. Embry welcome travelers with a tone as "positive and emphatic as a thunder-drum in affirming the determination to submit to oppression no longer."[43] One delegate suggests that all "resolutions relating to migration first be referred to the Southern delegates," likely the original cohort that called the meeting.[44] Another resolution declared that African American migrants need prior knowledge of localities before travel, along with enough savings to secure a safe journey and a home in which to settle. Another delegate recommends creating a commission of emigration advisors to choose homes for travelers, while yet another believes a single commissioner should be appointed to oversee all activities. Another delegate proposes a committee of three to visit the western states and territories to report on the "health, climate, and productions" of these areas. By the end of the conference, the delegation agrees to support thousands of southerners in flocking to "the free and fertile West" —with some stipulations in place.[45] Their stipulations in the form of social policies allow the distribution of the minutes to serve as print-based voices of counsel on the subject.[46]

The issue of poverty undermines migration support at the 1879 meeting, which reflects organizational tensions characteristic of the Colored Conventions movement. While less prominent in the minutes in comparison to emigration debates, detailed discussions about poor health and sanitation practices present a key debilitating factor in response to emigration supporters' arguments about the nature of Black people's social mobility in the South in comparison to those in cities in the West and North. These positions highlight the fundamental roles that delegates' assessments of Black populations play in presenting sound counsel on political topics in ways that represent the 1879 pamphlet as instructive guidance for public audiences. Delegate William Still, the prominent activist out of Ohio whose concerted work on the Underground Railroad substantiates his claims, argues that emigration will prove unsuccessful for some vulnerable classes:

> Now, I am compelled to say, with deep regret, that our poor people are not prepared to emigrate under any such encouraging aspects. They have been too long shut out from the light of knowledge to be ready for any en masse emigration movement.[47]

Still's position is compounded by statistics published in the proceedings that reflect the state of health among African American populations, making the data important indicators of the lack of Black populations' access to social services and creature comforts. According to the 1879 minutes, J. W. Cromwell, the convention's clerk, read an absentee physician's paper. The Howard University faculty member in medicine and Army veteran Alexander Thomas Augusta's paper, "A Sanitary Condition of the People of the United States," appears in the pamphlet's appendix. In it, Doctor Augusta argues that the Black population is growing but that the federal and state governments lack legal safeguards to grant proper access to census records, and "still less attention is paid to give correct reports of the colored people."[48] As a byproduct of this situation, these government record-keeping practices tend "to make no difference between whites and blacks" in vital and other social statistics.[49] Augusta's paper focuses on the District of Columbia's 1870s vital records. This time encompasses its transition to "Washington, D.C.," through phases of a commission-governed municipality and radical infrastructure revitalization. Moreover, Augusta's essay evokes the necessity of post-emancipation Black leadership thought concerning an area wherein the 1862 Compensated Emancipation Act had freed more than three thousand slaves and whose African American men gained access to municipal suffrage in 1868.

Black Literary Realism in the 1879 Convention Pamphlet

A key example of demography-based literature that may have stalled emigration arguments alongside delegate Still's anti-emigration position, Augusta's essay raises the enjoyment of good health as a primary goal to accompany acts of accruing wealth and civil rights. The essay indirectly promotes a Black–white racial reconciliation doctrine by considering poor health as a debilitating aspect in narratives of population decline. This comparative study emphasizes colliding social problems impacting not only "the colored race, but ... all others."[50] It uses vital statistics drawn from census records and annual municipal reports to describe the Black–white racial binary and comment on Black people's particular struggles. Augusta's frank and concerned style of discourse appeals to readers to consider the consequences of poor health, including the factors of yellow fever, premature death, despair, and other conditions. The health of these Americans is further menaced by "doctors and sanitarians" who had been overwhelmed and had "been taxed to their uttermost to apply means of cure."[51] Augusta also argues that the dearth of resources includes "sanitary measures, such as disinfectants, quarantine and isolation to stamp out the disease and prevent its recurrence." Among the paper's cited diseases are "small-pox, diphtheria, cholera, and the plague, or black fever."[52] The paper displays an overarching cautionary rhetoric, opening with a narrative of viral diseases among the "human family," including in armies, ship crews, and nations with famous struggles with mass contagion apparent in historical records.[53] Then follows a description of America's particular style of insufficiently documenting or misrepresenting vital statistics. Augusta cites overly high death rates for African Americans and undercounted death rates for white populations.

The essay focuses on sanitation and housing issues in Washington, D.C., during a time when the newly established territorial government of the District of Columbia struggled to manage advancements in its infrastructure following the Organic Act of 1871. Specifically, the essay shows the ways that Black people were severely impaired by area-wide social prejudices. The essay's citation of vital statistics substantiates claims of "fearful" mortality rates among District of Columbia communities as a case study in hygienic practices.[54]

Population totals by race, births (including still births and the birth of twins), deaths, marriages, and percentages of mortality of children under five years of age are given for 1874 to 1878. In one case, the author brings attention to disparities in mortality rates for the year 1877: "Deaths—White 2,102, being 1.82 per cent of white population, and 51.23 per cent. of the total mortality; colored 2,001, being 4.44 per cent. Of colored population, and 48.76 per cent. of total mortality."[55]

Augusta's representation of issues concerning Black constituencies presents likely causes associated with harmful lifestyle conditions. They include the housing conditions of "frame shanties" or rows of "small houses" without regulatory standards for sanitation that nonetheless fuel a high-rent housing market for Black people in the Washington, D.C., area. Augusta's essay especially focuses on Black impoverished communities living in shanties or, alternatively, "mean-cabin(s)," which serve as "temporary or permanent shelter(s)."[56] In the context of the 1879 pamphlet, Augusta's representation of a housing crisis seeks to raise alarm for his sense of a dystopian timeline in which "our wretched poor are born and exist and die in" these conditions in the United States.[57]

Augusta's first-person account offering demographic analysis is at the center of his notion of Black convention leadership. The essay's descriptive passages about Black people's sociopolitical conditions tie his exposé and the broader pamphlet to the larger American realism literary movement. However, his denouncement of housing conditions, which are presented as facts and are drawn from the course of the author's experiential work as a physician, seek to prompt social action from empowered governing bodies, rather than to convey an objective study without a philosophical stance for social change. The following passage describes Augusta's commentary on Black people's housing conditions:

> I found a one-story room about 12 by 12 to 12 by 16 feet, and about seven feet in height, composed of inch and a half boards, the top or roof being covered with felt or gravel. There were no water-spouts to lead the water from the roof, and consequently it ran close to the foundation and under the house, where it often remained for an indefinite period, combined with other surface water and refuse matters.[58]

He attributes such low-quality living conditions, in part, to bad architectural and material infrastructure. Another example points to homes in states of poor assembly:

> Down in the alleys, below grade, with combination roof of felt, tar, shingles, rags, tin, gravel, boards and holes; floors damp and broken, walls begrimed by smoke and age; so domiciled are families, with all the dignity of tenants having rent to pay; perhaps four or five, or may be eight dollars a month, and proud of the distinction though often greatly exercised to meet their obligations.[59]

In addition to Augusta's eye-witness accounts, testimonies referenced in the essay describe other conditions detrimental to occupants' health.

Citizen testimonies recorded in Augusta's "Sanitary Condition" paper heighten the pamphlet's engagement with the realist tradition. Testimonials from unnamed individuals cite wild swings in temperature over the course of a day from "75 to 85 degrees of heat, while at night, after the fire went out, the temperature would fall to the freezing point" due to a lack of plaster on shanty home walls. A typical family of a man, wife, three to six children, and a grandparent might inhabit such a home that was likely to have but one "small door" and a three-by-three window for ventilation.[60] Conversely, even large shanty cabins could cause extreme discomfort. A lack of proper sanitation and airing out of floors, carpets, and beds were cited as evidence of the housing crisis. The fact that cooking and waste production and containments were held or "done in the same room" also proved problematic causes of unhygienic living conditions.[61] After in-person debates and reading of papers such as Augusta's, the post-event 1879 pamphlet captures the National Executive Committee on Migration's ultimate decision to support emigration. In one statement that precedes its resolutions, the committee posits:

> This migration movement is based on a determined and irrepressible desire, on the part of the colored people of the South, to go anywhere where they can escape the cruel treatment and continued threats of the dominant race in the South.[62]

Nonetheless, Augusta's paper demonstrates the educational and political interventions that convention forums' literary production could promote. His proposal for good health as a central goal of convention-leadership formation and subsequent initiatives for racial uplift helped to diversify the pro-Black advocacy avenues available to reading publics.

Augusta's analysis reflects the educational capacities of CCM delegations' advocacy-based labor and subsequent collaboratively written publications. Characteristic of Black convention cultures, the 1879 pamphlet's appendix features a policy document, "Report of the Committee on a Permanent Form of Organization." The document proposes a permanent society inclusive of most standing delegate members to facilitate the enactment of agenda items "to Prevent Injustice to the Colored People."[63] This document resolves a future imagined body to pursue both emigration and the improvement of sanitary conditions, thus showing the power of in-person arguments given on the convention floor and classical argumentation rendered in essay form to build momentum for long-term Black activism.

The Literature of the Colored Conventions Movement

Nineteenth-century Black convention meetings' structures, performative aesthetics, and literary productions sought to amplify evaluations of Black communities' social condition for delegations, represented communities, and members of the public. Thematic threads that run through the movement's primary documents capture delegates' competing positions during processes of proposing racial uplift initiatives. In addition to competing stances that unraveled in movement documents over the linguistic authority of convention-naming practices, the power to provide sound advice necessitated a greater reliance on methods of literary realism among late-century delegations to contextualize and promote Black constituencies' needs. As the 1879 national meeting demonstrates, the basic tenets of most conventions carrying the "Colored Convention" moniker remained intact long after the movement's 1830 launch, even as some Black leaders sought to depart from the CCM tradition as the movement's end neared. Convention activities, including oral and written debates, votes, and the passage of resolutions, were mainly concerned with community- and constituency-building, streamlining political messages, and garnering Black people's full access to civil rights.

As a byproduct of my role as a co-founder and a former, long-term co-coordinator of the CCP and ColoredConventions.org, my research shows that the known corpus of CCM print proceedings endures as one of the movement's foundational literary achievements that reflects its practice of Black democratic theory and civic engagement. Like the movement's historical actors, we established research committees that created the framework and content for ColoredConventions.org. This organizational structure allowed us to borrow from the movement's editorial methods while also broadening public readers' access to a range of additional information that we compiled about the movement, including information about Black women's contributions to meetings, physical event spaces, and related documents apart from primary proceedings. In doing so, I and other CCP members helped to re-envision the idea of scholarly anthologies in the context of visual education in the age of contemporary digital humanism that concentrates on studies of Black intellectual history.

Notes

1. "Formalism," Britannica Online, accessed May 3, 2021, britannica.com/art/Formalism-literary-criticism.

2. "Stephen Greenblatt," Britannica Online, accessed May 3, 2021, britannica.com/biography/Stephen-Greenblatt.

3. Elizabeth Gloucester was married to James Gloucester, who served as a data aggregator for the 1843 statistical report in his capacity as a delegate for the 1843 National Colored Convention held in Buffalo, New York. While she did not appear to have served as a CCM delegate, her work with trade organizations and children's relief associations supplemented the work of the Black convention platform.

4. *Survey* was edited by Howard Holman Bell. Two volumes of *Proceedings of the Black State Convention* were edited by Phillip S. Foner and George E. Walker.

5. See Martin Kilson, *Transformation of the African American Intelligentsia, 1880–2012* (Cambridge, Mass.: Harvard University Press, 2014), 52.

6. *Proceedings of the National Conference of Colored Men of the United States, Held in the State Capitol at Nashville, Tennessee, May 6, 7, 8 and 9, 1879* (Washington, D.C.: Rufus H. Darby, Steam Power Printer, 1879), 29 (hereafter *Proceedings*).

7. *Proceedings*, 18.

8. *Proceedings*, 10.

9. "Great Migration," Britannica Online. Accessed February 3, 2022, britannica.com/event/Great-Migration.

10. *Proceedings*, 8.

11. The minutes compile delegate rolls and speeches, debates, voting tallies and resulting resolutions, committee reports, petitions, statistics, and an appendix of essays advocating for civil rights.

12. *Proceedings*, 9.
13. *Proceedings*, 34.
14. *Proceedings*, 107.
15. *Proceedings*, 107.
16. Derrick Spires, "Flights of Fancy: Black Print, Collaboration, and Performances in 'An Address to the Slaves of the United States of America (Rejected by the National Convention, 1843),'" in *The Colored Conventions Movement: Black Organizing in the Nineteenth Century*, ed. Gabrielle Foreman, Jim Casey, and Sarah Lynn Patterson (Chapel Hill: University of North Carolina Press, 2021), 126.
17. See my essay "'As the True Guardians of Our Interests': Black Demography at Colored Conventions," in Foreman, Casey, and Patterson, *Colored Conventions Movement*, 211–19.
18. *Proceedings*, 3.
19. *Proceedings*, 3–4.
20. *Proceedings*, 3.
21. *Proceedings*, 4.
22. *Proceedings*, 4.
23. *Proceedings*, 2.
24. *Proceedings*, 8.
25. *Proceedings*, 3, 98.
26. *Proceedings*, 4.
27. *Proceedings*, 4.
28. *Proceedings*, 7.
29. *Proceedings*, 7.
30. *Proceedings*, 8.
31. This line refers to Williams's actions toward an unnamed delegate.
32. *Proceedings*, 7–8.
33. H. D. F. Kitto, "The Greek Chorus," *Educational Theatre Journal* 8, no. 1 (1956): 2.
34. Nicole H. Gray, "Recording the Sounds of 'Words that Burn': Reproductions of Public Discourse in Abolitionist Journalism," *Rhetoric Society Quarterly* 41, no. 4 (2011): 364.
35. Gray, "Recording the Sounds," 370.
36. The 1843 convention is denoted as radical due to debates surrounding Henry Highland Garnet's speech "An Address to the Slaves of the United States" at a time when most antebellum conventions focused on the state of free Black people in the West and Northeast. The 1843 convention rejected the speech due to most delegates' belief that it encouraged insurrection among enslaved people in the South. The 1848 convention is denoted as radical due to it being the first known departure from an all-male delegation in the movement's run. The delegation accepted all colored attendees as delegates, including Black women.
37. *Proceedings*, 9.
38. *Proceedings*, 12.

39. *Proceedings*, 14.
40. *Proceedings*, 29.
41. *Proceedings*, 29.
42. *Proceedings*, 106.
43. *Proceedings*, 106.
44. *Proceedings*, 10.
45. *Proceedings*, 105.
46. *Proceedings*, 106.
47. *Proceedings*, 59.
48. *Proceedings*, 43.
49. *Proceedings*, 43.
50. *Proceedings*, 42.
51. *Proceedings*, 42.
52. *Proceedings*, 42.
53. *Proceedings*, 42.
54. *Proceedings*, 47.
55. *Proceedings*, 44.
56. *Proceedings*, 45.
57. *Proceedings*, 45.
58. *Proceedings*, 45.
59. *Proceedings*, 45.
60. *Proceedings*, 45.
61. *Proceedings*, 45.
62. *Proceedings*, 100.
63. *Proceedings*, 67.

CHAPTER 9

Not Reading the Edition

CASSIDY HOLAHAN, AYLIN MALCOLM, AND
WHITNEY TRETTIEN

We are literary scholars who do not read.

That is not entirely true, of course. We read all the time, but it is not always what we wish to do with books, professionally. When one of us goes to a rare book room and calls up an item, we pick it up and look at the binding, turning it over and around gently to examine the spine. We touch the leather cover to see if it is original or a later imitation. Setting it down, we open it up, running a finger between the flyleaf and the book board. The spine quietly creaks. Has it been repaired? We shine a light through a leaf, searching for watermarks or hair follicles, and into the gutter, searching for stitches. We smell it. Looking at the design of each page, we ask questions like: how does the text hang together? Is the text large or small, are the margins wide or slim? Are there page numbers, running headers, gauffered edges, or indices? What are the mechanisms for moving through the book? *Collate, map, scan, navigate, explore*—these are the verbs that explain what we do with an old book. Not, typically, *read*.

The scene we are describing is the bread-and-butter work of analytic bibliography: the close examination of a book as a material artifact in order to learn something about how and why it was made, by what processes and to what ends. Bibliography is tangled up with literary studies because it is the engine that helps textual scholars produce editions for us to *read*: editions that identify the literary work, fill out historical context, and neutralize dissonance across variations. As early as 1932, in an apologia that effectively founded the field of so-called "new bibliography," W. W. Greg cemented this relationship between the material text and literary studies: "Books are the material means by which literature is transmitted; therefore bibliography, the study of books, is essentially the science of the transmission of literary documents."[1]

Transmission is a key word here. Greg was attempting to convince textual critics who valued their own intuition of what an author's intentions were over the physical evidence offered through a careful collation of variants. In order to do so, he spent a great deal of his essay *narrowing* the purview of bibliography to include only those features of a document that contribute to the transmission of literary meaning, and thereby help the scholar identify the text. Binding, the aesthetics of typography, illustrations, provenance: "these branches" of the study of books, he writes, "whatever their own interest may be, are of bibliographical importance just in so far as they relate to the function of books as the preservers and transmitters of literary documents."[2]

In the decades following Greg's foundational work, textual critics have discovered the limitations of his narrow formulation of bibliography. In the 1960s, working at the same time as theorists like Michel Foucault and Roland Barthes and citing philosophers of science such as Bertrand Russell and Karl Popper, D. F. McKenzie challenged the idea that inductive reasoning, grounded in the close observation of physical documents, can tell us anything about the transmission of literature, since material evidence *alone* is not enough to make judgments about meaning.[3] "To observe at all is to bestow meaning of some kind of the thing observed," he writes; "To gather particular pieces of evidence is to seek those relevant to some preconceived notion of their utility."[4] Thus, "the very fixity of the physical bounds within which we are asked to work is inimical to the development of a sound methodology."[5] To understand physical evidence, the bibliographer must always place it within the broader sociological and cultural contexts extrapolated from other archival sources, like performance contracts. Building on McKenzie's critique of Greg and his "sociology of texts," Jerome McGann cites poststructuralist critics like Paul de Man when dismissing the notion of an authorial text entirely. Rather, he argues, all literary production is fundamentally *social*, occurring within a dense "network of symbolic exchanges"; "to participate in these exchanges is to have entered" what he calls "the textual condition," where the "only immutable law is the law of change," a "ceaseless process of textual development and mutation."⁶ Thus, by the end of the twentieth century, textual scholars might practice a version of bibliography that no longer had as its telos a singular, stable literary text, embracing instead the kaleidoscopic *material* text and related primary sources as evidence of culture, ideology, and social formations: entire worlds and ways of thinking.

In pursuing this new style of analytic bibliography, which was, by the 1970s or so, sometimes known as the "history of the book," scholars began to practice not *reading* material texts, but something more like close looking, touching, and observation, grounded in a deep appreciation for all aspects of book production, both print and manuscript. Quantitative methods pioneered by the French Annales school of history around the same time that Greg was writing fed into this new "new bibliography" through the work of later book historians like Roger Chartier and Robert Darnton, who emphasized the long history of texts, from the cycle of publication to the readers who bought, collected, and exchanged books. Methods from new media studies, too, fueled the field's rise, as foundational scholars such as Elizabeth Eisenstein drew inspiration from Marshall McLuhan's notion of a "Gutenberg galaxy" and "typographic man," as well as comparative work on film, television, and popular culture. And the book arts contributed a passion for structure, form, aesthetics, and what Johanna Drucker, a book historian and practicing book artist, has recently called "visual epistemology."⁷ The generations who grew up reading this diverse array of thinkers felt increasingly comfortable examining those branches of the study of books that Greg had dismissed as irrelevant to his particular version of bibliography, including bindings, type design, a book's paratextual apparatus, and the material design and structure of books across different formats. In doing so, they began to approach the codex not only as a means of transmitting literary texts, but as a technology with its own history, cultures, and affordances, just like any other. Or, as Wim Van Mierlo has put it: "Editing in the time of the history of the book requires editors to acknowledge at the very least that texts do not exist on their own."⁸ Thus, a century after its founding, we now have a bibliography *cum* textual studies *cum* book history that might be entirely untethered from literary studies, where physical archival materials are studied as one of many different mechanisms that humans have used to record, mediate, and share knowledge.

And so there now exist literary scholars who do not read.

The media environment that has made possible this shift is, of course, the digital. It did so, first, by making bibliographers see the physical book in a new light. Hypertext literature and theory in the 1990s spurred book historians to highlight the unique forms of interactivity enabled by the codex, as did more research into premodern interactive book design, like volvelles, flap anatomies, emblem books, and harlequinades.[9] Later, the digitization of books through platforms like Google Books or HathiTrust, where the dynamic codex becomes a vertical scroll of rectos, stimulated comparative work on what was increasingly being called not the *transmission* but the *remediation* of texts across different media.[10] These digitization projects also encouraged a return to letterpress printing, papermaking, and other book arts, which are now an integral part of pedagogy in book history.[11] At the same time, the actual material conditions of our networked environment have made it easier than ever to study rare books and other archival materials. These conditions include advanced technologies like multispectral imaging and artificial intelligence, used to reveal inscriptions not visible to the human eye alone, or DNA and protein analysis of biological materials like parchment; but they also include the more prosaic ways our daily work is supported by email, social networks, phone cameras capable of high-resolution photography, and cloud storage for saving and sharing them. More, the digital collections being built in individual research libraries are increasingly compatible with each other through the adoption of IIIF standards, as well as research tools for comparison, like Mirador (for viewing images) or VisColl (for encoding collation formulas). As a result, the twenty-first-century researcher who is approaching the book in conceptually new ways can now also see it in a literally new light, conducting advanced bibliographic research across dispersed libraries without leaving home.

Given the imbrication of digital technologies and book history, it is perhaps no surprise that the thinkers who helped unchain bibliography from literary studies are also some of the founding and most influential figures in digital humanities (DH), specifically digital editing and curation. McGann gave us the Rossetti Archive, which relied on the web to make visible Rossetti's multimedia publications, as well as a tool kit for thinking about the "radiant textuality" of the web.[12] Drucker, his colleague then at the University of

Virginia, developed bibliographical games like Ivanhoe, in collaboration with Bethany Nowviskie, a founding figure in DH, and urged us to think about visualizing digital information in *humanistic* ways, under the rubric of what she called "speculative computing."[13] And of course some of the longest-running and most successful digital editions, like the Dickinson Electronic Archives, the William Blake Archive, the Women Writers Project, and the Walt Whitman Archive, were founded in this early period of humanities computing explicitly to make accessible dynamic literary texts *and* multi-modal books that either had not been or could not be easily replicated in print. While this list is by no means exhaustive, the point here is that it was the *capacity* of networked digital media to readily take, share, and link image and text together that ironically helped to foment a fervor for the bookish-ness of books, a frenzy for studying and editing books as richly designed objects—over and above whatever literary texts they may or may not contain. Here, then, even amongst these digital editions of canonical authors, is bibliography and/as book history coming into its own as a field distinct from literature and literary studies.

While this history is known, it is not often made explicit within conversations about digital editing and its futures, where bibliography still implicitly plays the role in which Greg cast it. This is probably because, even as editors in the digital age have come to recognize the fundamental variance, *mouvance,* and fluidity of literary texts, it still seems almost impossible to imagine textual studies without a text at the center of the field's practice.[14] Yet, as this brief sketch of bibliography's transformation into book history and its relationship to digital humanities shows, this is exactly what some textual critics have been imagining for over twenty years now. The cumulative effect of these subtle shifts is evident in several recent projects that combine methods from book history, quantitative analysis, and DH to expand beyond the Anglophone tradition of digital textual editing. Consider, for instance, the digital Codex Mendoza, developed by the Instituto Nacional de Arqueología e Historia in Mexico. While the editors firmly name their work as a "digital edition," citing figures like McGann as inspiration, the website's explanatory notes stress that Mexican codices incorporating elements of pre-Hispanic cultures "clearly brea[k] with traditional Western notions of writing" and should not be read as "texts" per se, so much as multimedia, multimodal performances: a "repertoire" to the text's "archive," to adopt generative terms from Diana Taylor.[15] The design of the interface encourages the study of the book as such by layering over each page image a transcription of whatever text is on the photograph, viewable through a moving lens that never fully obscures the page; hypermedia, highlighted and explained in modal boxes; and a tab on the book's materiality. Maps and a timeline place the visual content within its cultural contexts. Pushing the boundaries of edition-as-performance even further is Gabriela Aceves Sepúlveda's *[Re]Activate Mama Pina's Cookbook,* a creative remediation of a family cookbook written by three generations of women in Guadalajara, Mexico, that presents the book through a video of a hand thumbing through its pages, overlaid with videos of hands cooking the recipes.[16] The reader can, if she wishes, access the recipes through a digitized index; but the juxtaposition of these texts with the video installation only tends to bring into relief how impoverished the index alone is as an experience of the book's meaning.

Other recent work has evacuated reading from digital textual studies entirely. In her project on the Scottish poet Edwin Morgan's scrapbooks, for instance, Bridget Moynihan and her network of collaborators have prototyped several speculative interfaces for visualizing and interpreting each page as a collage of abstracted visual and textual elements. Moynihan began by building a database of "rich information surrogates" for each clipping, including both traditional metadata and computationally extracted metadata, like the color values of each item.[17] This database serves as the underlying text from which more advanced visualizations can be generated as an alternative means of reading, exploring, or navigating the book.[18] For instance, from the color values of each clipping, Akmal Putra designed the Colour Collage prototype, representing each item's color content as a pie chart reflecting pixel size and page placement. Putra also used a game engine to construct a navigable 3D network of the relations between different items in the scrapbook. Moynihan and Putra do not call their prototypes "editions" and are adamant that their "interfaces are not . . . a direct remediation of the archive of the scrapbooks, but rather a creative interpretation of, and a contribution to, this archive."[19] Yet it is also clear from their work that scrapbooks like these *could not* be edited using methods from digital textual studies, even those attuned to textual difference, since their creativity inheres in the material juxtapositions between images and texts, between a cutting's source and its new context. Recognizing similar forms of creativity in women's writing, in 2016 the Women Writers Project developed Intertextual Networks, a three-year project funded by the National Endowment for the Humanities to explore, map, graph, and visualize different citational practices within its textual corpus.[20] The resulting collaborations offer visual "editions" of individual works or groups of works, often without any readable text.

At the extreme end of textless editions, numerous projects in digital book history are deploying machine reading to negotiate new scales of analysis. For instance, Asanobu Kitamoto has been using image matching technologies to collate and track the reuse of woodblock pages in *bukan*, bestselling books of the Edo period listing influential figures in Japan.[21] This form of "differential reading," as he calls it, might be seen as an automated version of stemmatics that seeks to identify a source text (or, in this case, a source block) and the relationship between versions. Similar technologies have been used to track the reuse of woodcut illustrations in European books printed before 1500 and in early modern broadside ballads.[22] Some projects are attempting to eliminate the need for an editor entirely. For instance, HTR2CritEd is using advances in handwritten-text recognition to build "a semi-automatic pipeline to produce a critical digital edition of literary texts with multiple witnesses."[23] Because HTR2CritEd seeks to produce an edition of a text for scholars to read, it is more traditional in its projected outcomes than the other experiments in digital book history that we gesture at here; yet the project's use of machine learning to bypass transcription—a process often seen as an important part of the intellectual work of editing, since it involves making decisions pertaining to the meaning of the text—points to a future for textual criticism where scholars work less with various versions of a work's texts and deal more with the design of interfaces that can represent this data and metadata in ways that reflect contemporary needs and interests. Similar initiatives can be seen in EarlyPrint, a project to enrich the markup of early English printed books in the Text Creation Partnership and Early English Books Online in order to make them more available for various forms of corpus analysis. In these projects, we begin to see an entirely new form of textual studies emerging, one deeply influenced by the concurrent rises of DH and book history.

Our own contributions to this emerging trend take the form of what we might call "material texts editions" made in Manicule, an open-source, web-based application built by software engineer and interactive fiction author Liza Daly in collaboration with Whitney Trettien. Whereas digital editing platforms like Edition Visualization Technology (EVT) or digital collections like HathiTrust treat the book as a sequence of flattened pages aimed at delivering content, Manicule attempts to capture and make visible something of what Drucker has described as the "phenomenal" book: the book as a multidimensional object experienced by embodied subjects.[24] In concrete terms, this means that the platform de-emphasizes reading or searching a text and instead brings into relief a book's navigational mechanisms, internal organization, and physical structure. Drawing on the rich traditions and debates within textual studies and bibliography, Daly and Trettien thus designed Manicule to serve a growing need for editing and publishing tools that take seriously the book *as a material object* bearing traces of its own history, as well as histories of textual production, reading, and reception. As such a tool, Manicule supports the call for more copy-specific research in book history and interest in the material text within textual studies by showcasing the depths and breadth of knowledge that can be gleaned from a close examination of *all* aspects of a document's making and design.

Manicule attempts to achieve this through a series of intentionally "hypermediate" navigational features, to borrow a still generative term from Jay David Bolter and Richard Grusin. "Hypermediacy" names when a platform makes visible its own layers of mediation, refusing to render its interfaces transparent windows onto content.[25] Many web-based book-browsing technologies deliberately do not do this. For instance, the Internet Archive's BookReader presents digitized books as a series of horizontally scrolling page openings, with a fake fore-edge and an animated page turn. In doing so, it attempts to mimic the experience of reading a physical book, encouraging readers to ignore the limiting, two-dimensional framework in which they are actually experiencing the material object.[26] By contrast, Manicule intentionally makes the "photographed"-ness of each page image obvious, even while attempting to provide a familiar perspective on the book as it might be perused in person. Thus readers can choose one of two different views in the main browser, both of paired pages that scroll horizontally: the book can be seen either as a series of openings or as a series of leaves, recto and verso set beside each other. The former offers a more natural view of the book as its makers intended it to be experienced, although a small gap is purposefully left between the two page images to avoid the illusion of transparency. The latter representation of each leaf presents a more artificial perspective, impossible to ever see on the physical object but important for certain types of bibliographical or codicological work. By offering these choices, Manicule aims to empower readers to explore the book not as a sequence of flattened pages, but as a series of relationships.

Toward this end, Manicule also offers readers several ways of orienting themselves within the larger codex. Below the main, two-page book browser, there is a filmstrip of thumbnails showing several page openings immediately before and after the loaded pages. Below that, a bird's-eye "map" of the book shows a color-coded, abstract representation of every page at once. The editor of each project can choose how to encode the pages and their color schema, depending on what they wish to highlight in the material text. For example, a scholar interested in marginalia may want to draw attention to pages with readers' marks, or further subdivide the marks into different categories. Another may wish to divide pages according to the genres of the text contained within the book, or to highlight subsections that organize the text as a document. The bird's-eye view allows the editor to direct readers' attention and in turn helps readers quickly spot these moments of variance within the codex, as well as the distribution of elements across it. Finally, on a separate page, readers can view the structure of the book: which leaves are attached, how they are nested, and any insertions or cancellations. An XML file authored using an earlier standard developed by the VisColl project currently feeds this structural visualization. In a newer version currently under development, Daly is building a pipeline from VCEditor, a tool for generating an XML file modeling the book's collation formula, to Manicule, so that editors will not need to write in XML.

Lastly, and perhaps importantly for most users, Manicule allows editors to build a tour of the digitized book. Tours are made up of stops, which are anchored to a page image. Viewing the tour on that page (noted by a bookmark icon) opens a modal box that delivers HTML content: text, image, video, sound. A JSON file assembles these stops into a linear tour, although the stops themselves may nonlinearly zigzag across the book, if the editor wishes. Clicking through a tour, the reader thus experiences a guided walk through important aspects of a book's design, structure, or layout, according to its editor and the goals of their edition. This feature was included in Manicule with pedagogy in mind, in the hopes that editors might use it to provide some direction and context to readers who otherwise would not know how to approach a material text or where to identify its uniqueness and import. For instance, one imagines a library curator might build a digital tour to accompany a physical exhibit of a book. Since the actual book may be opened only to one page spread at a time, Manicule takes advantage of digital media's affordances to offer a more nuanced view of an exhibit item. Or an editor of a literary text may build a tour of a digitized copy to show the interplay between the material and the textual in different versions. In the version currently under development, editors might also embed any page opening or a structural view of any quire as modular components within a multimedia essay, giving the editor more control over presentation. By thus negotiating various scales of knowledge, Manicule's book tours may help orient a novice within a difficult document, even as the platform offers the bibliographer more sophisticated tools of analysis. In these curational or instructional goals, Manicule differs from something like BookReader or HathiTrust, which merely present the book images as they are within a prefabricated technical infrastructure, without any editorial context. It is less a platform for presentation, and more a tool for curation and editing, drawing from the lessons of bibliography and textual studies.

To show how these features influence digital editing, we turn now to sharing two recent material text editions built in Manicule: Samuel Richardson's *A Collection of Moral Sentiments,* published in 1755 and digitally edited by Cassidy Holahan, and an astronomical anthology assembled in the late fifteenth century in Bavaria and digitally edited by Aylin Malcolm. The editors will describe their projects individually.

"Richardson's Moral Sentiments"

After the publication of his three popular novels, *Pamela* (1740), *Clarissa* (1748), and *Sir Charles Grandison* (1753), Samuel Richardson published a 1755 print commonplace book comprising quotations and maxims extracted from these novels, titled *A Collection of the Moral and Instructive Sentiments, Maxims, Cautions, and Reflections, Contained in the Histories of Pamela, Clarissa, and Sir Charles Grandison*. Produced in part as a bid to manage readers' interpretations of and reactions to his novels, the book is, according to Richardson, "the pith and marrow of nineteen volumes": a distillation of the novels' moral lessons, stripped of plot.[27] The "moral sentiments" are organized first by novel and then by alphabetized topic, including such topics as "Duty, Obedience" and "Advice and Cautions to Women." Built with Manicule, "Richardson's Moral Sentiments" (https://www.cassidyholahan.com/moral sentiments/) is a digital edition of this text erected upon a digitized facsimile of a copy held at the Kislak Center for Special Collections, Rare Books and Manuscripts at the University of Pennsylvania.[28] Rather than primarily aiming to recreate the text as isolatable from the codex form, the edition reproduces and emphasizes the mechanisms of the book's organization and its functionality, such as how it teaches the user to navigate its pages and read its content. Producing this edition thus enables a better understanding of the networked nature of the book, offering the user not just a readable text, but more importantly, insight into the historical reading modes and practices it encouraged.

Richardson's *Collection of Sentiments* is both a commonplace book and an index: each "sentiment" refers to the page number where it is sourced from in the corresponding novel. A digital edition of the *Collection,* therefore, would be better served by a hyperlink than it ever could be by a mere reproduction of those page references. An entirely hyperlinked edition of the *Collection* was out of scope for this project, given that there are nearly four hundred pages of commonplace material, each of which contains anywhere from five to a dozen sentiments. The digital edition does utilize, however, Manicule's "tour through the book" function to offer a sampling of sentiments linked back to their corresponding novel pages in HathiTrust copies. In doing so, it replicates the book's intended use, with the experience of leafing between multiple bound works replaced by a proliferation of browser tabs. By asking the reader to dip into the novel to read isolated lines and pages outside of the larger plot framework, Richardson encourages his readers to treat his novels as they would a biblical text, and in doing so not only strives to teach the reader *how* to read but also suggests an attempt to elevate the novel form and the *use* of fiction.[29] The sampled hyperlinked sentiments also illustrate how varied the maxims' relationships with their source material is. Take, for example, two sentiments found consecutively under the subject of "Penitence" in *Sir Charles Grandison*: "A generous person will make the generous confession of a fault easy to the contrite self-accuser, ii. 169 [270]" and "An error gracefully acknowledged, is a victory won, *ibid*." (358).[30] Of these two sentiments, one is a quotation found word-for-word on that page, and the other is not found on that page at all: it sums up some advice that is gleaned from reading that page. The hyperlinks thus recreate the disorienting experience of using the *Collection*: the reader is directed back to a single page—plunged into the novel and its event *in medias res*—hunting for an "extracted" quotation that might not even be there in the first place.

As an index, the *Collection* thus reorders the novels, imagining each one as composed of interconnected but detachable pieces of knowledge.[31] As Rachel Sagner Buurma argues is characteristic of the index, the *Collection* thus renders the original novels unfinished.[32] That is, by attempting to liberate scenes, dialogue, and narrative aside from the overall plot of the novel, the *Collection* might indeed accomplish the opposite of what is often cited as a major motive of Richardson's paratextual materials: to dissuade misreadings of his novels.[33] Moreover, as an index, the book continually redirects the reader away from its pages and back to the novels, ceding control and opening up the possibility of further readerly digression. The "Richardson's Moral Sentiments" Manicule edition highlights how some of the links even lead to further redirections. For instance, one maxim directs the reader back to *Pamela*, which in turn redirects, via a footnote, to a page from John Locke's 1693 essay "Some Thoughts Concerning Education" (13). The *Collection* thus imagines itself as part of a highly interconnected print culture: its intertextual network extends not just to Richardson's novels but also to other sources, including Locke and biblical Scripture. The mode of reading that the *Collection* teaches, in short, resists the closure and finality so often associated with print.

While the digital edition does not reproduce this external network, it does digitize the work's internal network. The organization and classification of information in the *Collection* is unmistakably influenced by the reference genres, such as dictionaries and encyclopedias, that were emerging in print during the eighteenth century. "Richardson's Moral Sentiments" contains a hyperlinked version of the work's internal index appended to the volume, as well as a remixed version of the original index, not divided by novel. By placing the original and remixed index side by side, the edition offers both an overview of the work's organizational structure, facilitating its intended use, *and* a new perspective on that structure. The remixed index does not indicate what novel is being commonplaced for each topic unless there are duplicate topics (all three novel sections have a section on "Love," for example). Only the *Clarissa* section of the work, perhaps surprisingly, includes sentiments on the topic of "Power"; Richardson thought readers looking for advice on "Female Education," conversely, were best to consult *Pamela*. The remixed index thus opens up new possibilities for reading the text without *reading* the text by offering insights into Richardson's decisions in commonplacing his novels, and thus even his attitudes towards their intended moral lessons.

Following, perhaps, in the footsteps of Denis Diderot's *Encyclopédie* (1751–1772), Richardson also included cross-references between the topics. A user looking to read about humility in *Clarissa*, for example, would also be advised to consult "Duty" and "Goodness." In the final *Grandison* section in particular, the cross-references proliferate: at the end of the subject on

Figure 9.1. The hyperlinked index for the digital edition of Richardson's *Collection*.

"Love" in *Grandison*, for example, the reader is redirected to thirty-two other topics (318).³⁴ The digital edition brings these cross-references to life by hyperlinking them in the margins. Allowing the user to instantly jump from topic to topic, these hyperlinks offer an alternative tour of the work, reinforcing the book's demands for the reader to navigate it nonlinearly. Richardson also included section headings existing only for redirection, suggesting, for example, that a reader who turns to "W" to read about "Wickedness" in *Sir Charles Grandison* should, not finding such a topic there, instead consult "Vice." These redirections are often quite self-evident and even redundant (the reader looking for sentiments on "Unhappiness," for instance, is redirected to "Happiness"), suggesting they exist not just to assist the reader, but to facilitate an understanding of the book as a complex interconnected system. In addition to these hyperlinked cross-references featured in the margins, the digital edition also features supplemental network visualizations of these cross-references, which offer an abstracted view of its organizational system, revealing patterns within the *Collection* and offering insight into how Richardson conceptualized his novels. The digitization of these

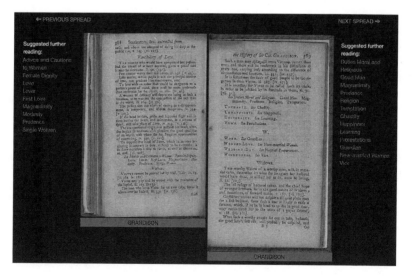

Figure 9.2. A double-page spread from the digital edition, with cross-references hyperlinked in the margins.

cross-references, in short, offers a way to move through and interact with the book without reading.

By treating the *Collection* primarily as a technology, rather than a text, the digital edition highlights the specific and historical modes of reading it demands of its user. It is a work uniquely suited to a digital edition because it is not meant, if we use the traditional sense of that word, to be "read." An eighteenth-century user of the *Collection* would be unlikely to read the book cover to cover, or in complete isolation from the novels: the hyperlinked nature of the digital edition thus not only better facilitates the book's intended use but also draws the user's attention to the methodologies behind this unique print object. Recreating the *Collection*'s modes of use, in short, offers layers of information about the book as an object and a reading technology, ones that are related to, but can even be more revelatory than, the textual contents alone.

"An Astronomical Anthology" (UPenn LJS 445)

Our second case study reveals that not-reading has a long history. We have seen that contemporary analytic bibliography and digital environments enable scholars to appreciate otherwise unremarkable books by focusing on form rather than content. These methods can also help us recognize fellow not-readers in the past—people who used books for reasons other than transmitting or studying texts.

The manuscript on which this edition, "An Astronomical Anthology" (aylinmalcolm.com/ljs445/), is based—known as LJS 445, currently held by the Kislak Center for Special Collections, Rare Books and Manuscripts at the University of Pennsylvania—presents abundant evidence of such historical non-readers. LJS 445 is a late-fifteenth-century Bavarian collection of astronomical and medical texts written in Middle High German and Latin. This codex is itself a remediated object, containing material copied from three printed books: Johannes Lichtenberger's *Prognosticatio* and two editions of Johannes Regiomontanus's *Calendarium* (Nuremberg, 1474; Venice, 1478). It has also been heavily annotated and irreverently damaged by later users. The Manicule edition strives to convey all of these elements of the manuscript while introducing new layers of interpretation and potential user interaction.

LJS 445 begins with the *Prognosticatio* (9r–61v), a collection of astrological predictions about the Church and the Holy Roman Empire. First printed by Heinrich Knoblochtzer in 1488 (ISTC i100204000), this text reflects the popularity of prophetic literature in the decades leading up to the Reformation; indeed, soon after printing the Latin first edition, Knoblochtzer produced a Middle High German version (ISTC i100210000) on which LJS 445 seems to be based.[35] Many of the remaining pages in LJS 445 are taken up by calendars, but this codex also contains: texts addressing the influences of seasonal and celestial phenomena on humans; a fragment of a treatise on the signs of the zodiac (147r–151r); a text on constellations, attributed to Kaspar Engelsüss and based on descriptions by the thirteenth-century scholar Michael Scot (178r–183r); a text on the planets (183v–190r); and medical texts on complexions (190r) and health regimens (198r–209v).

As this outline of its contents suggests, there are many reasons not to read LJS 445. Perhaps most obviously, it is written in two languages that are not used today outside of specialized contexts, and in scripts that few have been trained to decipher; researchers working on the Regiomontanus or Lichtenberger texts would likely begin by reading the more legible printed editions. Beyond these initial barriers to entry, premodern geocentric astronomy is both challenging to comprehend and, of course, obsolete, making it a niche research topic within medieval studies. The calendars in LJS 445 hold even narrower appeal, as they are specific to certain dates and regions. Finally, many elements of this codex were designed for purposes other than linear reading, such as its tables (e.g., 71v–72r), eclipse diagrams (111v–113v), and instruments for measuring time and lunar motion (70r–v, 114r–v).

As a *material* text, however, LJS 445 is extremely interesting. For instance, its incorporation of standard features of printed books, such as a title page carefully copied from Regiomontanus's 1478 *Calendarium* (97r), attests to the complicated relationships between print and manuscript in the late fifteenth century. The reproduction of print paratexts in LJS 445 suggests that print already held a degree of authority, but manuscripts remained a valid option for transmitting scientific writing; indeed, luxury printed books were often designed to resemble manuscripts and/or hand-colored, a practice that continued into the sixteenth century.[36] Complex astronomical images could be especially challenging to render in print; even printing eclipse diagrams in two colors was a labor-intensive process requiring multiple impressions or multiple woodblocks.[37] The Manicule edition encourages users to consider

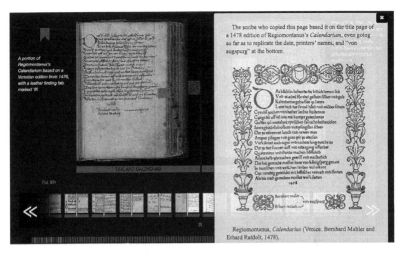

Figure 9.3. Tour stop from the digital edition of LJS 445, with the title page of a print edition that the manuscript imitates.

these issues through tour stops that compare the manuscript with its print sources.

LJS 445 also contains numerous signs of use that transform or simply ignore its astronomical content. A series of whimsical doodles adorns its first few pages, including human figures in period attire and sketches of doors and flowers (1r–2v). On the third folio are an alphabet and the name "Veit engel" copied in an unsteady hand; similar inscriptions recur several times throughout the codex, sometimes accompanied by "1589" (e.g., 95v–96r, 222v). As this date suggests, all of these doodles were likely produced by two children during the late sixteenth century: Georg Veit (1573–1606) and Veit Engelhard (1581–1656) Holtzschuher, the sons of a Nuremberg patrician.[38] These children's names (and variants thereof) frequently appear on otherwise blank pages (e.g., 125r, 130v, 177r), giving the impression that they approached the manuscript more as a convenient notebook for writing practice than as a text to be read.

In addition to highlighting these features of LJS 445 via a tour, the Manicule edition includes a "Structure" page providing a visual overview of the relationships between this book's construction and its contents, which are color-coded by topic (e.g., red for prognostication, dark green for medicine, bronze for calendars). The inconsistent structure of the codex indicates that it was planned and assembled section by section: the *Prognosticatio* section consists of three quires of sixteen leaves and a final quire of six; a calendar for Augsburg occupies a large quire of twenty-two folios; and the regimen text near the end is copied on one quire of twelve leaves. Extra pages containing astronomical instruments have been added to the two Regiomontanus transcriptions, each consisting of two leaves glued together for enhanced durability.

The "Structure" view also reveals that many leaves are missing from the sections on celestial bodies and constellations. One possible reason becomes apparent upon viewing these sections in the main browser: these texts include numerous drawings of the creatures and objects for which constellations and planets were named, often depicted on a grassy field beneath a blue sky (e.g., 179v–180r). Such drawings might have helped readers to remember and recognize constellations by relating them to terrestrial phenomena, but they also provided incentives for defacing LJS 445. Nineteen of thirty-five images in the Engelsüss text have been removed or damaged, and only four of those in the zodiac text remain intact. The text on the planets lacks all of its original illustrations, which may have depicted the planets' namesakes in classical mythology (as in another UPenn manuscript, LJS 463, 30r–37v).

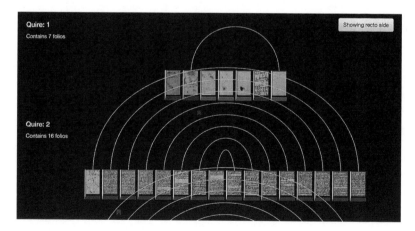

Figure 9.4. Structure of the first two quires of LJS 445, with attached leaves indicated by white lines.

In one intriguing case, a previous user has removed an image associated with the constellation Canis Minor (182v), or the Lesser Dog, by cutting along its outline, leaving only two front paws on the page. Here, the techniques of bibliography permit us to not-read what is actually not even there. The missing dog is one of this codex's evocative absences, inviting us to consider where this image might have traveled after leaving the book. Perhaps the Holtzschuher children used it as a toy, like a paper doll; perhaps a different reader removed it for inclusion in another volume, such as a commonplace book or scrapbook. No matter what its fate, the dog's extraction from LJS 445 would have altered its significance; outside of its original context, the image of a constellation named for a dog simply signifies a dog, a familiar earthly creature rather than a distant cluster of stars.

The missing drawing of Canis Minor also evokes our interactions with digital images in the twenty-first century—images that we might cut, save, copy, and reuse in ways far removed from their previous contexts. Like many other digital projects, the Manicule edition of LJS 445 encourages such practices, enabling users to download, transform, and share images from this manuscript. As an effort to make medieval texts accessible to a general audience, this edition thus not only reflects new developments in textual studies, but also participates in this manuscript's long history of adaptation, remediation, and creative desecration.

These examples show that non-reading is not only a digital phenomenon but also a historical practice that has always existed against and alongside reading. From flipping through pages to cutting out images, instances of not-reading the text challenge textual studies' understanding of what to *do* with a book. Digital editions that forefront the material text, such as those enabled by Manicule, rise to this challenge by showing how the evidence found in physical documents can tell deeper histories of reading, writing, and literature than can edited texts alone, even texts enriched with high-resolution images and digital markup. The digital editions not only expand public access to texts and archival material but also, in themselves, offer a critical interpretation of the material text by revealing larger structural patterns and guiding user interaction. In this manner, our digital editions encourage the reader to not-read again, in new ways.

Notes

1. W. W. Greg, "Bibliography—An Apologia," *The Library* 13, no. 2 (1932): 115.
2. Greg, 116.
3. Gabriel Egan points out the connection to French literary theory in *The Struggle for Shakespeare's Text: Twentieth-Century Editorial Theory and Practice* (Cambridge: Cambridge University Press, 2010), 84.
4. D. F. McKenzie, "Printers of the Mind: Some Notes on Bibliographical Theories and Printing-House Practices," in *Making Meaning: "Printers of the Mind" and Other Essays,* ed. Peter D. McDonald and Michael F. Suarez, S.J. (Boston: University of Massachusetts Press, 2002), 16.
5. McKenzie, 17.
6. Jerome McGann, *The Textual Condition* (Princeton, N.J.: Princeton University Press, 1991), 3, 9.
7. Johanna Drucker, *Graphesis: Visual Forms of Knowledge Production* (Cambridge, Mass.: Harvard University Press, 2014).
8. Wim Van Mierlo, "Reflections on Textual Editing in the Time of the History of the Book," *Variants* 10 (2013): 138.
9. Jessica Helfand, *Reinventing the Wheel* (New York: Princeton Architectural Press, 2002); Peter Stallybrass, "Books and Scrolls: Navigating the Bible," in *Books and Readers in Early Modern England: Material Studies,* ed. Jennifer Andersen and Elizabeth Sauer (Philadelphia: University of Pennsylvania Press, 2012), 42–79; Jacqueline Reid-Walsh, *Interactive Books: Playful Media before Pop-ups* (London: Routledge, 2018); Suzanne Karr Schmidt, *Interactive and Sculptural Printmaking in the Renaissance* (Boston: Brill, 2018).
10. Peter Shillingsburg, *From Gutenberg to Google: Electronic Representations of Literary Texts* (Cambridge: Cambridge University Press, 2006); Bonnie Mak, *How the Page Matters* (Toronto: University of Toronto Press, 2011); Michelle Warren, *Digital Holy Grail: A Medieval Book on the Internet* (Stanford, Calif.: Stanford University Press, 2022).
11. For example, see the BookLab in the University of Maryland's English department, Skeuomorph Press at University of Illinois, Urbana-Champaign, and Huskiana Press at Northeastern University.
12. Jerome McGann, *Radiant Textuality: Literature After the World Wide Web* (New York: Palgrave, 2001); Rossetti Archive, rossettiarchive.org.
13. Johanna Drucker, *SpecLab: Digital Aesthetics and Projects in Speculative Computing* (Chicago: University of Chicago Press, 2009).
14. John Bryant, *The Fluid Text: A Theory of Revision and Editing for Book and Screen* (Ann Arbor: University of Michigan Press, 2002); Marilyn Deegan and Kathryn Sutherland, eds., *Text Editing, Print and the Digital World* (Burlington, Vt.: Ashgate, 2009); Elena Pierazzo, *Digital Scholarly Editing: Theories, Models and Methods* (Burlington, Vt.: Ashgate, 2015).

15. Diana Taylor, *The Archive and the Repertoire: Performing Cultural Memory in the Americas* (Durham, N.C.: Duke University Press, 2003); *Codex Mendoza*, codice mendoza.inah.gob.mx/html/acerca.php.

16. Gabriela Aceves Sepúlveda, "[Re]Activate Mama Pina's Cookbook," critical mediartstudio.com/RemediatingMamaPina.

17. Bridget Moynihan and Akmal Putra, "Prototyping the Archival Ephemeral: Experimental Interfaces for the Edwin Morgan Scrapbooks," *Digital Studies/Le champ numérique* 9, no. 1 (2019): 16.

18. For examples of these visualizations, see the prototypes on Moynihan's site, Digital Decoupage: digitaldecoupage.llc.ed.ac.uk/prototypes.

19. Moynihan and Putra, "Prototyping," 16.

20. "About Intertextual Networks," Women Writers: Intertextual Networks, north eastern.edu/intertextual-networks/about.

21. Asanobu Kitamoto, "Book Barcoding: A Framework for the Visual Collation and Woodblock Tracking of Japanese Printed Books," presentation, Association of Digital Humanities Organizations, Tokyo, Japan, July 25–29, 2022.

22. Cristina Dondi, Abhishek Dutta, Matilde Malaspina, and Andrew Zisserman, "The Use and Reuse of Printed Illustrations in 15th-Century Venetian Editions," in *Printing R-Evolution and Society 1450–1500: Fifty Years that Changed Europe*, ed. C. Dondi (Venice: Edizioni Ca' Foscari, 2020), 839–69; Carl Stahmer, "Digital Analytical Bibliography: Ballad Sheet Forensics, Preservation, and the Digital Archive," *Huntington Library Quarterly* 79, no. 2 (2016): 263–78.

23. Daniel Ben Ezra Stoekl, Hayim Lapin, Bronson Brown-DeVost, and Pawel Jablonski, "HTR2CritEd: A Semi-Automatic Pipeline to Produce a Critical Digital Edition of Literary Texts with Multiple Witnesses out of Text Created through Handwritten Text Recognition," in *Digital Humanities 2022: Responding to Asian Diversity* (Tokyo: University of Tokyo, 2022), 689.

24. Johanna Drucker, "The Virtual Codex from Page Space to E-space," in *A Companion to Digital Literary Studies*, ed. Ray Siemens and Susan Schriebman (Malden, Mass.: Blackwell, 2007), https://companions.digitalhumanities.org/DLS/?chapter=content/9781405148641_chapter_11.html.

25. Jay David Bolter and Richard Grusin, *Remediation: Understanding New Media* (Cambridge, Mass.: MIT Press, 1999). On transparency in digital interfaces, see Lori Emerson, *Reading Writing Interfaces: From the Digital to the Bookbound* (Minneapolis: University of Minnesota Press, 2014), esp. x–xii.

26. Zachary Lesser and Whitney Trettien, "Material / Digital," in *Shakespeare / Text*, ed. Claire Bourne (London: Bloomsbury, 2021), 402–23; Dot Porter, "The Uncanny Valley and the Ghost in the Machine," *Dot Porter Digital* (blog), October 31, 2018, dotporterdigital.org/the-uncanny-valley-and-the-ghost-in-the-machine-a-discussion-of-analogies-for-thinking-about-digitized-medieval-manuscripts.

27. Preceding the publication of the *Collection of Sentiments*, Richardson published three novel indexes as appendices; much of this content is reused in the 1755

text. This included an eighty-six-page appendix of the 1751 *Letters and Passages Restored from the Original Manuscripts of the History of Clarissa* and two appendices to the 1753 edition of *Sir Charles Grandison,* an "Index, Historical and Characteristical" and "Similes, and Allusions, in the Foregrounding Six Volumes"; see William Sale, *Samuel Richardson: A Bibliographic Record of his Literary Career with Historical Notes* (New Haven, Conn.: Yale University Press, 1936).

28. Rare Book Collection, PR 3662.H5.

29. As Leah Price argues, the *Collection* attempted to dictate not just *what* readers gleaned from the novel, but more importantly, the pace of that reading: the text taught readers "not so much how to live as how to read" (*The Anthology and the Rise of the Novel: From Richardson to George Eliot* [Cambridge: Cambridge University Press, 2000], 22). By isolating the sentiments from the plot, the *Collection* attempted to reform readers hastily reading for the plot or habitually skipping passages by dictating an "enforced stasis" (21).

30. The numbers cited in the *Collection* are both part of the original text. The number before the brackets references the page number for the octavo edition of *Sir Charles Grandison,* and the number inside the brackets references the page number for the duodecimo editions. This schema follows throughout *Collection.*

31. Price notes that, by "substitut[ing] the paradigmatic for the syntagmatic," the *Collection* overturns "the significance of order" of the original novels, a reordering that becomes even more pronounced in the publication of a "set of entertaining Cards, neatly engraved on Copper-Plates, Consisting of moral and diverting Sentiments, extracted wholly from the much admired Histories of Pamela, Clarissa, and Sir Charles Grandison" in 1760 (*Anthology,* 17).

32. Rachel Sagner Buurma writes: "The index's powers of offering new discontinuous forms of access to the book—separating information from interpretation and argument, segmenting what was unified, reordering its priorities—thus decomposed the book into parts, rendering it unfinished and opening it to new meanings and new uses" ("Indexed," in *The Unfinished Book,* ed. Alexandra Gillespie and Deidre Lynch [Oxford: Oxford University Press, 2019], 384).

33. The attempt to detach the sentiments *from* the novels was, of course, not always fully possible: as Price notes, some of the *Collection's* sentiments need to include plot details in order to convey the moral lesson, as in a note in the section "Repentance" that clarifies that Lovelace "lived not to repent!" (*Anthology,* 23). For discussions of misreadings of Richardson's novel, see William Warner, *Licensing Entertainment: The Elevation of Novel Reading in Britain, 1684–1750* (Berkeley and Los Angeles: University of California Press, 1998).

34. The number of cross-references increased over time: *Clarissa,* the first novel to be commonplaced, contains 275 cross-references; *Sir Charles Grandison,* the last novel commonplaced, contains 674.

35. The *Prognosticatio* was clearly in high demand during the late fifteenth century, with eleven editions appearing before 1501. Jonathan Green links its popularity

to publishers' efforts to reach broader audiences via vernacular translations and images (which LJS 445 omits); see *Printing and Prophecy: Prognostication and Media Change 1450–1550* (Ann Arbor: University of Michigan Press, 2012), 65–71.

36. On the authority of handwritten texts in the era of print, see Siân Echard, *Printing the Middle Ages* (Philadelphia: University of Pennsylvania Press, 2008), and Peter Stallybrass, "Printing and the Manuscript Revolution," in *Explorations in Communication and History*, ed. Barbie Zelizer (New York: Routledge, 2008), 111–18.

37. Ad Stijnman and Elizabeth Savage, "Materials and Techniques for Early Colour Printing," in *Printing Colour 1400–1700: History, Techniques, Functions and Receptions* (Leiden: Brill, 2015), 11–22.

38. Regina Cermann links these drawings to the Holtzschuher children in her description of the manuscript (Berlin, 1997), available at manuscripta.at/docs/Cermann_Olim_Kreuzenstein_22170.pdf.

CHAPTER 10

Indigenous Publishing, Scholarly Editing, and the Digital Future

ROBERT WARRIOR

In 1963, the Kiowa writer and scholar N. Scott Momaday began his first academic job as an assistant professor of English at the University of California, Santa Barbara. Momaday was fresh out of graduate school at Stanford, where his mentor was poet and critic Yvor Winters. The author's photo on the back of Momaday's 1969 novel *House Made of Dawn* was taken in a UCSB office he shared with fellow Americanist Martha Banta, who discussed it with me when we met in the 1990s.[1] *House Made of Dawn*, of course, went on to win the 1969 Pulitzer Prize for Fiction, the first novel by a writer of color to win that award and a novel that is widely regarded as the most consequential in the history of Native American literature.

Momaday's subsequent books featured various headshots of the now-famous Momaday that variously captured his expansive personality and larger than life manner.[2] In the photo from his Santa Barbara faculty office, by contrast, Momaday sits at a desk, reading what appears to be a well-used paperback book with a cracked spine, his left hand holding it open while the right rests on the open pages as if following the text as he reads. The frames of his glasses are black plastic. He is clean-shaven, his dark hair short and tame. He wears a plain white or perhaps light-colored dress shirt and a dark cardigan. A brown drip-glaze ceramic mug sits on a file folder on the desk. Behind Momaday, where we might expect this professorial tableau to be completed with an overstuffed bookcase, hangs instead a wall-mounted weaving —almost certainly a Navajo rug—the book jacket's only obvious signifier of the indigeneity of the novel or the novelist.

This jacket photo captures Momaday on the cusp of international distinction, renown, and a career not only as a writer but as a literary figure who has uniquely embodied modern Native literary presence and sensibility. For my purposes here, though, I want to focus on Momaday as we see him at that moment as he approaches the cusp, for the photo offers a glimpse of the oft-mentioned but mostly undiscussed life of literary scholarship Momaday would soon be leaving behind in the wake of the success of *House Made of Dawn*. That scholarly life for Momaday was defined up to that point by scholarly editing.

Like most literary scholars, Momaday won his job at Santa Barbara in large part on the strength of his doctoral dissertation, which in his case was an edition of the complete poems of the nineteenth-century American writer Frederick Goddard Tuckerman. Oxford University Press, in fact, published the edition in 1965 with an introduction by Winters.[3] The Tuckerman edition was clearly connected to Winters's broader agenda as both poet and critic to bolster the case for the importance of form, rhyme, and meter not only in the history of poetry, but also in his exacting vision of the poet's vocation across all eras.[4]

Momaday's Tuckerman edition is far from the only case in Native American studies of significant work coming from scholarly editors, and some of the others have shifted the field considerably.[5] Vine Deloria Jr., the other towering Native American intellectual figure to emerge in the late 1960s, compiled (with Raymond DeMallie) the massive two-volume *Documents of American Indian Policy*, the first project pulling together treaties and other negotiated documents since Charles Kappler's 1904 *Indian Affairs, Laws, and Treaties*.[6]

Literary studies of Native authors have generated significant textual editing projects. Though nothing so ambitious or comprehensive as the Schomburg Library of Nineteenth-Century Black Women Writers has ever been done for Native writers, volumes such as Barry O'Connell's collected writings of William Apess, Joanna Brooks's edition of Samson Occom's writings, and Robert Dale Parker's *Changing Is Not Vanishing: A Collection of American Indian Poetry to 1930* and *The Sound the Stars Make Rushing through the Sky: The Writings of Jane Johnston Schoolcraft* have been essential to establishing and contextualizing critically generated versions of Native-authored texts.[7]

Smaller forays into scholarly editing, often contained within larger projects, are scattered across Native and Indigenous literary studies, including, for example, an appendix I included in my book *The People and the Word* in which I sought to establish an authoritative version of the 1881 Osage constitution, one that provides an apparatus through which I was able to discuss variants and other textual issues involved in this political founding document.[8]

As is true of most areas of scholarship, the growth of digital archiving has brought tremendous changes to Native American and Indigenous studies. Projects like the Yale Indian Papers Project, the Indigenous Digital Archive, and the National Centre for Truth and Reconciliation Archives (Canada) are all examples of the robust work that is bringing Indigenous archival materials into public light. These projects reflect many of the preoccupations and ideals of Indigenous studies, especially in their responsiveness to the perceived needs of Native people to access their own histories.

Clearly, a history of Indigenous scholarly editing awaits thoroughgoing recovery projects. However, these projects, as Phillip Round has argued, "will require a comprehensive theorization of the textual cultures of indigenous communities."[9] Rather than sketching more of what those projects might look like, I want to consider instead the history of Indigenous publication, which I see as an intriguing intersection that Indigenous scholarly editing helps to establish. In doing so, I am taking a cue from those, including Round, who have argued for the import and impact of material culture and textual studies on Indigenous research and writing, which is finding indigeneity as expanding our scholarly purview rather than sending us to the margins to find a small vein of knowledge that serves to add a little something to discussions at the discursive center.

For instance, Luis Cárcamo-Huechante argues: "Textualization is... a broader process, which can be grasped through the notion of 'inscription.' Practices of inscription, as a way to store information, have a long history in the Indigenous Americas."[10] Thinking in terms of inscription and information storage does more than proliferate materials and expand our archives. As Cárcamo-Huechante argues of codices and other New World forms of inscription, "even though they deploy the form and format of the book, many incorporate practices of textualization that exceed the framework of the Western book."

This notion of exceeding is what I see happening at the intersection of scholarly editing and Indigenous publishing. To tease out what that means, I want to forgo narrating more of the events, figures, and dynamics that inform the intriguing narrative arc that passes through Momaday's Tuckerman edition and discuss instead how that edition and publications adjacent to it show us some of the ways Indigenous forms and formats have, in fact, exceeded Western book history. As we figure indigeneity as a factor in that history, Matt Cohen has enjoined us to recognize that we are doing so while "once-familiar boundaries are blurring in productive ways. The rise of digital formats and delivery is a partial cause; the rise of forms of cultural inquiry that put pressure on the politics of media and archives is another. Both of these causes are parcel and part of larger geopolitical shifts."[11]

My examples run the gamut from self-published books by Native authors to what are now full-scale Indigenous publishing operations that produce, among other things, printed and digital publications that require scholarly editing, or at least something a lot like it. Coupled with the ongoing history of Indigenous journalism, Indigenous literary history, and the burgeoning world of Indigenous digital media, the examples I will discuss are part of an even bigger world of Indigenous media that, to me at least, makes the most sense when considered as a broadly construed whole.

This essay contributes, then, to an array of critical work from the past two decades that has opened the way toward fundamentally reshaping how to understand Indigenous participation in print culture and its development to the present. As Kelly Wisecup's recent book *Assembled for Use: Indigenous Compilation and the Archives of Early Native American Literatures* so ably demonstrates, this reshaping has been going on for a long time, and one of the challenges I want to place before those of us who continue on the arc of this work is to learn to see the vital resonances and synchronicities across publications like the ones Wisecup discusses, recent digital projects, and many other examples in between.[12]

The compilers Wisecup focuses on the act in their own ways as scholarly editors, joining the many other Indigenous writers who make themselves into scholars, editors, publishers, printers, marketers, and designers as they have "worked on behalf of their communities and nations, whether by defending land rights with petitions and letters or by using copyright and their own printing presses to determine representations of their communities and histories." Wisecup continues:

> Native people made compilations out of documentary forms that were designed to standardize information—as well as more readerly forms like scrapbooks and commonplace books—and in the process they turned those information-storing and -stabilizing functions to other ends. Indigenous compilers assembled medicinal, political, poetic, linguistic, and historical materials within lists, recipes, albums, and scrapbooks, in this way gathering environmental and linguistic knowledge, sharing poetry and songs in English and Indigenous languages, and circulating stories.[13]

Then and now, people in the Indigenous world have looked to modern publishing not only as something they might eventually catch up to or that might reasonably accommodate their needs, but also as something that could be, has been, and continues to be exceeded.

I will start with Kenneth Jacob Jump, an Osage writer who, in the 1970s, self-published books about the Osage world. Jump is one of many Native authors who have published their own books over the past two centuries, going back at least as far as Apess, the Pequot writer whose five books were privately published between 1829 and 1835.[14] Apess died in relative obscurity in 1839 only to be recovered as an important Indigenous voice 150 years later.[15] But in fact, he was more widely known in his own time than any of the self-publishing or alternative-published Native authors who have followed a similar path after him.[16] Because I have gotten to know something behind the story of Jump's books that has mostly escaped critical or literary historical notice, I will offer a somewhat detailed, though still brief, account of this self-publishing Indigenous author.

Jump, who died in 1980, includes this biographical note in his first book: "Kenneth Jacob Jump is an Osage Indian and a member of the Thunder Clan. Born and raised on the Osage Indian reservation, his Indian name is Shau^n-Gah^d-Lee, which means, 'Something that strikes a tree.' He is a former newspaper reporter and advertising sales manager."[17] In his second book, he includes that "he graduated from Pawhuska High School, [and] he attended Notre Dame University and Oklahoma State University," Pawhuska being the seat of government of the Osage Nation.[18] After he died suddenly on October 28, 1980, his relatives published a third book of his writings. An introductory note in it says that Jump was a World War II veteran of the U.S. armed forces who served in the Pacific.[19] While in the U.S. military, he was involved in the battle for Iwo Jima, and a song honoring that service is sung every year at the Osage In-losh-ka dance in the Pawhuska district. As his niece Meredith Drent pointed out to me, the song speaks to Jump's "role in the Osage community.... In his universe—in our universe—he has a place with us still."[20]

I did not know Jump, but I am related to him, and for several years in the 1990s, I would sometimes stay in the garage apartment where he lived in Pawhuska, Oklahoma. His sister, Arita Jump, was a relative whom I got to know in the late 1980s when I was in graduate school. Arita and her daughter Flora Jo Quinata were kind and gracious in offering me the garage apartment on several occasions when I stayed with them.

Figure 10.1. A portrait of Kenneth Jacob Jump, Osage author and publisher.

The apartment was mostly a large room plus a bathroom and kitchenette. The first time I stayed there I was pleased to find a desk where I could organize the reading and writing that I had brought along with me, and soon I realized that the desk not only was where Jump wrote, but also must have been where he designed, proofread, and did the other work it took to publish his books. He took up publishing after retiring from his newspaper job in Ponca City, forty miles west of Pawhuska.

It seemed clear to me from sitting at Jump's desk that he absorbed a lot of knowledge about publishing from working at the *Ponca City News,* and thus, as is often the case in the history of Indigenous writing, journalism played an important role in Jump's efforts to become a published writer. Based on my experience in school papers and professional journalism, I recognized various pencils, rulers, templates, and other tools of printing and publishing that I found in Jump's desk.

Jump's family—his sister Arita, niece Flora, and Flora's children Michael and Meredith Quinata—compiled a collection of his unpublished stories and poems after his death, and have arranged new printings of all three books as needed. Boxes of paperback and hardcover copies of the three books were stored in the apartment, and I recall seeing various mock-ups and early versions of cover art. When I would sit at his desk and read or write, I relished the opportunity to be in a quiet that was no doubt similar to the atmosphere he worked in, and I found inspiration from looking at the evidence of his success as a writer and publisher.

This was roughly the period during which I was developing the concept of *intellectual sovereignty,* and a fundamental aspect of that concept for me then was seeing how Native people have exercised Indigenous sovereignty and participated in promoting and strengthening it through engaging in intellectual work.[21] Jump's self-publishing is one of many examples of that aspect of what I was formulating. This is not to assert that Jump overtly addressed Osage politics in his published writings. He didn't, but I always intended intellectual sovereignty to be more expansive and nuanced than a straightforward political definition could contain. The erasers, markers, rulers, and other tools, in other words, were not only the tools Jump used as an entrepreneur to publish his own work. They were also tools he used in exercising intellectual sovereignty.

For Jump, according to his niece Flora, the impulse behind publishing his own books was that they would offer visitors to our reservation something they could easily take home with them, by which I took her to mean something different from a keychain, coaster, figurine, tissue box cover, or ashtray, something more specifically Osage.

All three of Jump's books were offset printed with black ink and measure 8.5 inches by 5.5 inches (a letter-size sheet folded in half). They have heavy-card-stock covers and stapled bindings. Illustrations, including many by Jump and some by another Osage, Pauline Allred, are all line drawings printed in black. Jump includes maps in the first two books, and photographs appear in all three. Along with these card-stock-cover versions, Jump produced library binding versions of the two books he completed, though the only place I have found them was in his apartment.[22]

Figure 10.2. Jump's first book, *The Legend of John Stink*, was first published in 1977. It is twenty-four pages with a card-stock cover; bound with two staples.

Jump's 1977 first book, *The Legend of John Stink, or Roaring Thunder "Child of Nature,"* is twenty-four pages (a single six-sheet block) with a card-stock cover; the block and cover were bound with two staples. The text recounts a true story of an Osage who rejected nearly all accoutrements of modern life, a choice all the more remarkable given the substantial oil wealth of Osages during the latter stages of Stink's life. In contrast to common images of oil-rich Osages of the period dressed like characters from *The Great Gatsby*, Stink lived by himself as a recluse outside Pawhuska in a spartan camp.

For tourists, Stink was an object of fascination, and for visiting journalists, a great story: the Indian eccentric who chose a spare lifestyle on his own rather than the luxury he could have afforded. What impresses me about Jump's version of the John Stink story is his thoughtful effort to dispel myths

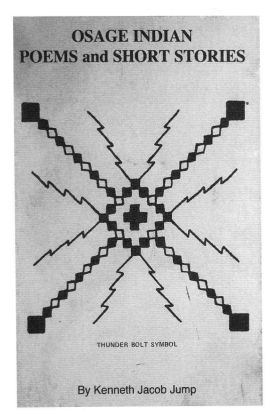

Figure 10.3. Jump's second book, *Osage Indian Poems and Short Stories*, appeared in 1979. The book is seventy-six pages long and features Jump's hand-drawn Osage symbols, five halftone photographs, and two maps.

about Stink that had grown up over the years, especially his supposed resurrection after freezing to death.[23] Insofar as Jump wanted his books to be something for people to take with them from their visit to the Osages, it seems he hoped to send them home with the most truthful version of John Stink's story as he could offer. *The Legend of John Stink,* then, functions as a souvenir while at the same time seeking to set the record straight.

Jump's second book, *Osage Indian Poems and Short Stories,* came out two years later, in 1979, the year before the author died suddenly of a heart attack. At seventy-six pages, it is over three times as long as his first. Along with Jump's own hand-drawn Osage symbols, the book features five halftone photographs

Figure 10.4. Jump left behind a significant amount of unpublished work; his *Osage Indian Anthology: Indian, Religious, General Poems* was published posthumously.

and two maps. The eight poems are formal in their rhyme scheme, their meter, and the length of stanzas.

The four short stories are notable for their range: nonfiction accounts of historical Osage migration and contemporary burial practices; a historically based fictional story about an Osage war party; and a story of a six-year-old Osage boy celebrating Christmas the year that Osages moved to our final reservation in 1873. The Christmas story is especially notable for its effective and imaginative telling of a story that seems particularly Osage that most readers would not expect.

The posthumous *Osage Indian Anthology: Indian, Religious, General Poems* is eighty-eight pages, demonstrating the significant amount of unpublished writing Jump left behind at the time of his death.

I was already a collector of first editions by Indigenous authors by the time I came to know Jump's garage apartment, and in the years since, I have kept an eye out for other self-published books by Native American writers. This has been anything but a systematic effort, and not even close to a comprehensive one, though elusiveness is by and large a constitutive aspect of these sorts of books, so I am not sure what being systematic or comprehensive might mean. And so, the fifty or so items in my collection demonstrate something important, I want to argue, about some of the basic impulses that have often motivated Indigenous people not only to take up pen and paper, but to find the means to put their writings between two covers.

As I have already discussed, Jump's work fits well into the concept of intellectual sovereignty that I formulated around the time I occasionally stayed in his garage apartment. Certainly Apess, as a foundational Pequot writer within the history of Indigenous self-publishing, evinced a clear commitment to the persistence and thriving of Indigenous peoples through the books he published. I would argue, though, that a much more practical concern has also been an important reason Native authors have had to become their own publishers: the lack of publishers interested in their work. This is certainly true of Native poets, who like most poets have scant opportunities to publish their work. Parker's anthology of Native poetry from before 1935 includes dozens of examples of unpublished poems or obscurely published poems.

Self-publishings like Jump's focus on distinctly local Native stories, but I would suggest that they also participate in broader currents in Indigenous intellectual life. Cohen has argued that "the objects we study are inherently furtive, more than local, beyond containment by any system or politics,"[24] and many if not most of the books discussed here more or less match that description. I include among these publications collective efforts through which various combinations of people from education programs, tribal governments, and local communities have responded to local needs by creating books. The self in these cases is a community program or church group, rather than an individual, as in the example of a volume of Blackfeet ghost stories published by a local educational program or a recipe book put together by a group of Osage Quakers.[25]

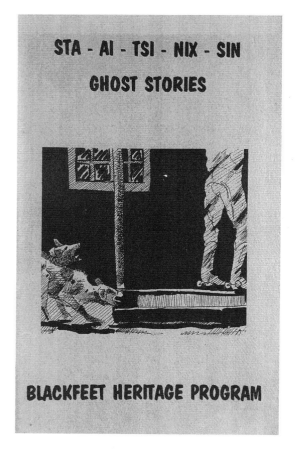

Figure 10.5. A volume of Blackfeet ghost stories published by a local educational program illustrates collective efforts at Native publishing.

Indigenous Publishing, Scholarly Editing, and the Digital Future 181

In some cases, these sorts of efforts have grown in relation to larger projects, such as the Navajo Community College Press, which operated from the early 1970s through the late 1990s. Little written history exists about the press, but available information indicates that it supported the work of the college (which became Diné College in 1997) in various ways, including publishing course materials, histories of the Navajo people, and books by Navajo writers.[26]

Another example is the Indian Historian Press, which was an enterprise of the American Indian Historical Society (AIHS), a San Francisco Bay Area organization founded in 1964. AIHS worked to support and further Native

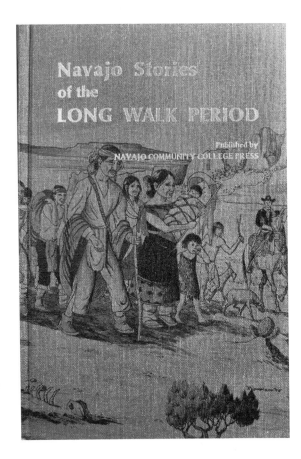

Figure 10.6. The Navajo Community College Press, which operated from the early 1970s through the late 1990s, issued books like the one pictured here, *Navajo Stories from the Long Walk Period*.

American self-determination through advocating for accuracy in history writing and in school curriculum. Rupert Costo (Cahuilla) was the society's founder, and it published a newspaper, and a journal.[27]

Communities in other parts of the global Indigenous world have also been sites of book publishing ventures, including Australia, Hawai'i, and Guatemala. Australia's history of Indigenous publishing is perhaps the most comprehensively chronicled, with Wiradjuri scholar Anita M. Heiss having written an account of that history. Along with looking at examples of Indigenous Australian authors publishing with commercial and alternative presses, Heiss recounts the development of the Institute of Aboriginal Development Press, which is Indigenous-run, and Aboriginal Studies Press, which began in the 1960s with a focus on non-Indigenous scholars' work on Indigenous topics. Heiss includes a brief account of a book of her own that she self-published. "Self-promotion and distribution does have its downfalls," she writes, "the most obvious being having to carry a box of books with you everywhere you go. . . . If you want your book to be out there, to be read, reviewed, and appreciated, . . . then you have to do a lot more than just write it."[28]

Hawaiian scholars have made significant use of a vast archive of Hawaiian-language newspapers that date back to the mid-nineteenth century, so the concomitant existence of a broad range of Hawaiian publishing is not a surprise.[29] The work of Manuel Tzoc Bucup, a Mayan poet from Guatemala, offers an instructive example from the Americas south of the Rio Grande River of the sort of "exceeding of the framework of the western text" that Carcamo-Huechante advocated. As Rita Palacios writes, Tzoc "is one of the founders of Maleta Ilegal, . . . a small, independent and handmade publishing outfit that carries out limited print runs."[30] Tzoc has self-published his work and worked with small, independent presses, finding exceedingly original formats, including printing poems on compact discs and placing poems printed on tiny pages folded and rolled to fit into prescription medication capsules, then bound inside a medicine bottle. The formats, Palacios argues, "shorten . . . the distance between creator and public. . . . For the poet, . . . the experience of handling the poetic object [prompts] the reader . . . to reflect on the fetishization of the book, and, ultimately, the word."

Before turning to some of the implications of this history of Indigenous publishing in considering the future of digital scholarly editing, the growing list of successful, sustained publishing efforts is worth a brief mention. This list is far from exhaustive, but hopefully provides a sense of the commitment Indigenous people have made to publishing the work of writers, artists, and scholars from their own communities. These Indigenous publishers include Theytus Books, founded as part of the En'owkin Center in Penticton, British Columbia.[31] Theytus is an independent, Indigenous-owned and -run press that publishes a full range of books, including fiction, poetry, and children's books. Another Indigenous publisher based in Canada is Kegedonce Press, founded in 1993 by Kateri Akiwenzie-Damm.[32]

Robyn Rangihuia Bargh and her spouse Bryan Bargh cofounded Huia Publishers in 1996 in Aotearoa / New Zealand to publish and promote books by Maori authors that reflect Maori worldviews.[33] In over thirty years since its founding, Huia has published over one thousand books by hundreds of Maori authors and others, with genres ranging across fiction, nonfiction, children's books, graphic novels, history, scholarly books, curricular works, and much more.[34] They now integrate much of their work with digital resources.

The Chickasaw Press, which the Chickasaw Nation established in 2006, is an impressive example of an Indigenous government engaging in publishing. The press publishes books and other materials on Chickasaw language, history, culture, and other topics and has spun off a separate imprint for creative work through which Chickasaw writers publish fiction, poetry, and other genres. Like Huia, Theytus, and others, the Chickasaw Press publishes the kind of work that non-Indigenous publishers, including academic and other nonprofit publishers, regularly decide they cannot or will not pursue.

This is especially true of work that supports Indigenous language revitalization programs. Many academic presses support Indigenous language dictionary projects, but might balk at publishing a dictionary aimed primarily at a student population that numbers at best in the hundreds and is more likely to be a couple of dozen—or even smaller. Yet, every Indigenous language revitalization program faces the need to develop curricular and pedagogical materials that support the work of saving languages.

Vi Hilbert, a fluent speaker of the Lushootseed language who died in 2008, worked for decades with other Lushootseed speakers to record stories and conversations, and she worked with credentialed linguists to develop grammatical materials and dictionaries. Eventually, she established Lushootseed

Research, which published the results of her work and continues to make her books available.³⁵ With a population of five hundred, the Upper Skagit people have nowhere near the resources of the Chickasaws, who are over seventy thousand strong and have casinos and other successful business operations.

Clearly, critical histories that need to exist of Indigenous publishing remain to be written. In concluding this essay, I want to suggest that spiraling out from the topic of what the Indigenous world brings to digital scholarly editing offers important insights that should be part of these as of yet unwritten histories. These insights are overlapping in lots of ways, but I have organized them into three points.

First and foremost, examples of projects involving scholarly editing or something very close to it run throughout the history I have sketched here. We can certainly see a history of editing across all these examples, and many of the works I have mentioned utilize methods and skills of scholarly and textual editing. The Indigenous language revitalization projects draw on specialized knowledge akin to that of textual editors.

Before getting further into the underbrush here, let me pivot to the shifts digital publishing brings to the discussion of indigeneity and scholarly publishing, which are considerable. Perhaps most importantly, digital publishing foregrounds the many collaborative, collective, and corporate conditions that have been part of modern publishing but have often remained obscure behind the focus on creative writing as best done by an individual, with the fetishization of single-author works remaining a strong current in the humanities. Thus, images often remain of writers as tortured geniuses crafting poems, novels, and other forms of creative writing.

Yet, the many people who typically take part in bringing the work of an individual poet, novelist, or scholar to a readership offer a reminder of the interpersonal worldliness of what we read and interpret. Even Jump and the other Indigenous self-published writers I have mentioned almost always of a necessity have involved others in producing a finished product, including illustrators, owners and workers of print shops, and booksellers and store owners who sell their books. Language, form, meter, and other elements of an author's craft and imagination are constitutive of what about a text makes it beautiful or significant or otherwise captures our attention. The apparatuses of editing, production, distribution, and marketing, however, are also necessary for making a literary text available to readers.

Digital publishing brings print culture more closely into alignment with visual and audio media in explicitly crediting and acknowledging the many people whose labor goes into making that work available. This is an important development insofar as it reveals some of the complex realities of the publication process. I am not suggesting that we attend to those complex realities at the expense of the writerly aspects of Indigenous texts. These digital formats make the work of editors, designers, marketing people, compositors, animators, and others visible, impacting not only the way audiences can see these publications as more than the work of an author or authors, but potentially also the way an incipient author perceives what it means to be a writer and author who works within a matrix of creativity, technical knowledge, and various forms of expertise in bringing a publication to its audience.

In my 2006 book *The People and the Word: Reading Native Nonfiction*, I wrote about the printer boys at American Indian boarding schools, students who learned to set type and print newsletters, student newspapers, and other materials as part of their training.[36] Something that drew me to the work of those boys in the boarding school print shops was imagining them (or at least some of them) looking critically at the things they printed and imagining themselves writing something better and more honest than did their teachers who wrote most of what they printed, or their fellow Native students—the few who actually made their way into print usually being the favored ones who were "representative" of the goals of the teachers, administrators, and policy-makers behind the ideologies of the schools.

That possibility of printer boys or girls working in offices aspiring not only to reproduce the words of others, but also to write them, seems by and large unimagined by those who designed these schools. That's all the more reason to realize now that those students could already begin to see something we are all still learning, which is that Indigenous presence is needed in all the jobs and at all the stages of the publication process. The goal, however, is not necessarily to demand that all those jobs at all those stages are filled by Indigenous workers, but to imagine Indigenous people in those roles and, further, to anticipate the time when that will be the case.

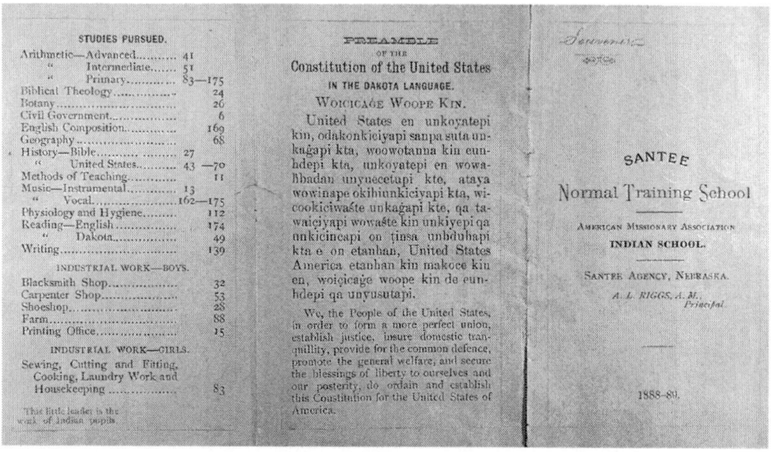

STUDIES PURSUED.

Arithmetic—Advanced	41	
" Intermediate	51	
" Primary	83	—175
Biblical Theology		24
Botany		26
Civil Government		6
English Composition		169
Geography		68
History—Bible	27	
" United States	43	—70
Methods of Teaching		11
Music—Instrumental	13	
" Vocal	162	—175
Physiology and Hygiene		112
Reading—English		174
" Dakota		49
Writing		139

INDUSTRIAL WORK—BOYS.

Blacksmith Shop	32
Carpenter Shop	53
Shoeshop	28
Farm	88
Printing Office	15

INDUSTRIAL WORK—GIRLS.

Sewing, Cutting and Fitting, Cooking, Laundry Work and Housekeeping	83

This little leaflet is the work of Indian pupils.

PREAMBLE
OF THE
Constitution of the United States
IN THE DAKOTA LANGUAGE.

WOICICAĠE WOOPE KIN.

United States en unkoyatepi kin, odakonkiciyapi sanpa suta unkaġapi kta, woowotanna kin eunhdepi kta, unkoyatepi en wowaĥbadan unyuecetupi kte, ataya wowinape okihiunkiciyapi kta, wicookiciwaŝte unkaġapi kte, qa tawaiçiyapi wowaŝte kin unkiyepi qa unkicincapi on ţinsa unhduhapi kta e on etanhan, United States America etanhan kin makoce kin en, woiçicaġe woope kin de eunhdepi qa unyusutapi.

We, the People of the United States, in order to form a more perfect union, establish justice, insure domestic tranquillity, provide for the common defence, promote the general welfare, and secure the blessings of liberty to ourselves and our posterity, do ordain and establish this Constitution for the United States of America.

Souvenir

SANTEE
Normal Training School

AMERICAN MISSIONARY ASSOCIATION
INDIAN SCHOOL.

SANTEE AGENCY, NEBRASKA.

A. L. RIGGS, A. M.,
Principal.

1888–89.

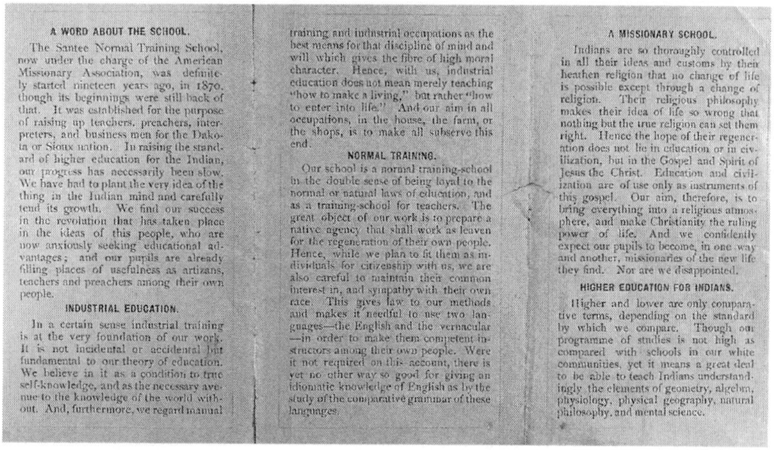

A WORD ABOUT THE SCHOOL.

The Santee Normal Training School, now under the charge of the American Missionary Association, was definitely started nineteen years ago, in 1870, though its beginnings were still back of that. It was established for the purpose of raising up teachers, preachers, interpreters, and business men for the Dakota or Sioux nation. In raising the standard of higher education for the Indian, our progress has necessarily been slow. We have had to plant the very idea of the thing in the Indian mind and carefully tend its growth. We find our success in the revolution that has taken place in the ideas of this people, who are now anxiously seeking educational advantages; and our pupils are already filling places of usefulness as artizans, teachers and preachers among their own people.

INDUSTRIAL EDUCATION.

In a certain sense industrial training is at the very foundation of our work. It is not incidental or accidental but fundamental to our theory of education. We believe in it as a condition to true self-knowledge, and as the necessary avenue to the knowledge of the world without. And, furthermore, we regard manual training and industrial occupations as the best means for that discipline of mind and will which gives the fibre of high moral character. Hence, with us, industrial education does not mean merely teaching "how to make a living," but rather "how to enter into life." And our aim in all occupations, in the house, the farm, or the shops, is to make all subserve this end.

NORMAL TRAINING.

Our school is a normal training-school in the double sense of being loyal to the normal or natural laws of education, and as a training-school for teachers. The great object of our work is to prepare a native agency that shall work as leaven for the regeneration of their own people. Hence, while we plan to fit them as individuals for citizenship with us, we are also careful to maintain their common interest in, and sympathy with their own race. This gives law to our methods and makes it needful to use two languages—the English and the vernacular—in order to make them competent instructors among their own people. Were it not required on this account, there is yet no other way so good for giving an idiomatic knowledge of English as by the study of the comparative grammar of these languages.

A MISSIONARY SCHOOL.

Indians are so thoroughly controlled in all their ideas and customs by their heathen religion that no change of life is possible except through a change of religion. Their religious philosophy makes their idea of life so wrong that nothing but the true religion can set them right. Hence the hope of their regeneration does not lie in education or in civilization, but in the Gospel and Spirit of Jesus the Christ. Education and civilization are of use only as instruments of this gospel. Our aim, therefore, is to bring everything into a religious atmosphere, and make Christianity the ruling power of life. And we confidently expect our pupils to become, in one way and another, missionaries of the new life they find. Nor are we disappointed.

HIGHER EDUCATION FOR INDIANS.

Higher and lower are only comparative terms, depending on the standard by which we compare. Though our programme of studies is not high as compared with schools in our white communities, yet it means a great deal to be able to teach Indians understandingly the elements of geometry, algebra, physiology, physical geography, natural philosophy, and mental science.

Figures 10.7. At American Indian boarding schools, students learned to set type and print newsletters, student newspapers, and other materials, as exemplified by this souvenir pamphlet printed by the students of the Santee Normal Training School in the late 1880s.

Frankly, my point here almost becomes moot when the category of the digital comes into play, insofar as digital publishing tends to follow the example of film, television, and video in revealing the scaffolding that supports its work through explicit credits that acknowledge the many people who play a hand in bringing work to publication. The differences I am highlighting here are the explicit ways in which the scaffold of labor that goes into film is typically available to a viewer or user of a digital resource, while books have traditionally not made that scaffolding nearly so visible.

Illustrating the significance of this first point becomes more straightforward by connecting it to my second point, which is that the fundamental Indigenous political concepts of sovereignty, autonomy, and self-determination hover over the Indigenous history of publication that I am imagining. The Chickasaw Press, for instance, directly invokes not just sovereignty, but "intellectual sovereignty," the term I developed in my earliest theoretical work as a way of articulating Indigenous intellectual work as an expression of Indigenous sovereignty. The press's goal

> is to preserve, perpetuate, and provide an awareness of Chickasaw history and culture. We accomplish this by generating and publishing research and scholarship about Chickasaw history and culture, making such scholarship accessible to Chickasaw people, exercising "cultural and intellectual sovereignty" by adhering to ethical and culturally appropriate research and publication practices, and providing an outlet for Chickasaw authors, scholars, and culture bearers.[37]

This articulation focuses on the Chickasaws as a people, as subjects of their own history and practitioners of their own culture, as an audience for scholarship about them, as judges of the appropriateness of what the press publishes, and as authors and producers of what the press publishes. Yet, the statement does not say that the press seeks only a Chickasaw audience or to publish only the work of Chickasaws. Plenty of non-Chickasaw authors are among those the press has published, and of course the Chickasaws benefit from non-Chickasaw people being able to access books and other materials that Chickasaw editors and publishers see as reflective of who they are.

My third and final, concluding point has to do with how everyone involved in publishing Indigenous projects navigates the professional demands of their work in light of history. I have mostly recounted this history in a positive, forward-looking way, focusing on the good work that Native writers, self-publishers, editors, and publication companies have done and are doing—and in recognition of the long history involving many non-Indigenous editors, publishers, and others who have supported their work in various ways. That history of work deserves to be understood, however, as also participating in a reparative process that addresses literally centuries during which Indigenous people were not considered able to speak for ourselves through writing, much less edit or publish that writing without the intervention of white people. The vast majority of non-Indigenous books, publishers, editors, and writers have represented the Indigenous world in tremendously damaging ways. In writing this essay, in fact, I have often felt haunted by awful examples of non-Indigenous editing such as Lucullus McWhorter's infamous torturous alterations to Mourning Dove's novel *Cogewea: The Half-Blood*.[38]

This difficult history, though, does not and should not change the basic responsibility of editors and publishers in considering Indigenous texts. That is, every author who publishes work focused on Indigenous peoples increases the possibility of producing meaningful and significant work by working with good editors and publishers. Indeed, I would suggest that the best response to that troubled history is helping to build a sustainable infrastructure for Indigenous publishing.

The starting place for most publishers in doing so has been and will most likely continue to be working with Indigenous authors. Non-Indigenous editors who have worked with Indigenous authors have written thoughtfully about how they have approached that work. Robin Freeman, a white Australian editor with experience working with Indigenous authors, argues that the differences Indigenous publishing highlights exist "against a background of some uncertainty, where [non-Indigenous editors] must be open to challenging the basis of their education and self-belief and their Eurocentric view of 'history,' that ... engagement with Indigenous texts may appear to be a daunting and intimidating task."[39]

Margaret McDonnell, another non-Indigenous Australian editor, calls that daunting task "consultation," by which she means the basic process of learning through conversation, research, and dialogue what issues will or might arise in a particular Indigenous project. That process "may not be easy; seeking out the appropriate person or people in a community can be difficult and time-consuming. The [editor] needs to be very clear about the processes involved and the implications of, for example, publication (in that sensitive or sacred material may become public knowledge) and copyright. Sufficient time must be allowed for consultation, and it must be remembered that the collaborator's priorities may not be those of the Indigenous community."[40]

All of this advice is worth considering seriously, but only if, I want to argue, what results from engagement and consultation is a space in which an editor is better able to do the tough work of editing. However obvious that might sound, I say it out of concern that respecting Indigenous protocol and cultural difference becomes the end point rather than one leading toward the goal of the publication of more and better Indigenous books and other projects. Related to this, I find it telling that neither of these non-Indigenous editors indicates much of an awareness of the publishing history Heiss writes about, and I don't think it's a stretch to wonder why Freeman, publishing six years after Heiss's book, doesn't cite it alongside the many books and articles by Indigenous writers and scholars she does cite. Gregory Younging, author of *Elements of Indigenous Style: A Guide for Writing by and about Indigenous Peoples,* a successful Cree author who devoted much of his career to developing the Indigenous publishing industry in Canada, describes that goal as creating "titles that reflect the highest levels of understanding, and authentic, meaningful stories, and truth telling."[41]

Aileen Moreton-Robinson, a Goenpul writer and scholar, has done important work as an editor, including the 2004 volume *Whitening Race: Essays in Social and Cultural Criticism* (Aboriginal Studies Press), which turns the tables on the assumed configuration of white editors and Indigenous writers as Moreton-Robinson takes on the role of Indigenous editor working with white scholars as they write about their own whiteness. Younging and Moreton-Robinson are important recent examples from a long history of Indigenous editors that complicate and complement the more familiar and expected configuration of white editors and Indigenous writers.

Thus, recognizing difference is a crucial step, but recognizing the power dynamics at play and changing them is important as well. Round has argued within this same set of issues, only when "our editorial practices and interpretive methodologies come to terms with this constellation of bibliographic 'difference' in Native texts may we embark on what John Bryant, in a recent volume of *Textual Cultures* has called, 'the ethics of editing.'"[42]

In short, I want to argue in concluding for publication ethics that prepare an acquisitions editor meeting with an Indigenous scholar for discussion of an editing project to be ready for the next Momaday to show up for the meeting. That Indigenous scholar might not be working on an edition of an underappreciated nineteenth-century white poet from the United States, but could very well be bringing to their project a set of *skills and perspectives* that are just as important to recognize as whatever *cultural or social differences* they might be bringing too.

Cohen points toward this sort of preparation when he says that his book-history version of this work "is going to require both engaging tribal intellectual traditions and using bibliographical elbow grease."[43] Those who work in textual and scholarly editing are familiar with these values, of course. Who, after all, dedicates elbow grease to editions of unimportant, mediocre texts? Along with those shared values, I want to suggest that very often the work that remains is related to something Freeman, speaking of her work with Indigenous authors, highlights: "Editors work within an ambiguous space, balancing the needs of the writer, the publishing house and the reader against each other, though always supportive of the text to which they owe their professional expertise to ensure that it becomes the best book it can be."[44]

Yet, while successful and experienced editors and publishers are always in need of coming to terms with various sorts of difference, they also need to continue being editors and publishers in the process. What this sort of engagement leads to, I think, is a recognition that the history of Indigenous publication is a prime example of how something from the Indigenous world can speak simultaneously to both the differences (cultural, linguistic) and the similarities (business, finance, technical expertise). As my examples of Heiss and Moreton-Robinson show, sometimes an Indigenous publisher (in Heiss's case, a self-publisher) or editor has already traversed the editorial landscape; the more focused on cultural differences we are, the less likely we are to recognize and acknowledge the legacy of Indigenous intellectual work.

Indeed, a prime example of this sort of work to keep in mind comes from the United States in the person of Wowaus, the Nipmuck man who came to be known as James Printer, translator and typesetter for John Eliot in

Massachusetts in the mid-seventeenth century. Printer brought not only who he was as a Nipmuck person to that work through his knowledge of his own language, but also through his knowledge of English and, crucially, his ability to set type.

So, I would suggest finally that some of that elbow grease Cohen urges us to use needs to be applied to the imagination, by which I mean this: those in the publishing world, including those who study it, need to imagine their corners of that world as places where people are learning to expect the unexpected, places where Indigenous people seeking to participate and share in the work of publishing that goes on there can roll up their sleeves and share in the application of elbow grease. In such a corner, perhaps the project the next Momaday I am imagining shows up to propose will be a digital edition of the collected works of Jump, or better yet an open-ended digital edition of self-published Indigenous authors. Wouldn't that be something?

Notes

Sincere thanks to the editors and readers of this essay, whose comments improved it immensely. I also want to express gratitude to Meredith Drent for helping with the section on the books by her great uncle Kenneth Jump. Finally, I would like to dedicate this essay to N. Scott Momaday, who passed away during the editing and production process. He was, indeed, the Man Made of Words.

1. N. Scott Momaday, *House Made of Dawn* (New York: Harper & Row, 1968). Banta was a highly regarded scholar of American literature, best known for her 1987 book *Imaging American Women: Ideas and Ideals in Cultural History* (New York: Columbia University Press). She was president of the American Studies Association (1990–1992) and editor of *Proceedings of the Modern Language Association* (1997–2000).

2. Through the 1970s, 1980s, and 1990s, Momaday's books feature an author photo of Momaday with a full beard and mustache wearing thin wire frame glasses with large rectangular lenses. Momaday squints in the photo, which was taken by Jim Kalett, who also shot author photos of Paul and Jane Bowles and published books of his photographs. That photo appears as early as the jacket of *The Names* (New York: Harper and Row, 1976) and as late as *The Man Made of Words: Essays, Stories, Passages* (New York: St. Martin's Press, 1997). In 1999, *In the Bear's House* features what appears to be a contemporary photo of Momaday, clean-shaven and hair white and short. He wears a sport coat and round wire frame glasses.

3. N. Scott Momaday, ed., *The Complete Poems of Frederick Goddard Tuckerman* (New York: Oxford University Press, 1965). For a detailed discussion of Momaday's work on Tuckerman, see poetryfoundation.org/poets/frederick-goddard-tuckerman (accessed 15 March 2023).

4. Revisiting Momaday's scholarly edition of Tuckerman for this essay over twenty years after I dug up the dissertation, the Oxford edition, and some correspondence between Momaday and Winters (and also Janet Lewis, Winters's spouse) from the libraries and archives at Stanford, I am struck by how much more remains to be thought through about Momaday's place in Winters's project. Clearly, Momaday forged his own poetics, and he stands on his own well beyond Winters. They shared, however, not only similar poetics, but also experience of and appreciation for the U.S. Southwest and Native American orality.

5. I use both Indigenous studies and Native American studies (sometimes shortened to Native studies) in this essay, differentiating between scholarly work focused on American Indian peoples within the United States and more recent comparative, synthetic, and theoretical work linking Indigenous peoples in various parts of the world to each other. One articulation of the emergence of Indigenous studies globally is *Critical Indigenous Studies: Engagements in First World Locations,* ed. Aileen Moreton-Robinson (Tucson: University of Arizona Press, 2016).

6. Vine Deloria Jr. and Raymond J. DeMallie, *Documents of American Indian Diplomacy: Treaties, Agreements, and Conventions, 1775–1979,* Legal history of North America 4 (Norman: University of Oklahoma Press, 1999); Charles Kappler, ed., *Indian Affairs: Laws and Treaties,* vols. 1–2 (1904; repr. Washington, D.C.: Government Printing Office, 1972). Kappler compiled and edited the first two volumes of what would become seven volumes that continued to come out until 1971. The Oklahoma State University Library hosts a digital collection of all seven volumes plus supplementary materials: dc.library.okstate.edu/digital/collection/kapplers/, accessed April 8, 2023.

7. The Schomburg Library of Nineteenth-Century Black Women Writers began publishing in 1988 under the general editorship of Henry Louis Gates Jr. The series has 50 volumes; see global.oup.com/academic/content/series/s/the-schomburg-library-of-nineteenth-century-black-women-writers-slbww/?cc=us&lang=en& (accessed March 15, 2023). See also Joanna Brooks, ed., *The Collected Writings of Samson Occom, Mohegan: Literature and Leadership in Eighteenth-Century America* (New York: Oxford University Press, 2006); Robert Dale Parker, ed., *Changing Is Not Vanishing: A Collection of American Indian Poetry to 1930* (Philadelphia: University of Pennsylvania Press, 2011); Parker, ed., *The Sound the Stars Make Rushing through the Sky: The Writings of Jane Johnston Schoolcraft* (Philadelphia: University of Pennsylvania Press, 2008).

8. Robert Warrior, *The People and the Word: Reading Native Nonfiction* (Minneapolis: University of Minnesota Press, 2006), 189–98.

9. Phillip H. Round, *Removable Type: Histories of the Book in Indian Country, 1663–1880* (Chapel Hill: University of North Carolina Press, 2010), 120.

10. Luis E. Cárcamo-Huechante, "The Long History of Indigenous Textual Cultures," *Textual Cultures* 6, no. 2 (2011): 44.

11. Matt Cohen, "The Codex and the Knife," *Textual Cultures* 6, no. 2 (2011): 109.

12. Kelly Wisecup, *Assembled for Use: Indigenous Compilation and the Archives of Early Native American Literatures* (New Haven, Conn.: Yale University Press, 2022).

13. Wisecup, 6, 9.

14. Scholarship on Apess is extensive. For these basic facts, however, see my chapter on Apess in Warrior, *The People and the Word*, esp. 1 and 4. Round has deftly and effectively argued that Apess's effort to maintain copyright of his own work, and thus embrace the model of "proprietary authorship," demonstrates the depth of Apess's connecting issues of Native political control and his own control as a Native author of the means of production and publication (*Removable Type*, 152–72).

15. Barry O'Connell led the effort to recover Apess's writings and published all his extant writings in a single volume (*On our Own Ground: The Complete Writings of William Apess, a Pequot* [Amherst: University of Massachusetts Press, 1992]).

16. Simon Pokagon, a Pokagon Band Potawatomi leader and writer of the late nineteenth and early twentieth centuries, also self-published, rose to a similar level of fame as Apess, with both being primarily known regionally.

17. Kenneth Jacob Jump, *The Legend of John Stink: Or, Roaring Thunder "Child of Nature"* (self-published, 1977).

18. Kenneth Jacob Jump, *Osage Indian Poems and Short Stories* (private-published, 1979).

19. Kenneth Jacob Jump, *Osage Indian Anthology: Indian-Religious-General Poems* (self-published, 1983).

20. See Jump, *Osage Indian Anthology*. Drent's quotation is from an email message to me dated February 11, 2024. Drent currently serves as Chief Justice of the Supreme Court of the Osage Nation.

21. See Robert Allen Warrior, *Tribal Secrets: Recovering American Indian Intellectual Traditions* (Minneapolis: University of Minnesota Press, 1995), esp. ch. 3.

22. These library-bound versions are rebindings of the card-stock-cover versions. Both books have buckram covers coated with acrylic. The spines are hollow. In both cases, the rebinding retains the back cover while the front cover has been removed, trimmed, and glued to the new front cover. The only difference in the rebindings is the color of the coating, with *The Legend of John Stink* being a milk-chocolate brown and *Osage Indian Poems and Short Stories* being black.

23. Jump, *Legend of John Stink*, 11.

24. Cohen, "Codex," 109.

25. *Sta-Ai-Tsi-Nix-Sin Ghost Stories* (Browning, Mont.: Blackfeet Heritage Program, 1979); Hominy Friends Meeting (Osage Reservation, Oklahoma), *Favorite Recipes* (self-published, ca. 1984).

26. A 2018 press release from the college indicates plans to revive the press: dine college.edu/news-release-dine-college-to-re-establish-college-press/ (accessed March 21, 2023). The history of Navajo Community College (NCC) / Diné College remains a mostly unwritten story, which is true of Navajo educational history in general. The college press's history, then, is perhaps not surprisingly also lacking documentation, analysis, or even mention. Fortunately, Wendy Greyeyes has recently published a full-length treatment of that more general history: *A History of Navajo Nation Education:*

Disentangling Our Sovereign Body (Tucson: University of Arizona Press, 2022). NCC was the focus of a 2020 dissertation by Merlee Arviso at Fielding Graduate University: "The Impact of Navajo Community College (Now Diné College) on Local Communities." Peter Iverson, who went on to a distinguished career writing primarily about Native history, taught at the college in its earliest days and published an article detailing his experiences there: "The Early Years of Diné College," *Journal of American Indian Education* 38, no. 3 (1999): 34–43.

One compelling example of the press's work is *Navajo Stories of the Long Walk Period* (Tsaile, Navajo Nation, Ariz.: Diné College Press, 1973). Ruth Roessel, director of the Navajo and American Indian Studies program at the college, is listed as having supervised the gathering of the materials for the book in the Navajo language, and she wrote the acknowledgments, making it seem that she was the person with primary editorial responsibility for the publication. The cloth-bound book is nine inches by six inches with glued-spine library binding. The title and name of the press is hot-stamped on the spine and front cover in silver, as is the logo of the press on the back cover. An illustration of the 1868 Long Walk by Raymond Johnson, one of the book's illustrators, wraps around the front and back covers and spine and is printed in black on fountain blue cloth. The inside front and back covers feature a map of the Navajo Reservation printed in black ink on pumpkin orange endpapers.

27. For a discussion of the society and the press it ran, see Rose Delia Soza War Soldier, "'To Take Positive and Effective Action': Rupert Costo and the California Based American Indian Historical Society" (PhD diss., Arizona State University, 2013).

28. Anita H. Heiss, *Dhuuluu-Yala: To Talk Straight: Publishing Indigenous Literature* (Canberra: Aboriginal Studies Press, 2003).

29. One example of contemporary Native Hawaiian independent publishing is Lilikalā Kameʻeleihiwa, *Nā Wāhine Kapu: Divine Hawaiian Women,* repr. ed. (Honolulu: Short Stack by Native Books, 2016). Short Stack, according to the copyright page of this reprint, "is a humble offering from Native Books, to put back into print, titles that have become out-of-print, rare, and as a result, inaccessible to community." Scholarly work that has relied on historical Hawaiian-language newspapers includes Noenoe K. Silva, *Aloha Betrayed: Native Hawaiian Resistance to American Colonialism* (Durham, N.C.: Duke University Press, 2004), and *The Power of the Steel-Tipped Pen: Reconstructing Native Hawaiian Intellectual History* (Durham, N.C.: Duke University Press, 2017). For other examples of scholarship that utilizes the newspaper-based Hawaiian-language work of Native Hawaiian editors, see kuʻualoha homawanawanui, *Voices of Fire: Reweaving the Literary Lei of Pele and Hiʻiaka* (Minneapolis: University of Minnesota Press, 2014), and Jamaica Heolimeleikalani Osorio, *Remembering Our Intimacies: Moʻolelo, Aloha ʻĀina, and Ea* (Minneapolis: University of Minnesota Press, 2021).

30. Rita Palacios, Introduction to "Manuel Tzoc Bucup's Queer Poetry," siwarmayu .com/manuel-tzoc-bucups-queer-poetry/. See also Emilʼ, Keme, *La Maya Qʼatzij / Our Maya Word: Poetics of Resistance in Guatemala* (Minneapolis: University of Minnesota Press, 2021), 173–92.

31. See theytus.com/, accessed March 22, 2023.

32. See kegedonce.com/, accessed March 22, 2023. Heiss includes a chapter on Canadian Indigenous literature in her history of Australian Indigenous publishing, featuring a section on publishers that covers Theytus, Kegedonce, and other publishers and writing organizations I have not mentioned (*Dhuuluu-Yala,* 174–88).

33. See huia.co.nz/, accessed March 22, 2023.

34. See e-tangata.co.nz/korero/robyn-bargh-building-the-wall-of-tino-rangatiratanga/, accessed March 22, 2023. Heiss has a chapter on Maori literature, including the publishers I have mentioned as well as others (*Dhuuluu-Yala,* 201–19).

35. See lushootseedresearch.org/about, accessed March 23, 2023.

36. Warrior, *People and the Word,* 95.

37. See chickasawpress.com/About/Chickasaw-Press.aspx.

38. See Alanna Kathleen Brown, "Mourning Dove's Voice in 'Cogewea,'" *Wicazo Sa Review* 4, no. 2 (1988): 2–15, esp. 11 and 13, doi.org/10.2307/1409273, accessed March 22, 2023.

39. Robin Freeman, "'We Must Become Gatekeepers': Editing Indigenous Writing," *New Writing* 6, no. 2 (2009): 135.

40. Margaret McDonnell, "Protocols, Political Correctness, and Discomfort Zones: Indigenous Life Writing and Non-Indigenous Editing," *Hecate* 30, no. 1 (2004): 89.

41. Gregory Younging, *Elements of Indigenous Style: A Guide for Writing by and about Indigenous Peoples* (Edmonton: Brush Education, 2018), xiv.

42. Phillip H. Round, "Bibliography and the Sociology of American Indian Texts," *Textual Cultures* 6, no. 2 (2011): 131.

43. Cohen, "Codex," 115.

44. Freeman, "'We Must Become Gatekeepers,'" 15.

CHAPTER 11

Preserving the Walt Whitman Archive

NICOLE GRAY

> I am he attesting sympathy;
> Shall I make my list of things in the house and skip the house that supports them?
>
> —WALT WHITMAN, "Song of Myself" (1855)

> It ends as it begins, in motion, in between various modes of being and belonging, and on the way to new economies of giving, taking, being with and for and it ends with a ride in a Buick Skylark on the way to another place altogether.
>
> —JACK HALBERSTAM, "The Wild Beyond: With and for the Undercommons" (2013)

As part of an assignment for a class on preservation in library school, I sat down in the summer of 2020 to give some thought to the long-term preservation of the Walt Whitman Archive. It was a strange moment to be thinking about preservation. Covid-19 had transformed everyday life for much of the globe, and my father was moving into the late stages of Lewy Body dementia, so my parents had recently made the move to be closer to me in Lincoln, Nebraska. I was also actually shifting off the Whitman Archive after several years of work with the project, having wrapped up work on a grant to create a digital edition (what we referred to as a variorum edition) of Whitman's 1855 *Leaves of Grass*. With all of this going on, I arrived at this challenge of thinking about preservation with something of an elegiac feeling, some sense that the world was changing in fundamental ways and that the work of preservation was a fragile effort, and possibly a futile one.

This wasn't a particularly unusual feeling to have when it comes to preservation, and especially digital preservation. It seems likely that if you topic-modeled discussions of digital preservation from the last two decades, "doom" would loom fairly large. Even William Kilbride's distinctly unhysterical 2016 assessment, critical of the exaggeration of so-called "snappy premonitions of digital doom," is somewhat lukewarm in its optimism: "it *may seem* that digital preservation is set to move from its early phase of anxiety to a positive future of tools, techniques, and capacity."[1] And even though digital preservation tools and techniques have evolved in recent years, "digital humanities [DH] collections are facing a widespread crisis of sustainability," as Katrina Fenlon has pointed out.[2] Some of the reasons for this, Fenlon and others have argued, include a history of funding opportunities designed to encourage innovation or expansion rather than maintenance, the often deeply collaborative and open-ended nature of such projects, and a lack of clarity about where the projects sit in relation to library resources and processes devoted to long-term digital preservation. James Smithies and his coauthors have provided a summary of other factors putting pressure on preservation considerations for digital projects: "A generation of legacy projects that need maintenance but are out of funding have reached critical stages of their lifecycles, an increasingly hostile security context has made DH projects potential attack vectors into institutional networks, heterogeneous and often delicate technologies have complicated the task of maintenance, and an increasing number of emerging formats have made archiving and preservation yet more difficult."[3]

Drawing and reflecting on these discussions, this essay considers the future of digital editing as a matter of digital preservation, but also uses the example of the Walt Whitman Archive and its transformations to think about preservation itself as concept and (perhaps poetic) orientation. As Fenlon and others have suggested, the challenges of long-term sustainability for DH projects continue to prompt us to meditate on value, on time and the notion of completion, and on the many ways that encounters with technologies and digital environments shape scholarly work and interests.[4] They might also provoke some reflections on what needs to be kept and by whom, what "keeping" means, and the structure and function of institutions like universities in relation to the attachments formed by communities to the digital resources they use and encounter.[5]

"To think How Eager We Are in Building Our Houses": Constructing Digital Projects

Editors and archivists alike have discussed how digital editions, digital archives, and digital thematic research collections are multifaceted entities subject to updates, expansions, transformations, obsolescence, failures, and migrations.[6] Under these conditions, editing and preservation both become the work of tending or long-term cultivation. Even a digital edition that is no longer actively expanding does not simply exist in the world. It requires effort to maintain: server space, security updates, and domain renewals. The claiming of the domain and the building and compiling and updating of the code are recurring and collective activities, often involving a collective that expands and changes over time. The proliferation of digital projects and the persistence of some, like the Whitman Archive, over decades also has helped to inspire conversations about project "sunsetting," or (as a Duke University ScholarWorks "Project Planning" document defines it), "thoughtfully ceasing to update or maintain a digital work."[7] This is practical, necessary, and also sometimes sad work: a 2019 roundtable on sunsetting was subtitled "on digital praxes of letting go."[8]

As is the case for many large-scale digital projects, the scope of materials that have come to make up the Whitman Archive is vast. Users are familiar with the website, whitmanarchive.org, divided into seven major sections and many more subsections and providing access to tens of thousands of files. Hosted by the University of Nebraska–Lincoln's (UNL) Center for Digital Research in the Humanities (CDRH), the Archive and its publication framework are currently under active reconstruction, but at the time of writing, the project still uses Apache Cocoon to dynamically transform XML files into HTML, with a Google-based site search and section searches powered by SOLR. Grant-funded work is now fueling the process of transforming it into a Ruby on Rails application that draws on the CDRH application programming interface (API) and leverages the center's custom publishing system. This change will align the project's web components much more substantively with principles of digital longevity like those articulated by the University of Victoria–based "Endings Project."[9] The Archive also curates scads of high-resolution TIFF files; lower-resolution JPG access derivatives; style sheets; scripts; Google documents; SharePoint documents; Excel files; wiki pages; databases (including a tracking database linking images and transcriptions and a database with bibliographical information about more than a century of Whitman criticism); electronic, printed, and handwritten correspondence, files and photocopies; journal issues; Git repositories, Post-it notes; objects accumulated over more than twenty-five years of meetings and Whitman camps (the familiar name for all-hands annual planning meetings); and more.

Preservation processes are in place for some of these materials, with more to come as digital capacities in the UNL Libraries expand. Most of the project's high-resolution scans of Whitman manuscripts and other materials have been deposited into Ex Libris Rosetta, a digital asset management (DAM) and preservation system. Lots of copies are made to keep stuff safe, some purposefully and some compulsively, from server backups to redundant copies on servers, hard drives, optical media, and individual computers. Printed copies of some records are generated and kept in file cabinets in the Whitman Archive offices. The files that make up two early versions of the Archive have been saved and can be accessed through the current interface. Two different versioning systems have been used in project workflows for various aspects of the work: Apache Subversion and Git. You'll notice the passive tense in this paragraph: the agents doing this work are so many and have changed so often over the years that each of these actions has truly been a cooperative effort, sometimes but not always guided by a clear plan or leadership intervention. And this description does not take into account the preservation processes also constantly happening among the project's large community of users, as people save images of poetry manuscripts for use in scholarship or because they are beautiful, or as they download the project's XML to use for various forms of computational analysis, or as they copy individual lines of poetry into essays or journals or notebooks.[10]

Sitting there in that summer of 2020, the more I thought through the scope of what constitutes the "Whitman Archive," the more overwhelming it seemed, particularly when thinking about preservation as a bulwark against loss. But recent work in archives and elsewhere suggests that maybe there are other ways of thinking about it. Resources like The Socio-Technical Sustainability Roadmap (STSR), developed by the Visual Media Workshop at the University of Pittsburgh, guide creators or inheritors of digital projects through a series of steps designed to produce documentation about a project's sustainability goals, essential features, and sociotechnical frameworks.[11] Key to the process as the Roadmap presents it are both an iterative approach and the recognition that there are various pathways and sustainability options available: "Digital humanities projects can, and should, have a variety of expectations of longevity."[12] Part of the work project representatives are asked to do in the first section of modules is to consider fundamental aspects of the project, including its scope, its mission, its community of users, and its priorities.

Preservation and editing both have the virtue, done carefully, of prompting some consideration and articulation of value. In reflecting on the spirit of the Whitman Archive and thinking about connecting preservation actions to values, some of what I wanted to figure out how to preserve was not just the technical or the content layers of the project, but less tangible or documentary things and more ephemeral ones, more ephemeral even than the digital materials or the links among them: the discoveries it had made possible, the moments of serendipity or surprise at recognizing something new in Whitman based on searches or juxtapositions of images and text on the Archive; the moments where, to paraphrase the poet, something startled us where we thought we were safest—"wonder at the resurrection of the wheat."[13]

I also thought about the social infrastructure of the Whitman Archive, the people who have been so fundamental to its construction and maintenance over the years. It's a lot of people, the staff page now featuring about two hundred folks who have contributed to the project. There are the codirectors: the project was shaped by the confident leadership and people-cultivating energy of Ken Price and the wisdom and poetic sensibility of Ed Folsom, both inheritors of the rich tradition of Whitman scholarship. In its more recent Nebraska- and Iowa-based iterations, the project has also been shaped by the leadership, organization, and people-wrangling accomplishments of Kevin McMullen, Stephanie Blalock, Brett Barney, and Elizabeth Lorang; brilliant design and dev management by the CDRH's Karin Dalziel; the programming prowess of Jessica Dussault, Greg Tunink, and others; the enthusiasm of contributing editors like Matt Cohen, Stefan Schöberlein, Jason Stacy, and Caterina Bernardini; sustained institutional support orchestrated by Katherine Walter; the labors of more extraordinary graduate and undergraduate students than I can count, who have gone off to do amazing things in a wide range of fields. There were consultants and supporters and advisors providing just the right words of caution or suggestion at just the right times. There were great strides in the wrong direction, good-natured corrections of course, and cosmic discussions over everything from authorship to the placement of a comma. These all have been, in so many ways, the heart of the Whitman Archive.

There are oral histories, too. I remember a moment when Brett, keeper of Whitman Archive lore, first told me about the "Price escape" and the "Folsom escape." Some impossible situation had come up (I can't remember what, now, one of many cruxes or interface lapses occasioned by Whitman's constant revision and vast assemblage of texts and re-texts and pretexts and contexts), and as we sat in silence staring forlornly at the screen, Brett said, "well, there's always the Folsom escape." First, there was the Price escape: that thing that needs doing can be done by some unspecified future people at some unspecified future time. And then there was the Folsom escape: whatever it was that couldn't possibly be captured or represented satisfactorily by the encoding or the web display would be okay, because a user could consult the associated images or explanatory text. And so, inch by inch, file by file, with care and compromise, the project moved forward. These escapes are things that speak beyond themselves: they are bridges, incantations, models, and habits of mind that move us from where we are to where we wish to go. They look at the stultifying pull of perfectionism in the eye, and then they move on.

What sort of thing is this that we are trying to preserve? How much of it can we capture with WARC files and bitstreams? How much of it do we need or want to capture? These are challenging practical questions, but they are also challenging theoretical, ontological, and ethical ones. The Whitman Archive, like editions in any medium, is a locus, a site of layered materiality around which relationships form and reform. Drawing on Kathleen Fitzpatrick's discussion of planned obsolescence, "Open Digital Collaborative Project Preservation in the Humanities" is a conference aligned with the Digital Humanities Summer Institute (DHSI) that has invited discussions of "a complex problem made more complex when environments are not static objects but rather dynamic collaborative spaces."[14] The sociology of texts is also the sociology of digital editorial projects.

And preservation, like editing, is world-building work. The impress of time is everywhere upon it. Alan Galey has explored some of the intersections, noting the temporality of both sets of activities: working in the present to preserve the materials of the past for the audiences and readers and users of the future.[15] Web archiving has often been described by archivists in terms of capturing "moments in time."[16] Time is at the heart of other methods and tools of digital preservation and access: emulation, versioning, migration and reformatting, DAM systems. Data-curation models like the one provided by the Digital Curation Centre (DCC) describe a lifecycle punctuated by stages and interventions, but the cycle is circular and (unlike the life of an individual) does not necessarily involve an endpoint.[17] Even the endpoint, as represented by guidelines like those described in The Socio-Technical Sustainability Roadmap or the Digital Documentation Process, or in principles like those articulated by the Endings Project, often isn't really the end: data, documentation, and other project materials are deposited into institutional or open-source digital repositories, or stored in some other secure location for continued access.[18] The work of sustainability and preservation is an ongoing and collective process, a set of specific actions, but also an orientation, a willingness to mediate in an open-ended way between technologies and people of the past and present and technologies and people of the future.[19]

This has driven calls to rethink not the ontology of the digital project, exactly, but rather the comparisons we use to try to imagine its persistence. A recent publication on what the authors refer to as "expansive digital publications" proposes: "If the scholarly community conceptualizes these projects as analogous not to a codex but to museum exhibits, for example, or the performing arts, then ephemerality becomes not an undesirable accident but an essential quality of the work."[20] They also raise the notion, often heretical to scholars if familiar to archivists, that not everything can be preserved, and (what's more) not everything *should* be preserved. I think of some of those lost things from the past whose felt absence is registered only by the incommensurate presence of other things, and our desire for them: the missing chapters of Martin Delany's serialized novel *Blake*; William Wells Brown's play *Experience*; the way some Indigenous words and languages used to sound. We project our own desires into these spaces at our peril, Saidiya Hartman reminds us, even as we must summon the courage and the compassion to do that work.[21] Before romanticizing ephemerality or embracing the lessons offered by its particular form of surrender, we must remember how often power has dictated what was preserved and what was not.

What do we save, of what we can save? In the case of a project like the Whitman Archive, not everything can be saved, and (we argue) not everything *should* be saved, and insofar as we have any agency in deciding—and capacity to balance the difficult work of building, managing, and preserving—it is practical and ethical work that deserves some attention. Time and backlogs being what they are, the work and resources devoted to saving one thing are taken from the work and resources devoted to saving another.[22] There are a range of ways in which digital editorial projects can be maintained, from fully functioning, database-driven websites and archival information packages, to a collection of static HTML pages, to a series of screenshots in a documentary description, to a snapshot on the Internet Archive. As the STSR suggests, "end-of-life" planning requires a project to go back to basics, to identify "significant properties," to think about the aspects that *mean* something to users, and how they might be sustained. It also suggests a need or an opportunity to reflect on key moments in the formation and development of a project and its connections to other projects, as well as broader conversations and initiatives, particularly for projects like the Whitman Archive that have emerged and evolved as part of the emergence and evolution of the field or subfield of DH.

"These Also Flow onward to Others . . .":
Preservation and Letting Go

Fenlon has noted that the distinction between *preservation* and *sustainability* is often not clear in discussions of DH projects. "One implication of this challenge," she suggests, "is the need for a stronger vocabulary for articulating the contributions of digital scholarship to support determinations about what needs to be kept 'alive' (and in what form, and for how long), and what can be effectively fixed in amber."[23] This distinction also speaks to the ways that the digital preservation practices that have developed for long-term maintenance of static materials often can only be partial, and maybe only address part of the question: "It is a good idea to archive the data from these projects," Christine Madsen and Megan Hurst point out, "but that will not sustain them."[24]

Scholars and practitioners in the libraries and archives world are profoundly aware of the difficulties attending digital preservation, but for many humanities scholars they are something new to be contending with, in part because digital materials require a kind of premortem. What's needed for these, preservation guidelines have suggested, is thinking about the end at the very beginning: building the project's sunset into its sunrise, into the laying of the foundations.[25] "Preservation action is needed at the start of the life of a digital object," the Digital Preservation Coalition's *Digital Preservation Handbook* advises, "not always at its end."[26] For digital editorial projects, this can be something of a melancholy activity not just because the end must be built into the beginning, not just because ultimately separating the two is, perhaps, impossible, but also because the broader context of the world is deeply unstable. We no longer have the luxury of thinking about sustainability as an intellectual exercise, if we ever did. Now, more apparently, it has become a matter of survival.

Whitman is a challenge and a joy to edit in part because he was so involved with the production of his books, testing any desire to circumscribe or project authorial intention. The 1855 edition of *Leaves of Grass* was brought about almost entirely as a matter of the relationships he had developed as a printer and newspaper editor, and the poet maintained that he had set some of the type for the edition himself. Material traces on surviving copies suggest the books probably were printed in stages between other jobs, their manufacture proceeding as a series of moments in time, a context-driven tempo of production.[27] When the 1860–1861 edition was being produced, Whitman installed himself in the Boston printing house, probably driving the printers crazy with his interventions. This involvement with the material production of his books combined with his newspaper experience to influence both his poetic metaphors and his sense of the fixity and finality of the codex and the printed page—which he saw as neither fixed nor final, but perpetually subject to transformation.

Digital editions and projects have been around long enough now that many of them have woven themselves deeply into the work and the psyches of scholars, and in some cases the sentiments. Having worked so closely with the Whitman Archive for so many years, it is difficult for me to imagine, for instance, the interface in any color but blue. But of course it wasn't always blue, any more than *Leaves of Grass* was always green: Whitman himself set the example with the many interfaces of *Leaves of Grass*.[28] Unless you owned more than one copy, your experience of Whitman's poetry was profoundly shaped by whichever book you bought. As fondness for a particular set of retro computer games can anchor a person in time, so too we might measure out our academic lives by our affection for the peculiarities of the printed and digital editions and collections we use.

One example of such a collection is Old Fulton New York Post Cards, an astonishing, idiosyncratic preservation effort in its own right that has served as a long-time resource for Whitman scholars and a range of other people interested in the history of New York.[29] This website, a labor of love by a retired IT professional, has long been a repository of millions of scans of New York newspapers, many of which could not be found elsewhere, and is equipped with a maddening but somehow charming interface that defies all current principles of usability and interface design.

The *Oxford English Dictionary*'s definitions of *preservation* are several, and they describe the preservation of many things: self, identity, health, antiquities, furniture, buildings, customs, language, remains. Preservation is also *against* many things: damage, decay, destruction, weather, disease, sin, extinction, dissipation, death. One of the definitions of "preservation" in the *OED* is "the state or condition of being preserved; intactness, keeping, repair":[30] *intactness,* as in the maintenance of a unified being as a whole (or perhaps the *seeking* of connections among things); *keeping,* as in "actively to hold in possession; to retain in one's power or control" (or perhaps "the *taking care* of a thing or person," "to *observe* by attendance, presence, residence"); *repair,* as in to fix (or perhaps "to *return* . . . to come back again").[31]

Following these words to their meanings, and imagining for them alternate, recursive meanings, begins to hint at the multiple valences of preservation, including a dark side that has registered in the literature and ruminations of archivists and theorists alike. In their book *The Undercommons,* a theoretical-poetic work grown out of the Black radical tradition and published as both a printed volume and an open-access PDF freely available for download, Stefano Harney and Fred Moten *repair* to the violence of the invocation of categories. "This responsibility for the preservation of objects," they write, "becomes precisely that Weberian site-specific ethics that has the effect, as Theodor Adorno recognized, of naturalizing the production of capitalist sites."[32]

As a rejoinder, they summon preservation as a mode of liberatory meta- or anti-critique, applied to self and community as protective positivity, a kind of reverberation within and resistance to the trap of institutional authority (including that gravitational pull of expertise, competence, credit, and critique that has often been the uninterrogated foundation of scholarly edition-making). In *The Undercommons,* Moten and Harney write: "Critique endangers the sociality it is supposed to defend, not because it might turn inward to damage politics but because it would turn to politics and then turn outward ... were it not for preservation, which is given in celebration of what we defend, the sociopoetic force we wrap tightly round us, since we are poor. Taking down our critique, our own positions, our fortifications, is self-defense alloyed with self-preservation":[33] preservation as something *given,* in celebration; self-preservation and self-defense as a matter of *taking down* fortifications. Preservation as/for sociopoetic force here is a matter of the self and a matter of the social. Moten and Harney also summon a kind of "militant preservation": "The multitude uses every quiet moment, every sundown, every moment of militant preservation, to plan together, to launch, to compose (in) its surreal time."[34]

And here we find a quandary, or perhaps an opportunity; and here editing and its discontents may help us. What, with respect to the temporalities of digital preservation, are we to make of this concept of "surreal time"? Digital editing challenges us to find our escapes, to become comfortable with states of incompleteness. Corrections are possible; versions can coexist; multiple stages of description might be part of a project's work plan; new sections of the Whitman Archive are added as new discoveries are made or new contributors with different interests develop grant projects. Digital preservation, too, draws our attention to moments. What we preserve is a series of fragments meant to represent or be summonable as the whole. But who better than Whitman to remind us that the unified, unchangeable whole or origin was always an illusion, even before the bitstream, even before software and its dependencies?

Here we split a definition of preservation into parts, tinker, and bring it back together again: in the surreal time of preservation, we might privilege movement rather than fixity, we might declare keeping as *giving* (as *taking care,* as continuous and careful *observation*), we might declare repair as *taking down* (as *return,* as *coming back again*). Here things are not necessarily *intact,* at least not in the way we have imagined. Here the *state of being intact* was a dream, a projection, more virtual than the virtual world itself,[35] but also a call into the future that imagines a group of people working to build the kinds of connections and foundations that can function as intactness within a given set of circumstances. Preservation, here, becomes not so much an effort to reconstruct exactly something that was, as to maintain the possibility of something that could be—even if that something looks quite different from how it did before.

The Genoa Indian School Digital Reconciliation Project, another project affiliated with the CDRH at Nebraska, has been working to digitize archival documents related to the Genoa U.S. Indian Industrial School, a boarding school that operated in Genoa, Nebraska, from 1884 to 1934, enrolling children from more than forty Native American tribes.[36] The meanings and set of practices comprising preservation in the context of this project are still evolving. They include: the digitization itself, which proliferates copies of and access to archival materials but also recontextualizes them with respect to the information most likely to be of interest to descendants and tribal communities; the plan to ingest high-resolution scans into a DAM system, and also the plan to copy images to hard drives to give to tribal representatives; work with the National Native American Boarding School Healing Coalition to aggregate metadata for documents related to boarding schools across the United States. There are also convenings of community advisors, plans to record interviews and speak with members of Indigenous communities about how to archive their own digital and analog materials, and ongoing conversations about reconciliation, acknowledgement, repatriation, and sovereignty.

This is only one small example of an ecosystem aspiring to sociopoetic, recursive modes of preservation. A wide range of postcustodial, participatory, and community-oriented approaches to archival work have started to put pressure on the idea of preservation itself, and the scope and imagination of what is being preserved. Preservation becomes an act of creation, both technological and social, a connection-building practice that considers all the many valences of sustainability, including minimal preservation and no preservation at all. "At a time of so much doom and gloom about the state of digital preservation," Laura Morreale has written, "it might be helpful to step back and ask why the loss of digital material is considered such a catastrophe."[37] "Knowing how to stop doing things is an important skill to learn," developer-librarian Matt Miller writes in a discussion of what he calls "repotting" digital projects. He concludes:

> I have one bonus example, something I really think of sunsetting, rather than repotting.... I made a site as a class project in graduate school to explore the possibilities of embedded metadata in digital assets. I had to evaluate the effort in repotting this tool or not. It could not be made into a static site because it is not a content site, you upload a digital asset and it will inform you of the embedded metadata present. I could possibly Dockerize it but it requires a special PHP module that was difficult to get working almost a decade ago, the thought of trying to get it functional today, even with Docker sounded extravagant. So I said farewell little website, you had a good run, someone even used it to write an academic paper but you can't do everything and this is something that can be let go. I made sure to make some videos of the site, do a webcapture of it, put all the source code on Github and redirected the domain to a page with all this information.
>
> It's sad to turn off something you spent time building but you also get the satisfaction of not having to think about it ever again. And maybe that little room that is freed up in your brain is the space needed to make it to the next thing.[38]

The STSR modules define a "state of graceful degradation," one example of an approach a project might take in its "Retirement" phase, as "defined by its utterly minimal interventions and accepting partial failures of the total system in due course."[39] Something about this formulation, perhaps the touch of drama added by the "utterly," seems to speak to the many kinds of emotional investment in a project, whether they manifest as fondness for it or relief at the prospect of being able to walk away from it (or both). The almost cosmic determinism of "in due course" also introduces a temporality that is not purely agent-driven, an acknowledgement of the way in which obsolescence proceeds as a function of the broader worlds of technology, links among digital resources, and communities of use and practice.

"The Preparations Have Every One Been Justified": Futures of Digital Editing

"To think the thought of death merged in the thought of materials," as Whitman puts it in the poem "To Think of Time"[40]—a poem that persisted, evolving, through all the editions of *Leaves of Grass*. He introduced a version of this line in the 1872 edition, where the poem appears as part of the section "Passage to India." House-building often becomes a figure for him, and here in this section of "To Think of Time" the speaker casts the passage of time and mortality against the building of houses (and possibly coffins, and possibly other things too):

> To think how eager we are in building our houses,
> To think others shall be just as eager, and we quite indifferent.
>
> (I see one building the house that serves him a few years, or
>   seventy or eighty years at most,
> I see one building the house that serves him longer than that.)[41]

But it is the *thought* of death that this poem is about, merged with the *thought* of materials—the poet observes the builders, but builds only the lines of the poem himself, one step removed from both the materials and the mortality.[42] And perhaps this is somewhere else the merge and the keeping can happen, here in the surreal space-time of poetry. The metaphor bridges two deeply human activities (building and dying) and looks for meaning in them, meaning shaped by the framing activity of the poem: "to think of time."

Preservation and editing both could be described in this way: to think the thought of death, merged in the thought of materials. Digital objects can seem immaterial, and deceptively so, as Matthew Kirschenbaum has pointed out.[43] The bitstream persists on material substrates, whatever the forms of transformation and mediation between those and the web page displaying on your computer screen, the interface that has shaped your explorations of poetry and your pursuits of understanding.

Preservation (or not, or how) is the unavoidable future of digital editing. The activities undertaken in pursuit of digital preservation sit, sometimes uncomfortably, between a set of established practices and an open-ended call continually to adapt, to include, to inquire, to desist. As Morreale points out, "in a cruel irony, even the digital preservation tools we create seem to become quickly obsolete."[44] (*I see one building the house that serves him a few years . . .*) More in certain ways than ever before, time is compressed—the end is always in sight—surreal time is upon us all, and it is demanding a reckoning and a reconciliation.

As the Whitman Archive is repotted again after almost thirty years, we might take the opportunity to think again of time, to think of building, to think of endings, to think of preservation. How do we work toward the sustainability of both a project and the imaginative and social and practical forces that fuel it? How might a project cultivate possibility for future transformations, for finding grace in its own endings, whatever those may look like, and its new beginnings? A digital edition is an investment not just in building and rebuilding but in keeping as care, in repair as return, in celebration and cooperation, in the willingness to work in moments. The preservation and maintenance of digital projects, like editing itself, is challenging and elegiac work, but somehow this seems like cause for joy as much as doom or despair, maybe because it necessitates a kind of thinking of time beyond the individual, outside possession and agency, past completeness and authoritativeness and perfection, that might serve us well as we move forward into the tumult of the twenty-first century.

Notes

1. William Kilbride, "Saving the Bits: Digital Humanities Forever?," in *A New Companion to Digital Humanities*, ed. Susan Schreibman, Ray Siemens, and John Unsworth (West Sussex, UK: John Wiley & Sons, 2016), 415 (emphasis mine).

2. Katrina Fenlon, "Sustaining Digital Humanities Collections: Challenges and Community-Centred Strategies," Conference Pre-Print, *International Journal of Digital Curation* 15, no. 1 (2020), dx.doi.org/10.2218/ijdc.v15i1.725.

3. James Smithies et al., "Managing 100 Digital Humanities Projects: Digital Scholarship & Archiving in King's Digital Lab," *Digital Humanities Quarterly* 13, no. 1 (2019).

4. See, e.g., Kilbride, "Saving the Bits"; Smithies et al., "Managing 100 Digital Humanities Projects"; Matthew G. Kirschenbaum, "Done: Finishing Projects in the Digital Humanities," *Digital Humanities Quarterly* 3, no. 2 (2009) (and other essays in this

cluster); Kathleen Fitzpatrick, *Planned Obsolescence: Publishing, Technology, and the Future of the Academy* (New York: New York University Press, 2011), 121–54; Julia Flanders and Trevor Muñoz, "An Introduction to Humanities Data Curation," *DH Curation Guide* (2012); Elena Pierazzo, *Digital Scholarly Editing: Theories, Models and Methods* (Surrey: Ashgate, 2015), 169–91.

    5. I should note that these reflections draw on conversations well underway in recent archival scholarship and practice. Work on postcustodial, participatory, and community archiving has interrogated concepts of possession and access that have long informed ideas about the structure and function of archives, proposing instead more recursive, community-based and outward-facing reformulations. For recent examples, see the essays in the June 2019 special issue of *Archival Science*: "'To go beyond': Towards a Decolonial Archival Praxis," ed. J. J. Ghaddar and Michelle Caswell. See also Katie Shilton and Ramesh Srinivasan, "Participatory Appraisal and Arrangement for Multicultural Archival Collections," *Archivaria* 63 (Spring 2007): 87–101; F. Gerald Ham, "Archival Strategies for the Post-Custodial Era," *The American Archivist* 44, no. 3 (1981): 207–16; Terry Cook, "Evidence, Memory, Identity, and Community: Four Shifting Archival Paradigms," *Archival Science* 13 (2013): 95–120; and Verne Harris, "The Archival Sliver: Power, Memory, and Archives in South Africa," *Archival Science* 2 (2002): 63–86.

    6. For a discussion of terms used to describe digital editorial and digitization projects, see Kenneth M. Price, "Edition, Project, Database, Archive, Thematic Research Collection: What's in a Name?," *Digital Humanities Quarterly* 3, no. 3 (2009). See also Pierazzo, *Digital Scholarly Editing*, 193–201.

    7. Duke University ScholarWorks, "Project Planning: Transitions," ScholarWorks, Duke University, accessed October 28, 2022, scholarworks.duke.edu/plan-and-build/project-planning/transitions/.

    8. "The Caribbean Digital VI," December 6, 2019, Barnard College Digital Humanities Center, last modified 2019, caribbeandigitalnyc.net/2019/program/.

    9. "The Endings Project: Building Sustainable Digital Humanities Projects," accessed August 31, 2022, endings.uvic.ca/index.html. The CDRH publishing system, which consists of three parts—Datura (a Ruby gem designed to manage and transform data), Apium (the CDRH's API), and Orchid (a Rails engine that configures new Rails applications to draw from the API and synthesizes functionality across apps)—is loosely based on the discovery system created by Project Blacklight.

    10. Recognizing the significant engagement of what she calls "research communities" in DH resources, Fenlon has proposed that some of the work of sustainability might involve consciously thinking about the role of those communities, a kind of "community-centred sustainability" in keeping with archival discussions more broadly about community and participatory archiving ("Sustaining Digital Humanities Collections," 9). Preservation efforts sometimes also involve creative leveraging of information networks both past and present, as a recent Whitman Archive grant proposal to reconstruct lost nineteenth-century newspaper issues from reprinted text suggests.

11. Visual Media Workshop at the University of Pittsburgh, The Socio-Technical Sustainability Roadmap (STSR), accessed October 28, 2022, sites.haa.pitt.edu/sustainabilityroadmap/.

12. STSR, "Welcome and Getting Started."

13. See the first line of the poem "This Compost," originally titled "Poem of Wonder at The Resurrection of The Wheat": "Something startles me where I thought I was safest" (Walt Whitman, *Leaves of Grass* [Brooklyn, NY: Fowler & Wells, 1856], 202). What startles need not be limited to content: The STSR notes that user studies suggest, "the more varied, and sometimes unexpected, the audiences for digital projects are, the more sustainable they might become."

14. Digital Humanities Summer Institute (DHSI) 2022 chair, Luis Meneses, "Open Digital Collaborative Project Preservation in the Humanities," June 7, 2022, accessed October 28, 2022, web.archive.org/web/20220607160251/https://dhsi.org/dhsi-2022-open-digital-collaborative-project-preservation-in-the-humanities/.

15. Alan Galey, *The Shakespearean Archive: Experiments in New Media from the Renaissance to Postmodernity* (Cambridge: Cambridge University Press, 2014).

16. See, for instance, "GPO Captures Moments in Time Through Web Archiving," 2021, accessed October 28, 2022, https://www.gpo.gov/docs/default-source/news-content-pdf-files/2021/typeline_spring-2021_gpo-captures-moments-in-time.pdf.

17. "DCC Curation Lifecycle Model," Digital Curation Centre, accessed October 28, 2022, https://www.dcc.ac.uk/guidance/curation-lifecycle-model.

18. Katherina Fostano and Laura K. Morreale, "The Digital Documentation Process," The Digital Documentation Process, January 31, 2019, digitalhumanitiesddp.com/. Module A2 of The STSR advises users to retain project documentation in its discussion of the "retirement" phase of projects, even if the project opts for removal: "The future will be interested in your work."

19. "Preservation," Fitzpatrick writes, "presents us with technical requirements but overwhelmingly social solutions" (*Planned Obsolescence*, 126).

20. David Hansen, Liz Milewicz, Paolo Mangiafico, Will Shaw, Mattia Begali, and Veronica McGurrin, "Expansive Digital Publishing," 2019, expansive.pubpub.org/pub/snb2tqyr/release/1. See also Christine Madsen and Megan Hurst, who describe research data produced in and by digital humanities projects as "more like a dictionary than 'traditional' research data," suggesting its availability for multiple uses and a reliance on long-term updates that reshapes the data's lifecycle ("Are Digital Humanities Projects Sustainable? A Proposed Service Model for a DH Infrastructure," Coalition for Networked Information Membership Meeting, December 10, 2018, slideshare.net/mccarthymadsen/are-digital-humanities-projects-sustainable-a-proposed-service-model-for-a-dh-infrastructure.)

21. Saidiya Hartman, "Venus in Two Acts," *Small Axe* 12, no. 2 (2008): 1–14.

22. This point deserves a full stop emphasis. The Whitman Archive is very well funded and supported compared to many DH projects. One pressing question preservation poses is how scholars, preservationists, administrators, funding agencies,

and users can help to make sure that well-funded projects affiliated with established DH centers and research institutions are not the only ones that are preserved, particularly when preservation assessment, planning, and action are so heavily resource-intensive and often emotionally charged.

23. Fenlon, "Sustaining Digital Humanities Collections," 6.

24. Madsen and Hurst, "Are Digital Humanities Projects Sustainable?" See also Pierazzo for a discussion of how the use of standards and the separation of data from interface have emerged as key aspects of preservation strategy, despite the often significant role of the interface in interpreting and mediating the data for users (*Digital Scholarly Editing*, 171–79).

25. From a (2008) Blue Ribbon Task Force on Sustainable Digital Preservation and Access: "The need to make preservation decisions can arise as early as the time of the asset's creation, particularly since studies to date indicate that the total cost of preserving materials can be reduced by steps taken early in the life of the asset" (quoted in Fitzpatrick, *Planned Obsolescence*, 125). See also Kilbride, "Saving the Bits"; STSR, "Welcome and Getting Started"; Fostano and Morreale, "The Digital Documentation Process"; and Smithies et al., "Managing 100 Digital Humanities Projects."

26. Digital Preservation Coalition, *Digital Preservation Handbook*, 2nd ed., dpconline.org/handbook.

27. Nicole Gray, "Introduction to the 1855 *Leaves of Grass* Variorum," The Walt Whitman Archive, ed. Matt Cohen, Ed Folsom, and Kenneth M. Price, 2020, whitmanarchive.org/item/anc.02135.

28. For photographs of the covers of the editions of *Leaves of Grass*, see Ed Folsom, *Whitman Making Books/Books Making Whitman: A Catalog and Commentary*, Iowa City, IA: Obermann Center for Advanced Studies, University of Iowa, 2005; for the colors of early versions of the Walt Whitman Archive, see "Earlier Versions of the Archive," The Walt Whitman Archive, accessed October 28, 2022, https://whitmanarchive.org/about/earlier.html.

29. Thomas M. Tryniski, *Old Fulton New York Post Cards*, last modified 2018, fultonhistory.com/. (An Internet Archive web capture of this site is available at web.archive.org/web/20221209114147/http://www.fultonhistory.com/.)

30. "Preservation, n.," *OED Online*, last modified December 2022, https://www-oed-com.libproxy.unl.edu/view/Entry/150719.

31. "Keep, v.," *OED Online*, last modified December 2022, https://www-oed-com.libproxy.unl.edu/view/Entry/102776; "keeping, n.," *OED Online*, last modified September 2021, https://www-oed-com.libproxy.unl.edu/view/Entry/102785; "repair, v. 2," *OED Online*, last modified December 2022, https://www-oed-com.libproxy.unl.edu/view/Entry/162631; "repair, v. 1," *OED Online*, last modified December 2022, https://www-oed-com.libproxy.unl.edu/view/Entry/162630 (emphases mine).

32. Stefano Harney and Fred Moten, *The Undercommons: Fugitive Planning and Black Study* (New York: Minor Compositions, 2013), 36.

33. Harney and Moten, 19.

34. Harney and Moten, 77.

35. N. Katherine Hayles has proposed a "strategic definition of 'virtuality'": "Virtuality is the cultural perception that material objects are interpenetrated by information patterns" (*How We Became Posthuman: Virtual Bodies in Cybernetics, Literature, and Informatics* [Chicago: University of Chicago Press, 1999], 13–14).

36. Susana D. Grajales Geliga, Margaret Jacobs, and Elizabeth Lorang, "Genoa Indian School Digital Reconciliation Project," accessed October 28, 2022, genoaindianschool.org/.

37. Laura Morreale, "Medieval Digital Humanities and *The Rite of Spring*: Thoughts on Performance and Preservation," BodoArXiv, July 2019, 4, osf.io/preprints/bodoarxiv/7p2t6/.

38. Matt Miller, "Repotting Old Digital Humanities Projects," January 31, 2020, https://thisismattmiller.com/post/repotting-old-digital-humanities-projects/.

39. The idea of "graceful degradation" was an anchor of a 2009 survey project aiming to better understand the stages of DH projects; see Bethany Nowviskie and Dot Porter, "Graceful Degradation Survey Findings: How Do We Manage Digital Humanities Projects through Times of Transition and Decline?," accessed October 28, 2022, nowviskie.org/Graceful_Degradation.pdf.

40. Walt Whitman, *Leaves of Grass* (Philadelphia: David McKay, 1891–1892), 333.

41. Whitman, 334.

42. Whitman revised toward "materials," both in this section and at the end of the poem, where death changes to materials in 1872 and later.

43. Matthew G. Kirschenbaum, *Mechanisms: New Media and the Forensic Imagination* (Cambridge, Mass.: MIT Press, 2008).

44. Morreale, "Medieval Digital Humanities," 3.

CHAPTER 12

Unsilent Springs

Dearchivizing the Data Choirs of Dickinson's Time-Shifted Birds

MARTA L. WERNER

To AS, who, long ago, sent me a sound of the night woods.
And to my Mother, who became a bird, August 2016.

+

bird, psuk *may be sound of birds taking-off;* psukses *little bird;* pussekesèsuck (Narr.); pissuksemesog *very small birds*
—FRANK WAABU O'BRIEN,
New England Algonquian Language Revival

+

UNDER THE CANOPY:
"THE MORNING LIT—THE BIRDS AROSE—"

In March 2020, in "the earliest ending of winter" and the long beginning of the pandemic, I spent more time than usual at my desk reading and watching the world outside.[1] The variorum of Dickinson's poems lay open before me;[2] beside it, H. L. Clark's 1887 *The Birds of Amherst & Hampshire County.* In the middle distance between laptop screen and windowpane, poems and birds and questions kept crossing. How could I make a book of Dickinson's birds—that is to say, her poems, that is to say, the birds of her world—addressed to readers of the Anthropocene that would not be a snare? How could a book of Dickinson's birds "conjure an awareness of what accepted categories cannot contain, what familiar taxonomies cannot order, what one medium cannot express"?[3] How could an archive not turn into an exhibit, with all its ties to the old cabinet of curiosities and, worse, the specimen case, but become instead a miscellany and a *murmuration*?[4]

Dickinson's Birds arose—and continues to arise—out of these unsettled questions. A digital-humanities (DH) work of the "third wave," it is necessarily hybrid in its nature, combining elements of the documentary archive and the scholarly edition but claiming neither as an identity. For, while we hope that, like the archive, as recently described by Arlette Farge, Dickinson's Birds will be experienced as a "spring tide" and a "forest without clearings," and further that, like the carefully prepared scholarly edition, it will remain responsible to the material forms and textual evolution of Dickinson's poems, in composing it we have let go of the gnostic desire to store and classify her works for eternity also characteristic of both these structures.[5] Instead, by gathering and disseminating digital surrogates of approximately 350 manuscript witnesses from Dickinson's oeuvre that name or allude to birds and 253 audio files and sonograms of Amherst's avifauna in relation to the unfolding hours of the day, the revolution of the seasons, and the calendar of her writing life, Dickinson's Birds embodies a letting go of both identities to imagine an archive turning into a sound installation and a thought experiment in speculative worlding.

Set quietly beside not only archive and edition but also before the unimaginably vast and inhuman scale of the Anthropocene itself, Dickinson's Birds is perhaps best described as a fragile mode of inquiry allied to a brief moment in the twenty-first century and the unthinkable stakes associated with it. It seeks to make possible a durational encounter with her poems that illumines them as part of the "flickering, shimmering field of forces without independent existence and in constant flux," and with Dickinson's lyric oeuvre itself as an entropic place in which the constant surging of time presages its eventual dissolution and passing away.[6]

It seeks to stir intensified concern with the smallest, most vulnerable, and most ephemeral of things, with poems and birds, in the belief that these things, too, have their infinity.

+

With the exception of only a few months, Emily Dickinson lived her entire life in Amherst, Massachusetts, deep in the Connecticut River Valley, where the primary biome is a temperate deciduous forest composed of oak, maple, beech, and elm. Above the forest canopy and hidden in its understory were the wild songbirds of Dickinson's world, the birds that still dart and whirr through her poems, letters, and fragments. Of the more than two hundred and fifty species of birds known to nest in this fertile valley or pass through it, she named a relatively small number, possibly just those she heard from her window or observed in her garden: robins, bobolinks, sparrows, jays, crows, eagles, cardinals, orioles, larks, phoebes, blackbirds and blue birds, hummingbirds, owls, eider ducks, whippoorwills, partridges, cuckoo birds, doves, linnets, and wrens, and a few that must instead have alighted from the pages of her books, lapwings, nightingales, swans, peacocks.[7] Yet unnamed birds also crowd Dickinson's work. Her fascicles shelter so many birds that they seem at times like nests; when she turns from fascicle gatherings to loose bifolium sheets, the birds migrate with her; and even her latest fragments carry birds or turn into them.

[Track: "June1864," *bird-weather-soundway.*[8]]

Just as birds are ever-present in her writings, so birdsong is arguably the most constant, evanescent sound she recorded through writing in the years before the first wildlife recordings had been made.[9] Birds' sound-making is also place-making: it orients humans to our own ecological emplacement in nature, locale, and time. As we have long known, for Dickinson the birds were harbingers of the seasons of the year and even the hours of the day. After the long New England winter, their dawn and dusk choruses broke open the biophony to sound the unaccountable fullness of our terrestrial condition in a "A Music + numerous as | space—."[10] While the birds' varied departures in late summer and fall for their wintering ranges and their many returns to Amherst in early spring with the ice still "in the pools" affirmed for Dickinson the cyclical, eternal nature of the life-forms of our planet, their brief lives and their often invisible (witness-less) deaths seem to have given her an exact imagination of our own similarly contingent, vulnerable, and common existence in time and weather.[11]

Such a world is beautifully hinted at in a simple map drawn from an archive not far from Dickinson's.[12] Made in April 1823 by fourteen-year-old Frances Alsop Henshaw for a class on geography and penmanship at the Middlebury

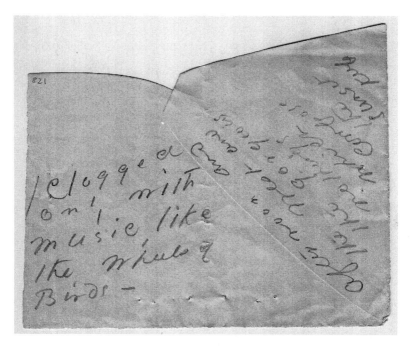

Figure 12.1. Emily Dickinson, "Clogged | only with | Music" (circa 1885), two fragments of envelope, originally pinned together. Amherst College Archives, MS A 821 (JL976n).

Female Academy, the rose- and charcoal-colored map of Massachusetts offers a spectral sense of emplacement. While the artificial borders look to have been traced from a printed map, large tracts of the interior remain empty. Amherst itself is nowhere on the map, and the few tremulously calligraphed place names she recorded seem to be erasing themselves in a sepia-dissolve. Perhaps Henshaw had become lost in contemplation as she worked on the assignment. Perhaps her mind had wandered and she had opened a window into the sudden spring migration. No legend or scale accompanies the map, but as the stroke of Henshaw's writing sweeps out, overtaken by the stroke of drawing, a sense of vastness breathes in the paper: the basalt mountain ranges (such as the Holyoke Range) that rose up at the end of the last Ice Age are rendered in charcoal scribbles and contour lines, and the rivers Merrimack (*Merruasquamack*), Narraganset (*Pettaquamscutt*), and Connecticut (*Quinnehtukqut*) materialize as dark arteries winding through the landscape. Through drawing's counterwriting, the map opens into the realm of the spatial

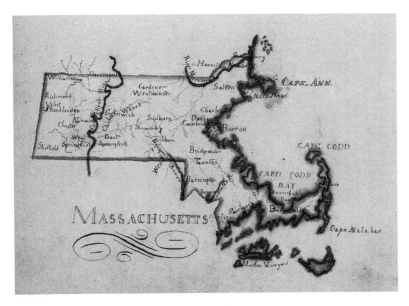

Figure 12.2. "Massachusetts," from "Frances A. Henshaw's Book of Penmanship Executed at the Middlebury Female Academy April 29, 1828." 16 cm (h) x 23 cm (w); scale: 1: 1,609,344. The David Rumsey Historical Map Collection.

imaginary. The empty spaces of Henshaw's map remind us that every map embodies only a tiny island of reality and leaves most of the world undisturbed by our representation; they invite us to conjure a quieter earth, its corridors lit up by birdsong.[13]

In Dickinson's nineteenth-century world, birdsong was certainly fuller and less masked than it is for inhabitants of the twenty-first century. Yet Dickinson also lived in the post-Industrial period, when new technologies were changing the sound of the world forever. Even the small site of Amherst, Massachusetts, reverberated with change. Between 1830 and 1870, the town's population rose by 53 percent and the sounds that entered Dickinson's windows suddenly included not only those of the old earth but also the din of the three to four thousand new human inhabitants and their occupations.[14] By 1850, Massachusetts had witnessed the loss of 60 percent of its forests, one of the most devastating ecological losses in American history, and in Dickinson's lifetime the quiet farms that had prevailed in the landscape were outnumbered by clamorous textile and paper mills, brickyards, and tool factories.[15] In 1853, the passenger train originating in Belchertown pierced the soundscape, a strange stimulus for birdsong: "A train went through a burial gate, / A bird broke forth and sang."[16]

+

Tapping into the oldest and innermost part of our brain, sound imparts immediate data telling us where we are and whether it is safe, along with relational data that tells us how far we are from other, familiar things. When sounds are missing, that, too, tells us something. Does the birdsong that, though already diminished, still welcomes us into Dickinson's world make us preternaturally aware of deeper silences in our own? How might we measure the ecological distances, the changed meters, between Dickinson's sound-world and our own while also attending to those soundings, however faint, that propose new pathways for moving forward in the altered world, new opportunities for attunement and ethical engagement with beings whose "otherness" is palpable but with whom we nonetheless share an uncertain future?[17]

[Track: "December 1864," *bird-weather-soundway.*]

While clairaudient access to the past is not likely to be possible even in a distant future, might the prospect of hearing again through the mind's more

Figure 12.3. An early "umbrella blind" constructed for observing birds. Photograph by Cordelia J. Stanwood, courtesy of Stanwood Wildlife Sanctuary, Margaret Sartor, and Alex Harris.

speculative ear one thin bandwidth of Dickinson's vanished soundscape by capturing, albeit incompletely, the calls and songs of the distant descendants of her birds, still be salutary?

+

FLYWAYS: *"AND FILLING ALL THE | EARTH AND AIR"*

Unlike the printed book bound by a gravity the process of writing does not have and a final form it is not meant to have, the virtual book is weightless, tuned to the sky.[18] And while the actual order of the pages of the codex never alters no matter how many times we mentally reassemble them in our memories, in the virtual book frames suspended in air allow for more speculative arrangements and interleafings (see Figures 12.4 and 12.5). By a sleight of hand, a touch—a tap—Dickinson's Birds metamorphoses from one archive into many possible archives generated on the fly: archives of fascicle bird-poems or bifolium-sheet bird-poems; of bird-poems sent across the miles or of those that never circulated beyond Dickinson's private papers; archives of beautiful fair-copy bird-poems and archives of still more beautiful rough-copy bird-poems; archives of blackbird, bluebird, or bobolink poems; archives of spring, summer, fall, and winter bird-poems, of morning and evening bird-poems; and archives of the birds themselves singing, nesting, migrating, endangered.[19]

This multiplicity of the archive calls to mind the image of murmuration, the phenomenon that results when hundreds, sometimes thousands of starlings fly in intricate aerial formations across the sky. In the murmuration, researchers believe, starlings behave mathematically like metals becoming magnetized. While studies of the starlings' velocity reveal the murmuration as a system poised at the edge of criticality, "like snow crystals in the moments before an avalanche," studies of their orientation reveal a topological system in which vast collective phenomena emerge from short-range interactions that ripple through whole flocks.[20]

The way of the murmuration is the way of what Michel Serres calls "the multiple": it is by immersion.[21] An intricate cloud of starlings, the murmuration (the multiple) also names a new mode of thinking, more grateful than confounded that we never experience or have access to the completeness of any phenomenon in nature or the world. From this perspective, Dickinson's birds, the cloud her poems make, are not manifest to us (any more so than they may have been to her) as a unity, but rather as a mobile, ever-changing figure, an "emergent unreadability."[22]

The way of the murmuration is also the way of the "meshwork": both ways belong to an ontological model of the natural world, and the archive-world, in which the "processes of formation," the "fluxes and flows of materials," have ascendancy over states of matter and even over materiality itself. Seen as meshwork, the world has not stopped worlding. The bird in the firmament and the poem in the current of composition or reading are not "objects" that can be set in motion, but rather movements that only ever intermittently resolve themselves in the "form of a thing." In the meshwork of Dickinson's

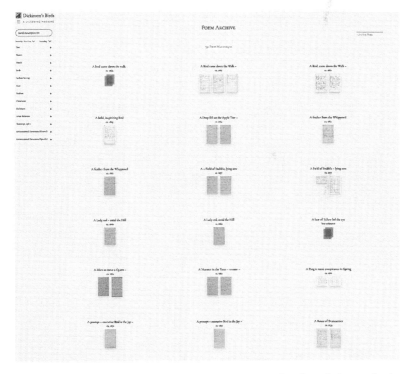

Figure 12.4. Poem Archive, opening scrolling page, screenshot from dickinsonsbirds.org, September 1, 2023.

Birds, moreover, relations between and among birds and poems cannot be conceived and plotted in advance of our encounters with them, but become manifest through our involvement in their circulations, metamorphoses, inherent variance, and potential for departure.[23]

Like the birds themselves, the bird-poems are without fixed abode: they offer a view of the earth from light-years away. For, while Dickinson's poems did not sing the ecological crisis we have named the Anthropocene (how could they?), still, by sounding new convergences between the lyric, birds, lateness, precarity, and the inhuman, they flew headlong from the nineteenth century into the cataclysm of the twenty-first. Like all works that reach us from other times, Dickinson's bird-poems do so in translation, touched by

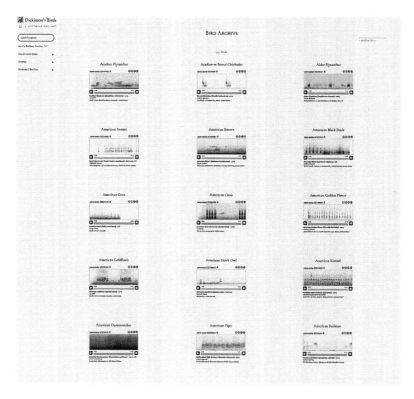

Figure 12.5. Bird Archive, opening scrolling page, screen shot from dickinsonsbirds.org, September 1, 2023.

the strangeness of their crossing. When they arrive—or rather, in their passing through toward another possible end—their *anachrony*, their readability in times, worlds, and ways that are not those of their own day, is part of the message they are unknowingly carrying.

+

The flying indices are one entryway to a knowledge of Dickinson's poems and birds. They are a summons to engage at the same in the protocols of both readings that are "distant," in the aggregation and scrutiny of vast amounts of data, and those of very close reading. Yet, while the indices encourage us to hypothesize new orders of poems and birds, in new scales, they never quite lead us to the end of the archive or its custodial logic. In the poem and bird archives, sight is still the guiding sense for sorting, with every searcher finding their singular way among the primary offerings and secondary data, both bibliographical and ecological, via a familiar set of signs. Look: we can follow poems by date, archive setting, state, medium, and circulation status; and lo, we can track birds by their presence across centuries, their habitats, their changing conservation statuses.

In the distance between the eyes and their targets, the analytic faculty arises and takes hold, holding open the possibility of a metaknowledge of poems and birds as disciplinary objects. Another portal is needed if we are to end our seemingly endless fall into archive logic and effect instead of our fall into worlding, becoming immersed in the meshwork, awareness of new sympathies conjoining us with the "light ethereal influences" beside and around us.[24] In choosing this second way, the searcher renounces the purchase of sight and enters the "other time" of sound, the time, as Salomé Voeglin tells us, of "ephemeral invisibility" and "always now." In this way, sound's way, the searcher is not separate from the world, but "placed in the midst of its materiality, complicit in its production."[25]

+

Sound-Ring: Data Firmament

Like the ancient astrolabe that inspired it, the sound-ring is at once calendar and wheel. Here, though, instead of capturing the brightest stars and deep sky objects visible in the northern or southern hemisphere in a given season and exact hour, it illuminates the bright arrivals and departures of birds and weather and poems across months and seasons of the year as observed from the coordinates of Amherst, Massachusetts. By means of this digital divining instrument, the archive's algorithms of classification are at last dispersed as currents of birdsong and proceedings of weather.

Against a fixed disk marking the intervals of the earth's rotation about the sun, two concentric rings spin around a common point. The inner ring is composed of data and sounds of those birds identified by a few natural historians who traversed the Connecticut River Valley and made their lists before ornithology was recognized as a science: Ebenezer Emmons in 1833, J. A. Allen in 1864, and H. L. Clark in 1887. The bird-ring does not illuminate a specific year of the nineteenth century, but rather those recurring patterns of the birds' arrivals and departures that remained unbroken, or appeared to, until 1914, when the extinction of the Passenger Pigeon troubles them forever. The outer ring is composed of the atmospheric data and sounds of nineteenth-century weather as they were recorded by Amherst College professor Ebenezer Snell and his youngest daughter, Sabra, in a five-volume journal spanning the years 1835 to 1902. Here, where time and weather reign, the average temperatures, the prevailing genres and directions of winds and clouds, the accumulations of rain and snow, the fall of meteors, the florescence of the Aurora Borealis are waymarks in an evanescent geography. Since the atmospheric phenomena of the Northern Hemisphere vary from year to year, we have mined the granular data of the Snells' records for 1864. This year is not selected at random. In addition to corresponding to the publication date of J. A. Allen's bird list, it is also the year in which Dickinson copied and bound her final fascicle and then turned to composing exclusively on unbound sheets, leaves, and fragments. At this moment, the weather of her work changed forever. Finally, incised into the inner ring are a few, fragmentary sounds from the world of the Industrial Revolution that reverberate through nineteenth-century Amherst into the meshwork.[26] The fleeting sounds from this world are among the only cultural references in the tracks of the soundscape: church and sleigh bells, the whistle of a train or factory, the shards of an Isaac Watts hymn, cartwheels and footsteps. Even together, they remain ambiguous signifiers; they do not let us get our bearings in Dickinson's world or our dream of it before being evacuated by the wind.

The turning of the ring around the seasons stirs the birds of nineteenth-century Amherst from the silence into which they have sunk in our collective unconscious. The early recorders' telegraphic notes of the first sightings of a bird in spring ("Bobolink. 4 April. Miss Morse") and last glimpses of it leaving for its wintering range ("Red Crossbill. Latest date seen, May 2") sound archives of inexpressible feelings and open our sense of another place and time when the most devastating effects of the Industrial Revolution were still unsuspected and the sound of the Anthropocene was still a sub-sub song in the bright Book of Nature. In this world where, to its most immediate ear-witnesses, all still seems well, where the passage of time and birds unfolds in humanly imaginable increments that still feel reconcilable with the deep time of creation, the calendar feels like a proof or at least a promise "against our vanishing."[27]

In studies of bird migration, ornithologists often compose graphs or maps marking where the migrating birds "fall out" in their long journeys over the earth. Here, the turning of the ring month by month also activates a visual depiction of its sonic data. In these scatterplots, small dots representing individual species of birds belonging to the chosen temporal interlude glow and pulse, their coordinates in the plot determined by their place in the migration cycle and their body weight in grams. Along the horizontal axis, waves of *arriving migrants* appear in the lower zone of the graph, while *departing birds* cluster in the graph's highest zone; *nesting migrants and year-long residents* glide across the mid-plane of the graph; and *rare* or *accidental migrants* flicker at random coordinates, small pinpricks of light in the graph. "Joy and Gravitation have their own ways," Dickinson wrote.[28] Along the scatterplot's vertical axis, the heaviest birds vibrate closest to the ground while the lightest migrants tremble nearest the horizon line of the sky. The scatterplot is a mist-net of unforeseen, *trembling* connections. Laid one over another in the order of the earth's yearly circuit, the scatterplots illuminate galaxies of birds moving in the meters and measures of the seasons.

In the ring's twelve tracks sounding the months of the year, each month sounds for a duration of two minutes; each season, then, sounds across six minutes, and a year's revolution sounds in just twenty-four hours—a single day. In the fall from archive into world, our translation from scholars into sonic subjects was seemingly accomplished. In our work curating the months'

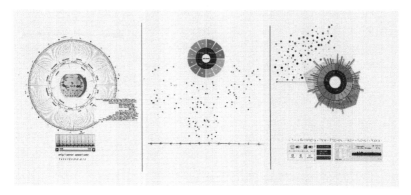

Figure 12.6. Sound-Ring: Data Firmament, preliminary designs 2020–2023.

scapes, we often felt like ringers working a net, unwinding the birds of the nineteenth century from the threads of time in order that they might sound again in our own. As a musical composition, the ring is variable and inconstant: shifting among registers, wavering, emergent, it does not produce a coherent order of birds or weather, but a chaology of orders. In some moments, we hear the sounds of a single species or the sudden swell or dissemination of a season's migrants following the arc of the sun. Sounding inside our bones, the small, unlasting homes of our bodies, these tracks may induce a restorative, impersonal feeling of tranquility or letting go. They may sound something heard forever in the mind of Nature, or only the sound of "a certain Slant of light" in trees.[29]

[Track: "September 1864," *bird-weather soundway.*]

In other moments in the ring we find ourselves immersed and estranged in a new sonic materiality, the commingled whirring of the meshwork beyond human organization. Here the ring that sounds the whorl of the present where time is weather also sounds the whirlwinds of the past and the future: not silent but spectral springs in which the song-souls of birds long-since extinct cross the northern zone alongside those whose vanishing is an unimaginable inaudibility still approaching us.

In the ring, Emmons's, Allen's, and Clark's bare taxonomies of birds on the verge of becoming disciplinary objects fall away in skeins of sound. In the ever-turning ring, the time-shifted, re-wilded birds are agents, vital guides to a moving, numinous, extensional world. The turning and returning birds attune us to a roaming knowledge, to a contingent and simultaneous inhabiting, to leitmotifs of wonder and difference.

Among its other potential classifications, Dickinson's Birds is a listening machine drifting just outside the poet's west-facing windows and our own window opening into the end of the world.[30] While many of the sounds transmitted from it are hauntingly beautiful, they do not offer an analytical understanding of her work but instead prize open the possibility of an affective, meditative, entangled, and present experience of it.[31] If the orientation of the archives of poems and birds is centripetal, rushing inward to the conservation of order, then the orientation of this digital divining instrument is centrifugal, rushing out toward an infinity of possible orders. Thus, while the ring is composed from the data of a place, with the records of birds and weather of more than 150 springs ago, it never offers a documentary sense of place. There is no totalizing schema by which to make conclusive sense of the data the ring holds or disseminates, only a plurality of sonic possibilities, multiple grammars of flight. Under these conditions the dream of restoring all of

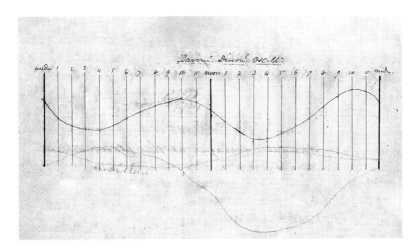

Figure 12.7. Ebenezer Snell, pencil drawing of an oscillating wave from his unpublished lecture notes headed "Meteorology." Amherst College Archives, Snell Family Papers, Series 5: Lecture Notes, circa1830–1876.

the sounds of the birds to Dickinson's writings in order to hear again her world as she heard it may be joyfully traded for an experience of inward listening to, and for, Dickinson's birds and words in the thinner air of the twenty-first century, not as still and finished archives but as data choirs: shimmering, conductive, moving-sounding in and out of focus, and passing on.

A line segment that goes from one point to another on a circle's circumference is called a *chord*. Below the ring a digital slide rule, a chord of "arrows," marks the advent of each new bird poem in Dickinson's lyric oeuvre linked to the year and season of its composition and to the fluttering sound of the bird/s within it. Like the wave machines of the nineteenth century, the timeline will make audible as wing-beats the larger rhythms of Dickinson's imagination of birds from the spring of 1854 to that of 1886.

By listening to the sounds along the line in their successive unfurling, we may be rewarded by a new capacity to hear the fragile and differentiated cadences of Dickinson's interior birdscape, while, by lightly tapping on points along the line to listen at once in and out of time to a single season of her writing life, we may receive both, on the one hand, a sudden intuition of the long durée in which the soundings of Dickinson's birds reverberate against the soundings of birds made outside the precincts of human history and memory, and on the other, a heightened experience of the present moment in which our finger-falls onto a keyboard are part of the manifold and ephemeral data of the world we listen to and create.

Figure 12.8. Emily Dickinson, Fascicle String, n.d. Amherst College Archives.

In 1804, seeking evidence that Pewees, now known as Eastern Phoebes, returned to the same nesting sites in successive springs, John James Audubon began the practice of bird-banding: "When they were about to leave the nest, I fixed a light silver thread to the leg of each." In the spring of 1805 two of the Pewees returned still trailing the silver threads.[32]

Among the wild songbirds named in Dickinson's poems, the Phoebe sings three times: once in the fascicles circa 1863, once more in an undated manuscript announcing the oncoming spring; and once circa 1865 on a loose bifolium sheet carrying a memo on fame: "I dwelt too low / that any seek—/ Too shy, that any / blame—/ A Phebe makes / a little print / Opon the Floors of / Fame-" (MS A 90-7/8 [Fr1009A]).

It is possible that acoustic information is part of our code from the beginning.[33] Sonic fibrils unfurl in the tremulous air between centuries. Birds and sounds, poems and fragments pass—*swerve*—through the eye of a needle.[34]

Murmur	*Trees*	*Thronged*	*Wheels*	*Birds*	*Glee*
lonesome	*puzzled*	*Wings*	*Afar*	*Myrmidons*	*Ghosts*
Acres	*Seams*	*gale*	*spell*	*wind*	*Body*
soul	*still*	*World*	*Swerves*	*Delight*	
Melody	*undone*	*Feather*	*Billows*		
Pang	*ripe*	*peal*	*Drums*		
Bells	*Bomb*	*Day*	+		

While the digital slide rule below the sound-ring tracks the linear unfurling of Dickinson's poems between the springs of 1854 and 1886, inside the ring it is not the poems' original connections to the author and her intentions, but rather their states and motions that first come forward, and then, in the forward scattered light, the fragments of the lively worlds within them. In the scattergraph they compose, the poems that were always already fleeing their lyric forms undergo a further luminous dissembly into impersonal, emergent vitalities. Here, "Out opon Circumference," the manifold data of the world they carry streams out as stars, suns, planets, seas, vales, hills, clouds, petals, stones, dust.

The continual bewildering of poems and birds in the ring, as well as on the site and in this essay, is not affirmation of their tropic interchangeability, as a

Romantic tradition of lyric reading would suggest, but rather an attempt to evoke the "inhuman lyricism" of both as they circulate not as laden tropes but as singular vitalities, semiconductors of sounds, and strange strangers to us and to one other.[35]

+

"SCATTERING AS BEHAVIOR TOWARD RISK"

In 2020, a study revealed that Robins are now beginning their migrations five days earlier every decade.[36] Birds, with their measurable responses to environmental perturbations, may literally be ec-static signals of the profound ecological changes in the era of the "sixth extinction."

A calendar marking the twenty-first century arrival and departure dates of the now distant descendants of Dickinson's birds would indicate that the cycles of the natural world perceived just two centuries ago as eternally unchanging are shifting year by year, perhaps second by second. Playing the disks carrying the birdscapes of the nineteenth- and twenty-first centuries one over the other would make audible the small variations and imperfect rhymings of the birds' altered migratory patterns. Would it signal the warming of the world and call on us to calibrate our passage in a new climate *in extremis*? In contrast, moreover, to the nineteenth-century calendar composed of the small data collected by a few naturalists with imperfect instruments, the twenty-first-century calendar sifts datasets too vast for human comprehension, measuring the otherwise unimaginable ways in which we have altered the world. Now the birds provoke a crisis of self-description: the imminence of the Anthropocene is evidence that the hours apportioned humans to offer an account of ourselves and our world may be run out.

In the face of such changes, it is little wonder that we are acutely reflective about endings of all kinds and how to forestall them. One manifestation of this reflectiveness can be seen in the work of a group of digital humanists at the University of Victoria whose anxious anticipation of the imminent coming of a "digital dark age" in which thousands of digital projects would be subject to degradation, deterioration, and ultimately death prompted The Endings Project.[37] Together, the members of the working group evolved a series of principles and protocols relating to the treatment of data, documentation, processing, and release designed to "future proof" DH resources.

Most importantly, sites sanctioned by The Endings Project must exhibit no external dependencies to stay functional, including server-side scripting or database software. Such DH projects thus achieve time-without-end through staticization.

In composing Dickinson's Birds, we too have often, perhaps very often, been subject to a twenty-first-century disquiet. So much of our work, especially our listening work but also our engineering work, intensified our awareness of the vulnerability of birds and poems, of the fragile circuitry of the digital meshwork, that small shelter we were weaving for them, and of their and our greater house, the singular, blue-spinning earth itself. The discovery of a broken link, a missing text or sound file, though signifying nothing essential, nonetheless triggered our Anthropocene anxieties not only of the project's end, but of the world's.[38]

Is "what | they sung for" all "undone"?

The Anthropocene is necessarily the dark blind from which we see our present reality. From the interior dark of the blind, small apertures give us birds and worlds as glimpses only, but the world's hiddenness—its maintenance of itself more in concealment than in revelation—remains as vast as it ever was. While more than ever before there are reasons for our belief that we live in the end-times, so a life involved in observing nature and reading poems prepares us to live in doubts and uncertainties, even to deeply desire and attend to them. Dickinson's time-shifted birds and lyrics may be emissaries of our untimely ending, but they may also be small reminders that the long arcs of change (poetic, technological, ecological) are not only longer than those of our individual human lives and memories, but discernibly nonteleological. We do not know what ends we or the world will come to. The ecological and epistemological orientation of Dickinson's Birds relinquishes the prospect of an Edenic restoration of the nineteenth-century poemscape and birdscape for a poesis of rewilding the sounds and words that composed it in and for our own times. Here a boundless vigilance for birds and poems caught forever in a common gravitational field is accompanied by hope for a future unendingly opened by uncertainty.

Ultimately, the perpetuation of Dickinson's Birds across time will be radically conditional. Like the sound art projects that are its nearest muses

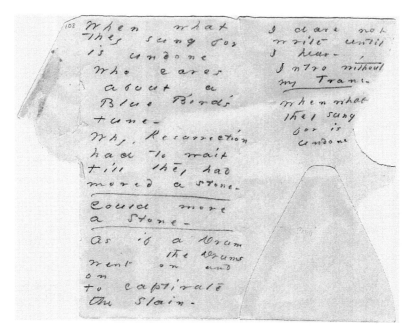

Figure 12.9. Emily Dickinson, "when what | they sung for | is undone" (circa 1881), Amherst College Archives, MS A 108 (Fr1545A).

(Douglass Quin's 2010 *Fathom*, Jana Winderer's 2018 *Spring Bloom in the Marginal Ice Zone*, Krista Caballero and Frank Ekberg's 2013–present *Birding the Future*), its existence will be intimately linked to the larger fate of the planet. And so its contingency and its possible vanishing, rather than its infinity, will be its message. Although we do not yet know how to bring about this conditionality (*pace techne*), we seek a mechanism whereby the existence of Dickinson's Birds is linked to changing climate conditions in the external world.[39] While the precise rates and scales of change triggering mutations in the project remain to be determined, rises in climate exceeding 1.5 degrees Celsius per year will initiate the first losses of local data—the erasure of the Linnean classifications of the birds, loss of information about their histories, habitats, and conservation status, as well as losses of bibliographical data related to the poems: their composition and copying dates, their fair and draft states, their archival locations—while annual rises in climate attaining or exceeding 2 degrees Celsius will trigger more widespread losses of conceptual data: the scholarly apparatus will fall away, our notes on the project's origins and aims, our introductions, paratexts, and indices to the archives of poems and birds, our annotations on the project's text and audio files, followed next by the decomposition of the digital surrogates of Dickinson's manuscript images and our transcriptions, as well as the spectrograms, those visual maps of the frequency energies and sound elements of the variant calls and songs of individual birds held for a moment in our machine. The extinction of any one bird species sheltering in Dickinson's Birds will trigger an immediate and irreversible collapse of the machine's substructure. In this end, in addition to the loss of content, random power surges will begin, causing broken links, memory errors, search function failures, and database corruption. The server account—the site's address—may disappear.

Until that time, however, no one end will be imagined as final.

And even "after the end," the sounds of birds and weather and poems will persist for an unknown epoch, streaming from the lost site en route towards an inhabitable otherness, or only the coordinates of a "quiet seeming | Day -".

+ The Flash between the
Crevices of Crash -

+Flare—+ Glare -
+Blare -

[Track: "April 1864," *bird-weather-soundway.*]

Notes

This essay is a revised and re-directed version of the first part of "Sparrow Data: Dickinson's Birds in the Skies of the Anthropocene," *The Emily Dickinson Journal* 30, no. 1 (2021): 45–84. This version updates materials on the digital instruments central to *Dickinson's Birds* and includes a new meditation on the notion of endings in digital and Anthropocene contexts. I am indebted to Ryan Cull, editor of *The Emily Dickinson Journal,* for his insightful recommendations for the revision of the first version of this work and for his kind permission to publish this new version in the present collection.

I am also grateful to Matt Cohen, Caterina Bernardini, and Ken Price for bringing us together in Nebraska for the symposium "The Digital Futures of Scholarly Editing" and for their wise and gracious editorial counsel. While my title is an evident allusion to Rachel Carson's critical work, the term "data chorus," altered here to "data choir," originates with my collaborator Caroline McCraw; it appears in her essay on this project in *Conjecturing a Climate: Reading Dickinson in the Anthropocene* (forthcoming). To all of my collaborators—Caroline McCraw, Danielle Nasenbeny, Abe Kim, Patrick Bryant, Rayne Broach, Will Sikich—I give thanks. We have worked together so long that the origin and circulation of thoughts about this project cannot be traced to any one of us but belongs to all of us. What is best in this work is as much theirs as mine; any fault in it, though, is wholly owned by me.

1. See Wallace Stevens's "Not Ideas about the Thing but the Thing Itself," in *The Collected Poems of Wallace Stevens* (New York: Alfred A. Knopf, 1954).

2. Quotations in this essay from Dickinson's poems are from their manuscript versions. Citations are to first line(s), date, current archival home, manuscript identifier, and poem number in *The Poems of Emily Dickinson: Variorum*, ed. R. W. Franklin, 3 vols. (Cambridge, Mass.: Belknap, 1998). Quotations from Dickinson's letters are also from the manuscript versions. Citations are to date, current archival home, manuscript identifier, and letter number in *The Letters of Emily Dickinson*, ed. Thomas H. Johnson and Theodora Ward, 3 vols. (Cambridge, Mass.: Belknap, 1958). All transcriptions in the body of the essay are from Dickinson's manuscripts and are my own. The "+" is the symbol often used by Dickinson to mark a variant reading in her work. See Emily Dickinson, "An awful Tempest mashed | the air -", circa spring 1861, Houghton Library, MS H 83 (Fr224A).

3. Lisa Pearson, *It is Almost That: A Collection of Image + Text Works by Women Artists & Writers* (South Egremont, Mass.: Siglio, 2011), 280.

4. In spring 2020, when I was just beginning to think about composing a book of Dickinson's birds, a group of scientists, soundscape artists, and global citizens were way ahead of me. Inspired by the work of bioacoustician Bernie Krause, the public soundscape project Dawn Chorus was born. The creators of the site describe its advent in the following way: "In the spring of 2020, we humans experienced an unprecedented, global break in public life, the 'Silent Spring.' This early phase of the corona pandemic meant the beginning of an extremely challenging time for millions of people. At the same time, this point in time was associated with a sudden, profound silence: cities, airports and industrial areas literally stood still, and there were numerous sightings of wildlife in suddenly deserted areas. The otherwise dominant sounds of human activities were temporarily silenced, leaving room for the sounds of nature. At the same time, global travel and exit restrictions literally forced us to pay more attention to things on our doorstep. Into this stillness, the project Dawn Chorus was brought to life by BIOTOPIA-Natural History Museum Bavaria and the Foundation Art and Nature, with the support of the Max Planck Society" (dawn -chorus.org).

5. Arlette Farge, *The Allure of the Archives* (New Haven, Conn.: Yale University Press, 2013), 4, 69.

6. Timothy Morton, "Ecology as Text, Text as Ecology," *Oxford Literary Review* 32, no.1 (2010): 9. See also Morton, *The Ecological Thought* (Cambridge, Mass.: Harvard University Press, 2010) and *Hyperobjects: Philosophy and Ecology after the End of the World* (Minneapolis: University of Minnesota Press, 2013).

7. While the Massachusetts Avian Records Committee records 510 bird species associated with Massachusetts in 2022 (maavianrecords.com/official-state-list/), the number of species inhabiting or passing through the geographical region of the Connecticut Valley in Massachusetts is closer to 260; see the comprehensive record provided by Aaron Clark Bagg Jr. and Samuel Atkins Eliot, *Birds of the Connecticut Valley in Massachusetts* (Northampton, Mass.: Hamshire Bookshop, 1937). Birds recorded in Amherst, Mass., constitute a still smaller set: in 1977, Peter Westover compiled a list of 234 birds known to have been sighted in or near Amherst (*Birds and Their Habitats in Amherst, Massachusetts, with Complete Annotated List of Amherst Birds* [Amherst, Mass.: Hitchcock Center for the Environment, 1977]).

8. I am deeply indebted to Danielle Nasenbeny and Rayne Broach for their work on the soundways, which were created with Audacity, an open-source multitrack audio editor. Although they cannot sound in this printed version of the text, the references may both allude to their absence and act as ghostly traces of lost melodies. See the Manifold version of the essay for access to the sound files.

9. The earliest known recording of a bird is Ludwig Koch's 1889 recording made in Germany on wax cylinder of a captive shama. The first sound recordings of wild birds were likely those of a song thrush and a nightingale made in England in 1900 by Cherry Kearton, also on wax cylinder.

10. The lines are from Dickinson's poem beginning "The Birds begun at | Four o'clock -" (circa early 1864), Amherst College Archives, MS A 81–8/9 (Fr504B).

11. The line comes from Dickinson's poem beginning "Before the ice is in the pools -" (circa late 1858), Amherst College Archives, MS A 80–1/2 (Fr46A).

12. The David Rumsey Historical Map Collection is available online at davidrumsey.com. Originally hand-drawn and colored by Henshaw on a loose leaf, it was later gathered into a slender volume containing eighteen additional maps along with descriptions of the Ptolemaic, Brahean, and Copernican Systems of Astronomical Geography, the Meridian, the Horizon, the Zones, and the Climates. While Henshaw's maps began as copies of the maps in Carey's 1805 *American Pocket Atlas*, they became singular and luminous objects. In his cataloging notes, Rumsey provides further information on Henshaw's sources: "The maps are copied from the 1805 edition of Carey's *American Pocket Atlas*, except for Ohio, which is from Arrowsmith and Lewis's *Atlas*, 1812, and Indiana, from an unknown source. The text is copied from Morse's *Geography Made Easy*, probably 1807, 11th edition, but certainly before the 12th edition (which was changed substantially); the text describing the maps is original. The only mystery is why she used such out of date sources if, in fact, she made this book in

182[3]" (davidrumsey.com/luna/servlet/detail/RUMSEY~8~1~214957~110004:Massachusetts; "Pub. Note"). The fusion of alphabetic and cartographic literacy found in Henshaw's maps clearly reflects the influence of Emma Willard, the educator and map-maker who led the Academy from 1807 to 1809.

13. The notion of the "ghost map"—a map that "make[s] visible the invisible traces of past human action in the landscape"—haunts our map; see Philip J. Ethington and Nobuko Toyosawa, "Inscribing the Past: Depth as Narrative in Historical Spacetime," in *Deep Maps and Spatial Narratives*, ed. David J. Bodenhamer, John Corrigan, and Trevor M Harris (Bloomington: University of Indiana Press, 2015), 72–101.

14. Much of this information is published at Digital Amherst, a pilot project developed by the Jones Library, Amherst, Massachusetts; see digitalamherst.org/exhibits. I am also grateful to Karen Sánchez-Eppler and her students for sharing their research on Amherst industry in the nineteenth century (2018 Dickinson seminar, Amherst College).

15. The contextual information here is from John Opie, *Nature's Nation: An Environmental History of the United States* (Boston: Cengage Learning, 1998).

16. See Dickinson, "A train went through a burial gate" (circa autumn 1863). The original manuscript has been lost, but was once part of fascicle 20. The transcription here is taken from Franklin, *Poems of Emily Dickinson*, Fr397[A]; Franklin's text derives from *Poems* (1890).

17. Dickinson's existence before the advent of recording technologies makes it impossible to hear the world of the mid-nineteenth century *as she heard it*. But even if new technologies could recover the sounds of this lost world, a still greater—indeed impassable—barrier to full sonic knowing would remain; for our powerlessness to hear Dickinson's birds *as she heard them* is not merely technological but profoundly perceptual, part and parcel of our twenty-first-century condition of loss and longing. Standing, even partly aware, on the shoreline of the Anthropocene and in the midst of the "sixth extinction" distorts our hearing. This need not lead us to lose heart. On the contrary, once we relinquish our fantasy of recapturing a perfect sonic memory of Dickinson's world and acknowledge that our auditory access to the past is necessarily strained and fragmentary, so perhaps can we also attune ourselves more keenly to those sounds that her world and ours still have in common and find new ways of commemorating time's passage as it is woven and measured in the cadences of birdsong.

18. The subtitle of this section heading appears in Dickinson's poem beginning "His Oriental heresies" (circa late 1881), Amherst College Archives, MS A 212 (Fr1562B).

19. In addition to providing detailed textual and material data on Dickinson's bird poems, Dickinson's Birds encourages attunement to the ways in which her poetry evokes the world(s) around her and her complex, sometimes uncanny experience of emplacement. Our encoding of the poems in the installation reflects their relationship to scale, place, motion, time, and sound. We began by inventorying the poems' scalar allusions to Universes, Worlds, and Solar Bodies. We then recalibrated

to catalogue all references to Nature, Landforms, Flora, and Fauna. We considered their climates, the meteorological and atmospheric processes they record, and their multiple temporalities. The central importance of sound in the poems is manifest in our attention to three interlacing registers in Dickinson's work: the geophony, the biophony, and the anthrophony.

20. Of course, the first meaning of *murmuration* is sonic: the action of murmuring—making a soft, indistinct sound, sometimes at a distance. For a brief but interesting note on starling murmuration, see wired.com/2012/03/starling-flock-dynamics/. For a video of this phenomenon, see petapixel.com/2020/04/02/this-video-captures-the-mesmerizing-patterns-traced-by-a-flock-of-starlings/.

21. See, especially, Michel Serres, *Genesis*, transl. Genevieve James and James Nielson (Ann Arbor: University of Michigan Press, 1995); see also Serres, *Branches: A Philosophy of Time, Event and Advent* (New York: Bloomsbury Academic, 2020).

22. See, especially, Timothy Clark, *Ecocriticism on the Edge: The Anthropocene as a Threshold Concept* (New York: Bloomsbury Academic, 2015).

23. See Tim Ingold, "Bringing Things to Life: Creative Entanglements in a World of Materials," *ESRC National Centre for Research Methods*, 2010, 4, accessed 1 March 2021, eprints.ncrm.ac.uk/1306/. Ingold's most crucial distinction is between the "object" that "stands before us as a fait accompli ... defined by its very 'overagainstness' in relation to the setting in which it is placed" and the "thing" that is "not ... an externally bounded entity, set over and against the world, but ... a knot whose constituent threads, far from being contained within it, trail beyond, only to become caught with other threads in other knots."

24. It is Henry David Thoreau who wrote of the "light ethereal influences" of nature in a journal entry of July 23, 1851 (*A Year in Thoreau's Journal: 1851*, ed. Daniel Peck [New York: Penguin, 1993], 126).

25. See Salomé Voeglin, *Listening to Noise and Silence: Towards a Philosophy of Sound Art* (London: Continuum, 2010), 5.

26. In the present tracks, a few fragmentary sounds from the human realm are incised into the bird-and-weather-scapes. We continue to experiment with the sonic interpenetration of "natural" and "human" realms, with the larger aim of reimagining their respective thresholds.

27. This line-fragment is drawn from Allen Grossman's poem "Of the Great House," the title poem in his book of the same name (New York: New Directions, 1982).

28. The line is drawn from a late prose fragment in the Amherst College Archives and special collections. The entire text reads, "Spirit cannot be | moved by Flesh—| It must be moved | by spirit—| It is strange | that the most | intangible is the | heaviest—but Joy | and Gravitation | have their own | ways. My ways | are not your | ways -" (MS A 871 [JL PF44]).

29. The part-line cited here opens Dickinson's poem "There's a certain Slant of light" (circa early 1862), Houghton Library, MS H 74 (Fr320A).

30. The site might also be imagined as a "possible world": neither Umberto Eco's "small world" nor W. H. Auden's "secondary world," the "possible world" into which Dickinson's Birds lifts/launches us is autonomous; for more on these "worlds," see Salomé Voegelin, *Sonic Possible Worlds, Revised Edition: Hearing the Continuum of Sound* (New York: Bloomsbury Academic, 2021).

31. As Caterina Bernardini noted in an early reading of this essay, the same principle applies to the reading and studying of poetry, which calls for a methodological shift toward poetic experience rather than poetic "understanding."

32. John James Audubon, *Dictionary of American Biography,* audubongalleries.com/education/audubon.php.

33. See Andrea Moro, "Why You can 'Hear' Words inside Your Head," BBC, September 29, 2020, bbc.com/future/article/20200929-what-your-thoughts-sound-like.

34. The words appearing here are all drawn from Dickinson's bird poems.

35. The phrase "inhuman lyricism" is Virginia Jackson's; see *Dickinson's Misery: A Theory of Lyric Reading* (Princeton. N.J.: Princeton University Press, 2005).

36. The line of poetry that opens this section is the title of Susan Howe's poem "Scattering as Behavior Towards Risk," in *Singularities* (Middletown, Conn.: Wesleyan University Press, 1990).

37. The Endings Project (University of Victoria, 2018–present) began as "a five-year project funded by the Social Sciences and Humanities Research Council (SSHRC) that is creating tools, principles, policies and recommendations for digital scholarship practitioners to create accessible, stable, long-lasting resources in the humanities" (https://endings.uvic.ca/about.html). For more on its origins and aims, see endings.uvic.ca/principles.html.

38. The quoted lines in the following section heading, which imagine this possibility, are from a partial draft of Dickinson's poem beginning "A Pang is more conspicuous in Spring" (circa 1881), Amherst College Archives, MS A 108 (Fr1545A); for a complete draft of the poem, see MS A 109 (Fr1545B).

39. The setting, once determined, could not be changed by us, lest some sudden regret, some anthropocentric need to save our work might urge us to intercede and stop its alteration or dissolution.

Afterword

JOHN UNSWORTH

I am happy to be included in this collection, and honored to be asked to provide some closing observations. The Whitmaniacs have done a great job in calling together this collection of experts in that vital field of scholarly endeavor, "digital scholarly editing." And even granting the editors' expressed suspicion of the term "scholarly" in their introduction, and everyone's qualms about the metaphorical use of the term *archive*, I haven't yet heard anyone express doubts about the currency of, or need for, editing. On the contrary, these essays have opened new vistas on the scholarly edition, from Stephanie Browner's "generous editions," to Elena Pierazzo's "distant editing," to Julia Flanders's social editions, to Dirk van Hulle's genetic editing of Beckett's gestalt, to Marta Werner's murmuration of bird poems and Robert Warrior's important introduction to the history of Indigenous publishing and editing, from the seventeenth century's James Printer to the contemporary work of N. Scott Momaday, and Warrior's own work.

I am reminded of Frank Kermode's Wellek Library Lectures, published in 1985 as the book titled *Forms of Attention,* in which he explains why we keep paying attention to certain writers and texts. I wrote/spoke about Forms of Attention at "The Face of Text: Computer-Assisted Text Analysis in the Humanities," the third conference of the Canadian Symposium on Text Analysis (CaSTA), at McMaster University, in November 2004. In that paper (available online from my home page), I wrote:

For as long as there has been humanities computing, humanities computing has been about the representation of primary source materials, and about building tools that either help us create those representations or help us manipulate and analyze them. Source materials might be—and have often been—texts, but they might also be drawings, paintings, architectural or archaeological sites, music, maps, textiles, sculptures, performances, or any of the other forms in which the record of human culture and human creativity can be found. Under that description, it might seem that we've been working steadily at more or less the same thing, for quite a long time now—more than half a century. But it would be a mistake to make that assumption, and a disservice to impute mere stasis or repetition to the field. In fact, over the half-century leading up to now, there have been significant accomplishments and significant changes. As a result of them, and (even more) as a result of changes in the world around us, . . . I think we are arriving at a moment when the form of the attention that we pay to primary source materials is shifting from digitizing to analyzing, from artifacts to aggregates, and from representation to abstraction.

By "abstraction," in that talk, I meant things like transcription, indexes, social networks, and even games (the Ivanhoe Game, specifically). Coincidentally, 2004 was also the year in which the Google Books project was launched, and from that followed a whole new scale of abstraction, based in the quantitative analysis of massive numbers of machine-readable texts, which would lead to a pivot in the direction of text analysis, machine learning, and eventually artificial intelligence (AI) as well—lead, indeed, to the collision between those two cultures of error pointed out by Fotis Jannidis. I didn't know that particular computational turn was about to happen, but I could tell that we hadn't exhausted the generative possibilities of the computer in 2004, nor had we yet, in 2022, when the symposium from which these essays emerged was held.

It occurred to me then that 2022 was the thirtieth anniversary of digital humanities (DH) at my university, the University of Virginia. In 1992, the library at UVA made a commitment of space (thanks, Kendon Stubbs) to a new Electronic Text Center, to the Institute for Advanced Technology in the Humanities (IATH), and also to the Rare Book School (RBS), which was moved in that year from Columbia to UVA. When I talked recently to Kendon about 1992, he said that the RBS was a hedge against the possibility that all this digital stuff would blow over, but he was joking, of course: RBS itself has had a significant impact on teaching digital methods (for example, Matthew Kirschenbaum's courses on the analytical bibliography of digital media). It seems appropriate here to note that what made UVA such a force in DH in the 1990s and the early 2000s was the fact that the digital work of projects like the Whitman Archive, the Blake Archive, the Dickinson Archive, and the Rossetti Archive was grounded in decades of scholarship on the history of the book, on bibliography, and on the need to understand how these things are made and why they are made that way. Cassidy Holahan, Aylin Malcolm, and Whitney Trettien certainly illuminate this point in their essay, and I thought of Jerome McGann's influential 2001 book *Radiant Textuality*, in which he explains why the digital edition is a better lens for understanding the book than another book could ever be, which is still true today, as it always will be.

This brings us to the problem of publication. Publishing has always had an important role in scholarship: to fix scholarship in durable book form and to make its dissemination feasible and sustainable. We know how to publish books, and as has been pointed out here, we understand what we might call the "total cost of ownership" of these objects. On the other hand, the publishing of digital scholarship and digital scholarly editions is more of a challenge, though it has its own long history in our field, from Wilhelm Ott's Tübingen System of Text Processing Programs (TUSTEP) to UVA's Rotunda imprint, to the University of Minnesota Press's Manifold. UVA's Rotunda was something I helped to start because I saw the necessity of formal publication for digital editions. But before writing the Mellon proposal that launched Rotunda, I had worked for a couple of years with the University of Michigan Press to try to get them to publish the Rossetti Archive. Ultimately, they could not wrap their minds around publishing something that was a perpetual work in progress, and I now understand that, because I now see that same problem from the perspective of preservation. The scholarly edition, the object of attention, needs to change hands at these key points in the life cycle of information, in order to allow these different agents to perform their functions: first publishers, then libraries, then archives. The Rotunda imprint, too, did not end up publishing the Rossetti Archive, precisely because it remained a work in progress until recently. Rotunda has, however, published a number of other important (and finished) digital editions, including John Bryant's "Fluid Text" edition of Melville's *Typee* manuscript (rev. ed. 2009).

Jerry McGann is not a contributor here, but his work informs the whole volume. His generosity of spirit, his instinct for upsetting the apple cart, his ideas about the social production of literary and scholarly objects, and his sheer playfulness were all crucial ingredients in the early days of IATH. He brought us the Blake folks, the Dickinson folks, and the Whitman folks too. His social network was formative for IATH and for UVA's impact on this emerging field of digital scholarly editing. I got to know Jerry when I invited him to be a member of the editorial board of the first peer-reviewed electronic journal in the humanities, *Postmodern Culture,* and much to my surprise, he said yes and committed his reputation to this sketchy idea. And all of these essays, in inventive and adventurous ways, are extending that spirit of generosity. I think particularly of Ed Folsom's remark during the symposium: "Digital Humanities to me means Collaborative Humanities." Collaboration—real-time versus serial—is indeed the hallmark of DH. UVA's first web page went up in 1992: it was a report to the Mellon Foundation on the serials crisis, and (as a hopeful aside) if you look hard enough, you can still find it on Brewster Kahle's Wayback Machine, archive.org. Publishing that one page was a collective effort involving Kendon Stubbs, Jim O'Donnell, Anne Okerson, and John Wilkin. The work of DH has always been the work of many hands, and always will be. The first UVA web page is a small example; at the other end of the scale is the Text Encoding Initiative (TEI), the world's largest and longest-lasting ontological undertaking, which Julia Flanders described as a metastandard for organizing arguments about texts. It is also known as an international and multilingual set of guidelines for encoding all kinds of literary and linguistic texts for the purpose of interchange and analysis, and incidentally, preservation. TEI represents collaboration on a large scale.

To that point, Marta Werner said during our exchanges at the symposium that, "without my students, I could not do what I do," and Ken Price noted that the Whitman Archive really began when he found Charlie Green and other grad students at William & Mary who understood how to use computers for something more than word processing. I'm still not sure whether those students were the clover or the bee, but in my own experience, the truth about DH is and always has been that it is dependent on intergenerational collaboration. The editor of a digital scholarly edition is not only a maker of connections among texts, as Dirk van Hulle says, but also a maker of connections among people, and at its best, that has resulted in the intergenerational transfer of intellectual, institutional, and reputational capital. As I suggested earlier, I was the beneficiary of that, as a junior professor working with McGann. But the importance of students in DH projects cannot be overstated, especially graduate students; and the importance of DH experience to those grad students is very real as well. Many of them, including two of this volume's editors, have become faculty or have gone on to other successful careers. From UVA, there was a DH diaspora, spawning not only individual careers but also centers (the Maryland Institute for Technology in the Humanities, the Center for Digital Research in the Humanities), which in turn have had their own generations of diaspora.

We also witness in these essays important insights into archival preservation. I am thinking here particularly of K.J. Rawson's excellent piece on the preservation of the records of trans people in archives, and the important question of what is missing from the archive, but also the equally important question of whether archives should "out" their subjects, or "deadname" them, or both, or neither. These questions have always been with us (many archival collections have stipulations about the time that must pass after the death of their subjects before their records are made available, for example), and Rawson mentions the analogy of respectful handling of Indigenous materials not intended for the uninitiated. But in that same spirit, Sarah Patterson shows how the preservation of an archival record, in this case the minutes of Colored Conventions, makes possible an analysis of a movement that might look uniform or even monolithic from a distance but that proves to be riven with factions and competing agendas when seen up close. Daniel Pitti's Social Networks and Archival Context project (SNAC; a.k.a. Facebook for the Dead) comes to mind as a project that is both collaborative and necessarily confronting the kinds of questions raised by Rawson and Patterson. You'll find it at snaccooperative.org/; and be warned, it is an almost bottomless rabbit hole that allows you to traverse many archives, following the records of people in relation with other people—a social network, indeed.

The transformations described here in scholarly practice and the emphases of DH work may be found in the institutions I have been describing, as well. As of July 1, 2022, the Institute for Advanced Technology in the Humanities became a unit of the UVA Library, and when our renovated main library building reopens, it will be co-located with the Scholars' Lab. We're now beginning the process of coordinating their missions and programs, and we will be preserving the identity of each in the process and looking to the future of both. This is thanks in large part to an external review by Ray Siemens, Trevor Muñoz, and Miriam Posner, who recognized that this small but significant change could be key to the future of DH at UVA.

And another development, the beauty and terror of which may be divined from the issues raised in Nicole Gray's essay, is that, after a formal process and due deliberation, the archives and special collections unit in my library has committed to collecting the history of DH, beginning of course with UVA's history in the field, but most definitely not ending there. I am certain that the folks in archives and special collections at UVA would agree with Gray's point that we must balance the attention paid to this effort against the attention taken away from other tasks: those invisible dollar signs, as Steve Ramsay described them during one of the symposium discussions, in querying our contributors about the economics of their endeavors. Deanna Marcum's aphorism that "preservation begins at creation" comes to mind, and I think ruefully of the fact that I didn't understand this very well when I was helping to make the many projects now unprepared for preservation.

Save the records of your DH production processes, because we want them. Before I left IATH in 2003, I did send fifteen thousand emails (printed on acid-free paper, in archival boxes) from the Blake Archive to the University of Minnesota's Babbage Institute, an actual archive focused on the history of information technology, so that fifty years from now there would be a record of at least this small part of the history of the transformation of scholarly publishing. Now I and my colleagues, and perhaps many of you, can step up to the challenge of preserving the history and the products of DH, or as I have been thinking of it lately: I can do something in this final chapter of my UVA career to clean up the huge mess I created in an earlier chapter.

Thank you—contributors, editors, readers—for bringing your brains, your hearts, and your digits to this meeting of the minds on the subject of digital scholarly editions: it is a rich subject with a fascinating past, a formidable present, and far-reaching future.

Contributors

CATERINA BERNARDINI is lecturer in the Department of English at the University of Nebraska–Lincoln. She is author of *Transnational Modernity and the Italian Reinvention of Walt Whitman, 1870–1945*.

STEPHANIE P. BROWNER is university professor at The New School in New York City. She is founder and coeditor of The Charles W. Chesnutt Archive and the general editor of a multivolume print edition of Chesnutt's complete writings.

MATT COHEN is professor of English at the University of Nebraska–Lincoln. He codirects The Walt Whitman Archive and coedited The Charles W. Chesnutt Archive. He is author of *The Silence of the Miskito Prince: How Cultural Dialogue Was Colonized* (Minnesota, 2022).

JULIA FLANDERS is professor of the practice and director of the Digital Scholarship Group at Northeastern University, where she also directs the Women Writers Project. She also serves as editor in chief of *Digital Humanities Quarterly*. She is coeditor of *The Cambridge Companion to Textual Scholarship* and *The Shape of Data in Digital Humanities: Modeling Texts and Text-Based Resources*.

ED FOLSOM, the Roy J. Carver Professor Emeritus of English at the University of Iowa, is editor of the *Walt Whitman Quarterly Review*, codirector of the online Whitman Archive, and editor of the Whitman Series at the University of Iowa Press. He is author or editor of twelve books.

NICOLE GRAY is a programmer/analyst in the Center for Digital Research in the Humanities at the University of Nebraska–Lincoln.

CASSIDY HOLAHAN is assistant professor of English at the University of Nevada–Las Vegas.

FOTIS JANNIDIS is full professor for computational literary studies at the Julius-Maximilians-Universität in Würzburg, Germany. He is coeditor of the historical-critical edition of Goethe's *Faust* (2018) and coeditor of *The Shape of Data in Digital Humanities: Modeling Texts and Text-Based Resources*.

AYLIN MALCOLM is assistant professor of English at the University of Guelph.

SARAH LYNN PATTERSON is assistant professor in the Department of English at University of Massachusetts–Amherst. She is cofounder of the digital archive ColoredConventions.org and coeditor of *The Colored Conventions Movement: Black Organizing in the Nineteenth Century*.

ELENA PIERAZZO is professor of digital humanities and director of the Centre d'Études Superieures de la Renaissance, University of Tours, where she directs the masters in digital humanities. Her most recent publication is *Digital Scholarly Editing: Theories, Models and Methods*.

KENNETH M. PRICE, Hillegass University Professor at the University of Nebraska–Lincoln, has codirected The Walt Whitman Archive since 1995. At Nebraska, he also codirects The Charles W. Chesnutt Archive and the Center for Digital Research in the Humanities. He is author of *Whitman in Washington: Becoming the National Poet in the Federal City*.

K.J. RAWSON is professor of English and women's, gender, and sexuality studies at Northeastern University. He is also the founder and director of the Digital Transgender Archive, and he is the cochair of the editorial board of the Homosaurus.

WHITNEY TRETTIEN is associate professor of English at the University of Pennsylvania. She is author of *Cut/Copy/Paste* (Minnesota, 2021).

JOHN UNSWORTH is dean of libraries and professor of English at the University of Virginia. He is coeditor of the *Companion to Digital Humanities* and *The New Companion to Digital Humanities*.

DIRK VAN HULLE is professor of bibliography and modern book history at the University of Oxford and director of the Oxford Centre for Textual Editing and Theory (OCTET) and of the Centre for Manuscript Genetics at the University of Antwerp. He is codirector of the Beckett Digital Manuscript Project. His publications include *Textual Awareness, Modern Manuscripts, Samuel Beckett's Library, The New Cambridge Companion to Samuel Beckett, James Joyce's Work in Progress,* and *Genetic Criticism: Tracing Creativity in Literature.*

ROBERT WARRIOR is Hall Distinguished Professor of American Literature and Culture at the University of Kansas and a member/citizen of the Osage Nation. He is author of *Tribal Secrets: Recovering American Indian Intellectual Traditions* (Minnesota, 1995) and *The People and the Word: Reading Native Nonfiction* (Minnesota, 2006), and coauthor of *Like a Hurricane: The Indian Movement from Alcatraz to Wounded Knee, American Indian Literary Nationalism,* and *Reasoning Together: The Native Critics Collective.*

MARTA L. WERNER is Martin J. Svaglic Chair of Textual Studies at Loyola University Chicago and author or editor of many works, including *Open Folios: Scenes of Reading, Surfaces of Writing*; *Radical Scatters: An Electronic Archive of Dickinson's Late Fragments and Related Texts*; *The Gorgeous Nothings*; *Writing in Time: Emily Dickinson's Master Hours*; and *Dickinson's Birds: A Listening Machine.*

Index

accessibility, xviii, 103, 111–17
agency, 24
AI (artificial intelligence), x, xix, 4–5, 6, 10, 79, 244
AIHS (American Indian Historical Society), 181–82
Allen, J. A., 228, 231
Allen, Reverend Richard, 121
Amherst, Massachusetts, 218–19, 228
analytic bibliography, 145, 147, 159
Anderson, Jane, 107, 112
Andrews, William, 55
Anthropocene, 218, 226, 229, 234–36
Apess, William, 170, 173, 179
API (application programming interface), x
Assembled for Use: Indigenous Compilation and the Archives of Early Native American Literatures (Wisecup), 172
Astronomical Anthology, An, 159–63
audience, xxi, xxiv, 133–34
Audubon, John James, 233
Augusta, Alexander Thomas, 137, 138–41
automatic collation, 3

Baker, Houston, 58
Banta, Martha, 169
Bargh, Bryan, 183
Bargh, Robyn Rangihuia, 183
Beam, Myrl, 104
Beckett, Samuel, 43–44
Benjamin, Ruha, 108–9, 117
Black archival practices, xvii, 51, 53, 55, 61, 65, 121–22, 206–7
Blake; or, The Huts of America (Delaney), 62
blockchain, 21, 29
boarding schools, American Indian, 186
Bontemps, Arna, 53
books of hours, 5–6
Bowers, Fredson, 35, 56–57, 62
Brayboy, J. A., 135–36
Brilmyer, Gracen, 24
Brooks, Joanna, 170
Brown, Elspeth, 104
Browner, Stephanie, xvi, xviii
Brüning, Gerrit, 87–88n2
Bryant, John, 38, 66, 190
Bucci, Richard, 61
Bucup, Manuel Tzoc, 182
Buurma, Rachel Sagner, 156

Cable, George Washington, 65
Calendarium (Regiomontanus), 159, 160
Camps, Jean-Baptiste, 6
Canterbury Tales, The (Chaucer), 55
Canterbury Tales Project, 14
Cárcamo-Huechante, Luis, 171, 182
Caswell, Michelle, xiii, xvi, xvii, 23–25, 26–28, 101, 103–4, 105
CCP (Colored Conventions Project), xi, 28, 30, 121–22, 141–42
Changing Is Not Vanishing (Parker), 170
Chartier, Roger, 147
Chesnutt, Charles W., 51–54, 56–59, 61–62, 63–64, 65–66
Chesnutt, Helen, 53
Chicksaw Press, 183, 187
Christen, Kimberly, 107, 112–13
Cifor, Maria, xvii, 24–25, 26–28, 101, 103–4, 105
Civil War, American, 121
Clark, H. L., 228, 231
Clérice, Thibault, 6
CLS (computational literary studies), xix–xx, 73–74, 75–77, 83, 86
Codex Mendoza, 149
Cogewea, The Half-Blood (Dove), 188, 195
Cohen, Matt, 90, 93, 172, 190, 191
collaborative humanities, 94
collation, 3, 55–56, 60–61
Collection of Moral Sentiments, A (Richardson), 154–59
Colored American, The, 60
Colour Collage, 150
communities of practice, 3
community, xxi, 26
Company (Beckett), 43–44
computational linguistics, xxii, 4, 7–9
"Conjurer's Revenge, The" (Chesnutt), 57–58, 60, 61

Connolly, Thomas C., 42
consent, 116–17
"Considering the Scholarly Edition in the Digital Age," 17
Cook, Terry, xiv
copyright, 109, 173
Cortelazzo, Michele, 10
Crane, Gregory, 5
Crane, Stephen, 57, 62
creative ecologies, 40, 42
Cromwell, J. W., 129, 137
Cushman, Ellen, 112
Custo, Rupert, 182
CWE (complete-works edition), 33–35, 38–40, 42

Dahlström, Mats, xxv
Daly, Liza, 152, 153
Dante, 46–47
Darnton, Robert, 147
DCC (Digital Curation Centre), 203
de Biasi, Pierre-Marc, 39
decolonial approaches, x–xi, xx
Deegan, Marilyn, xiii
deep hermeneutics, 39
Delaney, Martin, 62
Deloria, Vine, Jr., 170
Devonshire manuscript, 15–16, 17
dialect fiction, 58–59, 60
Dickinson, Emily, 91, 217, 218–19
Dickinson's Birds (Werner et al.), 218
Diderot, Denis, 157
digital, definition of, xxiv–xxv
digital asset management, 200
Digital Documentation Process, 203
digital edition, 37, 40–41
Digital Preservation Handbook (Digital Preservation Coalition), 205
discourse, freedom, 123
distant reading, 4, 76, 227
Documents of American Indian Policy (Deloria and DeMallie), 170

Dove, Mourning, 188
Driscoll, Matthew J., 13–14
Drucker, Johanna, xi, 147, 149–50, 152
DTA (Digital Transgender Archive), xviii, 101–2, 104–11, 112
Du Bois, W. E. B., 53, 58
dysteleology, 40–41

EarlyPrint, 151
Eastern Phoebes, 233
Eaves, Morris, xvi, xx
ECDA (Early Caribbean Digital Archive), 26, 28
Eggert, Paul, 59, 61
Eisenstein, Elizabeth, 147
Electronic Textual Editing (Burnard, O'Brien O'Keeffe, and Unsworth), xxiii–xxiv, xxv
Elements of Indigenous Style (Younging), 189
Embry, J. C., 136
Emigration. *See* migration, human
Emily Dickinson Electronic Archives, 90, 149
Emmons, Ebenezer, 228, 231
emotion detection, 84–85
empathy, xvii, 27–28
Encyclopédie (Diderot), 157
Endings Project, 199, 203, 234–35
ephemerality, xvi, 201
error culture, xix, 87
eScriptorium, 7
ethics, xii–xiii, xxi–xxii, 4, 10–11, 24, 27, 190, 204; of access, 111–17; of care, 101–2, 103–5, 111, 117–18
EVT (Edition Visualization Technology), 152
Ezell, Margaret, 18

FAIR (Findable-Accessible-Interoperable-Reusable), 5

Farge, Arlette, 218
Faust edition, 39, 74–75, 77–78, 82, 84
Fayetteville Educator, 54
Felski, Rita, xxiv
feminism, 101–4
Fenlon, Katrina, 198, 204
Fernald, Anne, 63
Ferrante, Elena, 10
Fitzpatrick, Kathleen, 202
Flanders, Julia, xvi–xviii, 246
fluid text, 38
flying indices, 227
Folsom, Ed, xv, xviii, 202, 246
Foner, Eric, 61
formalist framework, 123
Forms of Attention (Kermode), 243–44
Freeman, Robin, 188, 189, 190
"Frisk's First Rat" (Chesnutt), 54
"From Human Rights to Feminist Ethics" (Caswell and Cifor), 103–4
funding, xxiii, 27, 114–15, 198, 248

Gabay, Simon, 6
Gabiola, Joyce, 24
Gabler, Hans Walter, 38
Gadamer, Hans-Georg, xxvi
Galbraith, Robert, 4, 10
Galey, Alan, ix, 203
Gardner, Eric, 54
gender, 10, 101, 107–11, 113–16
generous edition, 54–55, 60–61, 62–63, 68
genetic criticism, 38–39, 41, 42–43, 44–46, 64–68
Genoa Indian School Digital Reconciliation Project, 208
gestalt, 37
Gilder, Richard Watson, 65–66, 67–68
Gilligan, Carol, 103
Goethe, Johann Wolfgang, 75

Gontarski, S. E., 36
Gray, Nicole, xviii, xxi, 92, 135
Great Migration, 127
Greenblatt, Stephen Jay, 123
Greetham, David, xxvi
Greg, W. W., 146, 147, 149

Ham, F. Gerald, xiii
Hansberry, Lorraine, 53
Harney, Stefano, 206–7
Harris, Verne, xiv
Hartman, Saidiya, 204
HathiTrust, 155
Heiss, Anita M., 182, 189, 190
Henshaw, Frances Alsop, 219, 221–22
Hilbert, Vi, 183–84
Holahan, Cassidy, xx, 154
Holm Nelson, Theodor, 19–21
Homestead, Melissa, xxii
House Behind the Cedars, The (Chesnutt), 65–68
House Made of Dawn (Momaday), 169
HTR (handwriting text recognition), 4–5, 151
Huia Publishers, 183
Hurst, Megan, 205
hypermediacy, 152–53
hypertext, 148

IATH (Institute for Advanced Technology in the Humanities), 92–93, 246
IIIF (international image interoperability framework), 5–6, 148
In a Different Voice (Gilligan), 103
Indian Affairs, Laws, and Treaties (Kappler), 170
Indian Historian Press, 181–82
Indigenous archival practices, xvii, xx, xxiii, 107, 109, 112, 114–15, 169–71, 172

Indigenous language revitalization, 184
information loss, 105–6
INKE (Implementing New Knowledge Environments), 15–16, 17, 19, 21
Institute of Aboriginal Development Press, 182
intellectual sovereignty, 175, 187
interoperability, xxiii
intertextuality, 39, 151

Jannidis, Fotis, xix, xxii, 244
Jockers, Matthew, 4
Joula, Patrick, 4
Jump, Kenneth Jacob, 173–80, 184
Juxta, 55

Kappler, Charles, 170
Kermode, Frank, 243–44
Kestemont, Mike, 4–5
Kilbride, William, 198
Kirschenbaum, Matthew, 210
Kitamoto, Asanobu, 151
Knoblochtzer, Heinrich, 160

Latour, Bruno, xxiv
Leaves of Grass (Whitman), 91–92, 95, 197, 205–6, 210
Legend of John Stink, or Roaring Thunder "Child of Nature," The (Jump), 177
Leung, Sofia L., 117
Levenshtein distance, 79
Lichtenberger, Johannes, 159–60
Lieberman, Erez, 8
Liu, Alan, xix
LJS 445 (astronomical manuscript), 159–63
LOD (linked open data), x
López-McKnight, Jorge R., 117
Lushootseed Research, 183–84
Lynch, John R., 132, 133
Lyons Render, Sylvia, 53–54

machine reading, 151
Madsen, Christine, 205
Malatino, Hil, 104–5
Malcolm, Aylin, xx, 154
Manicule (software), xx, 152–54, 155
Marcum, Deanna, 248
masculinity, 126
material texts editions, 152
Matienzo, A., 105–6
McCarty, Willard, 40
McDonnell, Margaret, 188–89
McGann, Jerome, xiii, 14, 18–19, 55, 62, 146, 148, 149, 245, 246
McGill, Meredith, 94–95
McGrail, Anne B., 101
McKenzie, D. F., 14, 18–19, 146
McLuhan, Marshall, 147
McPherson, Tara, 63
McWhorter, Lucullus, 188
medieval studies, 160
metadata, 104, 150
Micheaux, Oscar, 65
Michel, Jean-Baptiste, 8
migration, bird, 229, 234
migration, human, 127, 129, 135–37, 138, 140
Miller, Matt, 209
Momaday, N. Scott, 169–70, 172
Moreton-Robinson, Aileen, 189, 190
Moretti, Franco, 4
Morgan, Edwin, 150
Morreale, Laura, 209, 211
Morseau, Blaire, xx
Moten, Fred, 206–7
Moynihan, Bridget, 150
Mrs. Dalloway (Woolf), 63
Mukurtu (software), 115
murmuration, 224–25
mutual aid, 104–5

National Native American Boarding School Healing Coalition, 208

Native American literature, 169–71, 172
Navajo Community College Press, 181
new bibliography, 146, 147
Nieves, Ángel, 101
NINES (Nineteenth-century Scholarship Online), 55
NLP (natural language processing), xix, xxii, 73–74, 79
Nowviskie, Bethany, xii, 103, 104, 149
nucleic core archive, 122

Occom, Samson, 170
O'Connell, Barry, 170
OCR (optical character recognition), 3–4
Old Fulton New York Post Cards, 206
open access, xvii, xxiii–xxiv, 113
Open Digital Collaborative Project Preservation in the Humanities, 202–3
oral history, 202
Osage constitution, 171
Osage Indian Anthology (Jump), 179
Osage Indian Poems and Short Stories (Jump), 178–79
Ott, Wilhelm, 245

Palacios, Rita, 182
Pamphlets of Protest, 121
Parker, Robert Dale, 170
Patterson, Sarah, xviii, xxiii
People and the Word, The (Warrior), 171, 185
People, Practice, Power (McGrail, Nieves, and Senier), 101
Petrie, Paul, 58
Pewee (or Phoebe, bird), 233
phylogenetic approaches, 3, 4
Piece of Monologue, A (Beckett), 43–44, 45–46

Pierazzo, Elena, xvii, xix, xxii, xxiii, 13–14
Pinchback, Pinckney B. S., 126, 131, 132, 133
Pinche, Ariane, 6
planned obsolescence, 202
Pokagon, Simon, xx
politics, ix
postcritical movement, xxiv
postcustodial archiving, xi, xiii–xiv, xviii, xx, xxi
poststructuralism, 146–47
poverty, 136–37
power, 204
Pratt, Caroll, 37
preservation, xi–xiv, 203, 204–20, 245, 247
Price, Kenneth, 89–90, 92–93, 246
Printer, James, 190–91
print paradigm, 34
privacy, 108
Proceedings of the Black State Conventions, 1840–1865, 125
Proceedings of the National Conference of Colored Men of the United States, held in the State Capital at Nashville, Tennessee, May 6, 7, 8, and 9, 1879, 122–23
Prognosticatio (Lichtenberger), 159–60, 162
protest, 122, 125
Putra, Akmal, 150

Race After Technology (Benjamin), 117
racial passing, 65
Radiant Textuality (McGann), 245
radical empathy, 24–25, 104
Rainey, James, 129
Rapier, James Thomas, 126
Rawson, K. J., xviii–xix, xxi, xxiii
RBS (Rare Book School), 244–45

[Re]Activate Mama Pina's Cookbook (Sepúlveda), 150
Regiomontanus, Johannes, 159, 160
"Rena Walden" (Chesnutt), 65–68
repotting, 209, 211
representation, xvii, 3, 4, 106, 113, 130; of audience, 26, 102, 107–8, 111
resilience, 112
rhyme detection, 85–86
Richardson, Samuel, 154–59
Riemer, Friedrich Wilhelm, 82
Riffaterre, Michael, 39
Robinson, Peter, 29, 55
Rossetti Archive, 148, 245
Rotunda, 245
Round, Phillip, 171, 189–90

Sahle, Patrick, 13–14, 17, 38
Santa Barbara Statement on Collections as Data, xii
Schnitzler, Arthur, 36, 38
scholar, 13, 243
Scholarly Editing in the Computer Age (Shillingsburg), xxv
Schomaker, Lambert, 4
Schomburg Library of Nineteenth-Century Black Women Writers, 121, 170
Schwartz, Joan M., xiv
Sedgwick, Eve, xxiv
semantic distance, 79
Senier, Siobhan, xx, 101
Sentence-BERT, 79–80
sentiment analysis, 76
Sepúlveda, Gabriela Aceves, 150
Serres, Michel, 224
Sharpe, Christina, xxvi
Shillingsburg, Peter, xxv–xxvi
slow archives, 107
Smithies, James, 198
SNAC (Social Networks and Archival Context), xviii–xix, xxiii

Snell, Ebenezer, 228
Snell, Sabra, 228
social edition, 15–19, 20, 22–23, 24
Social Edition of the Devonshire Manuscript, A, 18
social geometry, 13–14
social justice archive, 124–25
social media, x
"Song of Myself" (Whitman), 97
Sonic Color Line, The (Stoever), 59
Souls of Black Folk, The (Du Bois), 58
sound-ring, 227–32
soundscape, 222, 224–26
Sound the Stars Make Rushing through the Sky, The (Parker), 170
Spärck Jones, Karen, 7–9
speculative computing, 149
Spires, Derrick, 130
statistics, 137, 138
Steward, William, 130
Still, William, 137, 138
Stirrings Still (Beckett), 45–47
Stoever, Jennifer Lynn, 59
Stokes, Peter, 7
STSR (The Socio-Technical Sustainability Roadmap), 200–201, 203, 209
Stubbs, Kendon, 244–45
Stutzmann, Dominique, 5
stylometry, 73, 76
Sullivan, Hannah, 67
Sullivan, Lou, 108
Sundquist, Eric, 58
sunsetting, 209
surreal time, 207
Survey of the Negro Convention Movement, 1830–1861, A, 125
sustainability, 204–5, 209
Sutherland, Kathryn, xxiv

Tai, Jessica, 24–25
Tales of War (Crane), 62

Tanselle, G. Thomas, xxvi, 57
Taylor, Diana, 150
TEI (Text Encoding Initiative), xxi–xxii, 5, 6–7, 16, 52, 77–78, 246
teleology, 40–41
temporalities, 207, 209–10
textualization, 171–72
Theytus Books, 183
topic modeling, 75–76
Transkribus, 4
Trettien, Whitney, xx, 152
Tuckerman, Frederick Goddard, 170, 172
TUSTEP (Tübingen System of Text Processing Programs), 245

Undercommons, The (Harney and Moten), 206–7
Underwood, Ted, x, 76
Unsworth, John, xviii–xix

van Hulle, Dirk, xvi, xviii, 247
Van Mierlo, Wim, 147
variants, 78–80, 81–82, 83
virtues, 17–18
Voeglin, Salomé, 227

Walt Whitman Archive, xiv–xv, xviii, 68, 89–91, 92, 93, 125, 149, 197, 199–211
Warrior, Robert, xviii, xx
web archiving, 203
Werner, Marta, xvi, 90, 246
Whitening Race (Moreton-Robinson), 189
Whitman, Walt, 95–97, 205–6, 210
Wideman, John Edgar, 58–59
William Blake Archive, 149
Williams, B. F., 133
Wilson, David, 136
Wilson, Ivy, 130
Winko, Simone, 84

Winters, Yvor, 169
Wisecup, Kelly, 172–73
women, Black, 124, 126, 142
Women Writers Project, 149, 151
Woo, Jewon, 54
Woodson, Carter G., 53
Work of Revision, The (Sullivan), 67
Wowaus, 190–91
Wyatt, Thomas, 15

Xanadu (platform), 19–22, 29

Young, John, xvi
Younging, Gregory, 189

Zavala, Jimmy, 24
Zeller, Hans, 35